THE M. & E. HANDBOOK SERIES

ECONOMIC GEOGRAPHY

THE M. & E. HANDBOOK SERIES

ECONOMIC GEOGRAPHY

H. ROBINSON, B.A., M.Ed., Ph.D.

Head of Department of Geography, Geology and Environmental Studies and Dean of the Faculty of Arts, The Polytechnic, Huddersfield

SECOND EDITION

MACDONALD AND EVANS

MACDONALD & EVANS LTD.
Estover, Plymouth PL6 7PZ

First published 1968
Reprinted 1968
Reprinted 1969
Reprinted 1971
Reprinted (with amendments) 1972
Reprinted (with amendments) 1973
Reprinted 1974
Reprinted 1975
Second edition 1976

©

MACDONALD AND EVANS LIMITED
1976

ISBN: 0 7121 0558 1

HANDBOOK *Conditions of Sale*

*Printed in Great Britain by Richard Clay (The Chaucer Press), Ltd,
Bungay, Suffolk*

PREFACE

ECONOMIC and Commercial Geography is a popular examination subject and many institutions, among them the Institute of Bankers, the Chartered Institute of Transport, the Town Planning Institute, the Institute of Chartered Secretaries and Administrators, the Institute of Costs and Management Accountants, the Institute of Grocers, the Co-operative Union Ltd., the Royal Society of Arts and the Civil Service, often require the study of Economic and Commercial Geography. This HANDBOOK has been prepared to meet the needs of students taking the examinations of the above-mentioned, and other, bodies and those students in Colleges of Commerce and Technology who are taking National Certificate and National Diploma Courses in Business Studies. It will also be of value to students in schools who pursue courses in Economic Geography and who take some of the special options of the Associated Examining Board, *e.g.* the Geography of Agriculture, the Geography of Industry and Commerce.

Economic Geography is important because of its relevance to human activities and to modern life. Economic realities affect us all and, as the world becomes increasingly smaller and happenings in any part of the world may have serious repercussions for us or any other people, it is important—one might say essential—for us to know something of the geographical, human and economic conditions which occur in other parts of this planet. If international problems are to be solved, they can come only through international awareness of them. In the past it was possible, like the ostrich, to smother one's head in the sand and ignore those things we did not wish to know about: today it is impossible to do this.

This HANDBOOK gives the basic essentials of Economic and Commercial Geography but clearly it is impossible to cover every aspect of the field, for examination syllabuses vary quite considerably and often lay emphasis upon particular areas of study. Thus, it is especially important for the student to familiarise himself with the particular syllabus with which he is concerned. For a fuller treatment of many of the topics dealt with in this HANDBOOK the student is recommended to read another text such as the author's *Geography for Business Studies* (published by the publishers of this HANDBOOK) or *A Geography of Resources* by E. Stringer and J. S. Davies or *Economic Geography* by R. Hope.

Economic Geography is a dynamic subject: it is constantly changing. Keeping up to date is something of a problem, but if the student reads a daily paper or a weekly periodical (such as *The Economist* or *The Statist*) he will keep in touch with changes and developments. For figures of production, population and new geographical developments, Philips' *Geographical Digest* is invaluable.

A selection of examination questions taken from recent examination papers by the undermentioned bodies is given in Appendix II and I am grateful to them for permission to use selected questions from their papers:

> Institute of Bankers;
> Chartered Institute of Transport;
> Institute of Chartered Secretaries and Administrators;
> Welsh Joint Education Committee;
> Northern Counties Technical Examinations Council; and
> Associated Examining Board.

A guide to the answering of questions is given in Appendix I. The student is advised to read this very carefully and to heed what is said. Many years of experience as an examiner and chief examiner have shown quite clearly where students frequently fall into error and, all too often, do not do justice to themselves.

H. R.

January 1968

NOTE TO SECOND EDITION

ALTHOUGH with earlier reprints statistics were revised, it has been felt desirable to bring this HANDBOOK even further up to date. The statistics in most cases have been brought up to 1972 figures, and new sections added to the text on such currently important topics as natural gas and oil production.

H. R.

April 1976

NOTICE TO LECTURERS

Many lecturers are now using HANDBOOKS as working texts to save time otherwise wasted by students in protracted note-taking. The purpose of the series is to meet practical teaching requirements as far as possible, and lecturers are cordially invited to forward comments or criticisms to the Publishers for consideration.

P. W. D. REDMOND
General Editor

CONTENTS

LIST OF ILLUSTRATIONS

LIST OF ILLUSTRATIONS

PART ONE

THE BACKGROUND OF
ECONOMIC GEOGRAPHY

CHAPTER I

WHAT IS ECONOMIC GEOGRAPHY?

MEANING OF ECONOMIC GEOGRAPHY

1. Modern geography. In a broad way the study of modern geography may be defined as "the exact and organised knowledge of the distribution and organisation of phenomena on the surface of the earth." Geography attempts to describe, relate and interpret the varied features of the earth and to study the interacting relationships between human distributions and activities and the physical environment.

2. Value of geography. Geography is studied and is of value for many reasons, but it is especially important because:

(*a*) We live in a world of increasingly rapid transport and new methods of communication which mean, in effect, that the world is becoming smaller and peoples everywhere are becoming more closely linked together.

(*b*) Anything that happens anywhere in the world, *e.g.* a war, a revolution, a natural disaster, an economic recession, is likely to have repercussions elsewhere; countries these days cannot be sufficient unto themselves and live in complete isolation.

(*c*) Many countries, of which Britain is a typical example, live by what they grow on their farms or make in their factories and rely upon the export of their products for their livelihood.

(*d*) The world is divided into the so-called "have" and "have-not" countries, *i.e.* the advanced and the underdeveloped countries, and if the latter are to be helped and the peace of the world ensured it is essential that we learn something about them and their problems.

In essence, geography is necessary for effective economic development and for the understanding of international relations.

3. Economic geography. Geography is a very wide subject and has many aspects of study. One of the most important and most practical of these aspects is the branch known as

Economic Geography. Briefly described, *economic geography is concerned with the ways and problems of making a living and with spatial interaction*. Elaborating this statement we may say that it is concerned with the human exploitation of the earth's natural resources, the production of commodities, whether raw materials, foodstuffs or manufactured goods, and their transportation, distribution and consumption. The study of these matters may be said to constitute the field of economic geography.

FUNCTIONS OF ECONOMIC GEOGRAPHY

4. The function of economic geography. Economic geography seeks to provide answers to a number of questions:

    (a) *What* kind of economic activities are carried on?
    (b) *Where* are economic activities carried on?
    (c) *Why* are economic activities carried on?
    (d) *When* are economic activities carried on?
    (e) *How* are economic activities carried on?

It will help us in our study of economic geography if we continually bear these questions in mind and repeatedly ask what? where? why? when? and how? in considering any aspect of economic geography.

5. A dynamic subject. In earlier times economic geography was often confused with commercial geography. The latter, which is really but a part of economic geography, is mainly concerned with the production, transportation and marketing of commodities. Commercial geography tends to be a rather dull subject in so far as it is essentially factual, and the mere learning of facts (though often necessary to build a skeletal framework) can be tedious.

Economic geography, however, probes deeper.

    (a) it goes behind the facts;
    (b) it seeks causes and notes effects;
    (c) it tries to discern trends and patterns in economic activities;
    (d) it attempts to explain trends and patterns; and
    (e) it relates production to the manifold influences which are likely to have some bearing upon it.

Economic geography is not a dead or static study: conditions in the world are constantly changing, so the subject is very much alive—it is so much alive it is often difficult to keep abreast of the changes and developments that are taking place. But much of the interest in economic geography comes from this constant change: it is at once interesting and instructive to follow the changes taking place in the use of commodities, in industries and agriculture, in the growth of countries, in the developments in transport and communications and in the flow of trade.

6. Production, manufacture and distribution. Economic geography may be said to concern itself with three stages of economic production:

(a) *The production of raw materials*, whether they be foodstuffs, such as wheat, meat or fruit, or industrial raw materials, such as coal, timber, cotton or wool. The production of such simple, unprocessed commodities from the rocks, the soil or the sea is called *primary production* and mining, forestry, farming, fishing and hunting are known as *primary activities*.

(b) *The processing, fabrication and manufacture of primary commodities*. This involves the preparation, working and changing of primary produce into states or forms required by the user or consumer: for example, iron ore is turned into sheet steel, wheat is converted into flour and timber is made into furniture; the making of metal goods, textiles, furniture, cigarettes and so on, is known as *secondary production*.

(c) *The distribution of commodities* is the third stage in economic production. This aspect of economic activity is concerned with the ways and means by which foodstuffs, raw materials and manufactured goods reach the consumer. It involves the use of systems of transport, techniques of communication and the services of merchants, brokers, bankers and financiers. These various activities are often called *tertiary activities*.

7. World inter-dependence. Exchange between communities is age-old and all countries to a greater or lesser degree engage in trade exchange. The degree to which some countries, such as the United Kingdom, depend upon outside resources and supplies is truly astonishing when one comes to think carefully about it. It is surprising how many people are unaware of the extent to which their lives and the life of the country in which they live are linked with, and are dependent upon, the outside world.

This inter-dependence of countries, one with another, is of course the basis of international trade. The more sophisticated an individual's or a country's life becomes, the more varied and more exacting do their wants become. These, in turn, result in both a greater *volume* of trade and a greater *complexity* of trade.

Since the peoples and countries of the world are, by and large, developing and their wants are becoming increasingly sophisticated, world trade is not only growing in volume and complexity but these peoples and countries are becoming more and more dependent upon each other. Many thinking people at the present time believe that the world's problems, political and social as well as economic, will be solved only when all peoples and all countries realise that the world is one and that they are all mutually dependent upon the understanding, help and goodwill of each other.

PROGRESS TEST 1

1. Explain why the study of geography is of value. (2)

2. Describe the field and function of economic geography. (3, 4)

3. Economic geography may be said to concern itself with three stages of economic production. What are these three stages? (6)

4. What is meant by saying that economic geography is a dynamic subject? (5)

5. Explain briefly the meaning of the following terms: "have-not" countries; primary production; secondary production; tertiary activities. (2, 6)

CHAPTER II

THE PHYSICAL ENVIRONMENT

IMPORTANCE

1. The physical basis. Man lives in a physical environment and although he has often modified this, sometimes in a drastic way, this physical basis is of great importance and from the economic point of view, man's activities depend upon it to a very considerable extent. It is sometimes averred that the role of the physical environment in influencing man and his activities has been, and continues to be, overstressed and that the social, economic and political conditions and factors are the ones which most strongly influence society and the activities of man in a given area.

Although these cultural aspects—using the term in its widest sense—are of very great significance, we should never lose sight of the fact that this cultural pattern or super-structure, call it what you will, is grounded upon, and so inevitably influenced by, the physical conditions. In emphasising this we are not suggesting the play of geographical determinism but merely paying due respect to the basic influence of the physical environment. It is true that man's ever-increasing scientific knowledge and technological mastery are slowly lessening the influence of physical conditions, but day still follows night, the seasonal cycle persists, the continents are anchored, the winds blow whither they will, used mineral resources are irreplaceable. And time and again man has learned, through bitter experience, that he cannot fly in the teeth of Nature. If man is wise he will recognise his limitations and try to co-operate with Nature.

2. The chief components. The chief factors which make up the physical environment are seven; these are:

    (*a*) Geographical location.
    (*b*) Topography or relief.
    (*c*) Geological structure.

(d) Climate.

(e) Soil.

(f) Vegetation.

(g) Animal life.

COMPONENTS

3. Geographical location. The location of a place is important. Geographical location implies two things; the first of
these is constant, the second is alterable:

(a) *Absolute location* as defined by lines of latitude and longi-
tude: this is mathematically determined and unalterable.

(b) *Relative position,* that is, position in relation to other
areas, such as land areas or bodies of water. Relative position
also includes *accessibility* which is of particular importance.
For example, an area, *e.g.* a country or part of a country, may
have its development retarded because it is remote, isolated and
inaccessible—think, for instance, of Bolivia, Tibet and the
northern parts of Canada or the Soviet Union or even Australia
until about one hundred years ago.

4. Examples of changes in relative position and accessibility.
The relative position and accessibility of a place are not constant; they may change as a result of new communications
developments. Think of the changes which have occurred as a
result of the elimination of obstacles or the introduction of new
means of transport. Three illustrations may be given to show
how the relative position and accessibility of areas have
changed:

(a) *In Roman times* the effective centre of the known world
was the Mediterranean and in those days Britain lay remote on
the edge of that world. With the discovery of the Americas,
around A.D. 1500, the commercial centre of gravity moved to
Western Europe and Britain then came to lie in the midst of the
most important portion of the earth's surface—a position which
she continues to hold and which brings enormous advantages
with it.

(b) *The cutting of the Suez and Panama Canals* brought great
benefits to many countries: not only was travelling time, and
therefore cost of carriage, greatly reduced between certain
countries but, as a result of these ship canal developments,
economic production and trade were greatly stimulated, *e.g.*
along the Pacific coasts of North and South America, regions

which, hitherto, had been rather remote, isolated and economically backward.

(c) *The advent of the aeroplane,* a completely new means of communication which soon developed speeds undreamed of in land-bound or water-surface transport, shortened drastically the travelling time over long distance and also made accessible regions which formerly had been extremely difficult of access. There are, even today, many places which are unconnected by either rail or road transport but which are served by aircraft, *e.g.* many of the Soviet arctic settlements fall into this category.

5. Relief. Relief, through its altitude and its degree of ruggedness, exerts many different effects on man.

(a) *Where the land is too high, too steep or too rugged,* farming is severely handicapped and may often be precluded, for the climate may be too harsh, the soils too thin and stony, and the slopes too steep for the use of a plough, *e.g.* in many parts of Alpine Austria and Switzerland, Tibet and the Andes. On the other hand, level or gently undulating plains, such as the Great Plain of North China, the American prairies and the English Lowland, are likely to have deep and better soils and mechanised agriculture is greatly facilitated.

(b) *The pattern of the relief may affect industrial and commercial development,* encouraging it on the one hand, inhibiting it on the other. For example, hydro-electric power resources are more likely to be present in areas of strong relief where there are many streams than in lower lying regions. Where there is a natural convergence of routes a place will come to have *nodality* and this will assist it to become a centre of exchange. Such centres become collectors of produce from the surrounding region, function as exchange markets, and become distributors of goods. Because of their commercial function they may, as indeed they often do, become manufacturing centres also, *e.g.* Paris, Vienna, Chicago.

(c) *Transport and communications* are closely influenced by topography. Roads, railways and canals are built over plains, follow valleys and take advantage of gaps and passes in order to avoid steep gradients and other physical obstacles which create construction difficulties and cause running and maintenance costs to be heavy. Where the land is relatively flat, movement is easy unless, as in Holland or the Yangtse delta, it is impeded by a multiplicity of water courses. Although, as was inferred above, aircraft are freer agents than railway engines, motor cars and canal barges, it must be remembered that they need airfields, considerable stretches of level land for taking off and landing.

(*d*) *The configuration of the coastline* may also exert a considerable influence upon human activities, stimulating or withholding fishing, mercantile activities, port development and human settlement. Although one should scrupulously avoid any deterministic interpretation, it is of interest to compare the deeply indented estuarine, ria and fiord coastline of northwestern Europe with its notable maritime developments with the straight and often block-faulted coast of much of Africa, which is deficient in good harbours and which has seldom stimulated mercantile activity.

6. Structure and geology. The geological structure and the types of rocks found in any locality are likely to have important effects upon human settlement and human activities.

(*a*) *Structure* expresses itself mainly in the build of land areas, in folding and faulting which give rise to particular landforms but it may also influence other things of importance to man, *e.g.*:

    (i) sites for dams and hydro-electric power plants;
    (ii) surface and sub-surface supplies of water;
    (iii) the occurrence of mineral wealth and mining; and,
    (iv) to some extent, the tourist industry.

(*b*) The various *types of rock*, of which the earth's surface is composed, have an important influence upon human activities for they are intimately linked with the supply of metals, non-metallic minerals, fuels, water, building stones, soils. To quote two examples:

    (i) *Coal and oil* are both "fossil fuels" of major importance in the world today and both are associated with particular types of sedimentary rocks, while the occurrence of oil is also closely related to specific geological structures.
    (ii) *The composition and internal structures of rocks*, *e.g.* their porosity, their fissuring, determine their water-holding and water-bearing capacity and may also affect the quality of the water, *e.g.* whether it is "hard" or "soft" or is mineralised.

7. Climate. Climate is one of the most important, perhaps *the* most important, of all the factors of the physical environment and it influences man and his activities in numerous ways. In some sense, it is true, man has been able to modify the effects of climate, *e.g.* by such simple expedients as wearing clothes, living in houses, using fires and using artificial lighting, or in the field of agriculture by practising irrigation, draining land or using glasshouses, but extreme climatic conditions present great difficulties which cannot easily be overcome. There is, for instance, little man can do to combat arctic cold or assuage torrential tropical rains. Broadly speaking, where extreme climatic conditions prevail man is unable, on any scale, to mitigate their effects and his activities are limited thereby.

Soils, plant growth, animal husbandry, house types, out-of-door activities, communications are all, to a greater or lesser extent, influenced by the conditions of temperature, rainfall and sunlight experienced in any region. One can illustrate this by recalling that wheat on the Canadian prairies must be spring sown because of the killing frosts of winter; that cotton will not mature where summer temperatures are less than 77°F (25°C); that where the rainfall is less than approximately 10 inches (255 millimetres) concentrated in the growing season crops cannot normally be grown except by irrigation; that soil erosion is likely to occur in hot, dry areas with strong winds or regions of torrential rainfall if there is no protective vegetative cover; and that communications and transport can be seriously affected or interrupted by snow, ice, fog, etc.

8. Soil. The soil is the uppermost layer of the earth's land surface and has been produced by the combined action of several inter-acting factors or conditions:

(*a*) mineral matter supplied by rock which is the *parent material*;

(*b*) the action of climate which actively alters the soil;

(*c*) vegetable matter which supplies most of the *humus* in the soil;

(*d*) biological activity which causes changes in the chemical and physical characteristics; and

(*e*) time, which is a passive agent, assisting soil formation and accumulation.

Soil is especially important to man for all agriculture is based upon it. Since, moreover, the greater part of the world's peoples depend upon agriculture for their livelihood, as well as their very existence in many cases, it will be appreciated how important soil is and why it should be most carefully conserved. The importance of soil is illustrated by the fact that, apart from certain industrial concentrations largely based upon coal-fields, the most densely populated areas are those possessing fertile, frequently alluvial, soils, *e.g.* the North European Plain, the Plain of Hindustan, the Great Plain of North China.

9. Vegetation. The natural vegetation of the earth's surface is largely determined by the climate and the soil. Much, it is true, of the original natural vegetation cover has gone, having been largely destroyed by man. Artificial vegetation or the crops grown by man have replaced the natural vegetation over large areas.

(*a*) *Vegetation,* whether it be natural or artificial, *influences man* in many ways, *e.g.*:

(i) it supplies him with many foodstuffs and raw materials, *e.g.* grain, fruits, vegetable oils, fibres, beverages, medicines;

(ii) it provides him with timber, both soft and hard timber, used for constructional and manufacturing activities; and

(iii) it provides him with pastures on which he can rear his flocks and herds.

The natural vegetation has also influenced man in numerous other ways, especially in the past; it has, for instance, often formed a refuge for peoples, served as a barrier to human movement, and affected man's spiritual and artistic life.

(*b*) It may also be noted that *man, in turn, has influenced the natural vegetation* by:

(i) *clearing away the forest cover,* as in Western Europe, eastern USA, and over much of China;

(ii) *draining land,* thereby driving out water-loving plant species;

(iii) *transplanting species* from one area to another, *e.g.* maize from the Americas to the Old World and the coffee tree from the Old World to the Americas;

(iv) *restricting growth* to the plants required, as in areas of arable farming;

(v) *producing changes in plants* by selection or hybridisation; and

(vi) *afforesting* large areas, often by species which are different from those which originally grew in those areas.

10. Animal life. There is an obvious relationship between animal life and vegetation, no matter whether we think of wild animals or domesticated creatures. Most animals are herbivorous creatures depending upon the plants that grow either on the grasslands or in the forests. Even the carnivores are indirectly dependent upon vegetation for they live off the herbivorous creatures. Some communities (now becoming rapidly reduced), such as nomadic pastoralists, are completely dependent upon the natural pastures, which support their animals, for their existence. The cattle farmer and the sheep farmer is just as dependent upon the presence of suitable pastures as is the Bedouin camel herder or the Lapp reindeer herder.

Many of the smaller creatures, however, are of great significance; *e.g.*:

(a) *The locust is a great menace in many semi-arid areas* and, though much less of a nuisance nowadays than formerly because of a greater measure of scientific control, occasionally locust plagues devour the crops over wide areas.

(b) *Many small insect pests attack and sometimes destroy crops:* one can think of the boll-weevil which attacks the cotton plant, the Colorado beetle, aphis and many others which may be destructive.

(c) *Some insects are carriers of disease:* one of the best examples is the mosquito which is responsible for the spread of malaria, a disease from which more people have suffered and died than perhaps any other.

(d) *Some insect pests are destructive to animals:* one of the best examples is the tsetse fly which makes cattle rearing an impossibility over wide areas of the tropical grasslands of Africa.

(e) *Rodents are very destructive* and a considerable proportion of the food that is produced by man is eaten or made inedible by rats, mice and other infestors.

Thus animal life is at once an asset to man, providing him with meat, milk, hides, skins, furs, ivory, fat and, in some places still, carriage and draughtage, and an enemy, especially when creatures carry disease, ruin his crops or attack his herds and flocks.

11. Reciprocal influence. In the foregoing sections we have tended to stress the influences which the various factors or components of the natural environment have exerted upon man and his activities. But man is a creature with a mind, he is a thinking animal, capable of adaptation, selection and of instituting changes. As his command of science and technology increase, so he becomes less and less dependent upon his natural surroundings. Slowly but surely, he has come to exert an important reciprocal influence upon his environment: for example, he has come to modify the surface features and the soil by terracing and fertilising, by building bridges and tunnelling, by embanking and drainage; he has come to modify the weather and the climate by introducing irrigation and dry farming techniques and by using glasshouses and quick-growing varieties of plants; he has modified vegetable and animal life by cutting down the forest and afforestation, by introducing new breeds of plants and animals, and by using scientific aids such as pesticides, fungicides and the like.

It is likely there will always be *some* limits to human control of the environment but after several thousand years of pitting his wits against nature and, more recently, of *co-operating with* nature, he has found ways and means of overcoming some of the obstacles and handicaps of his natural environment and even found some ways of turning what, initially, were disadvantages into advantages.

PROGRESS TEST 2

1. What is meant by the expression "the physical environment"? (2)

2. Show how the relative position and accessibility of areas may change in time. (3)

3. Explain how relief may affect (*a*) agriculture, (*b*) communications. (5)

4. Why is climate often said to be the most important of all the factors of the physical environment? (7)

5. What is soil and how is it formed? Why is it important to man? (8)

6. In what ways has man modified the natural vegetation of the earth's surface? (9)

7. Explain the importance of animal life in the life of man. (10)

8. Explain briefly the meaning of the following: absolute location; fossil fuels; herbivorous animals. (3, 6, 10)

CHAPTER III

ECONOMIC AND SOCIAL FACTORS

1. Means of earning a living. Generally speaking, the capacity of any area or country to support its people is related to two sets of conditions: natural and human.

Natural conditions determine the resources available; and *human conditions* will determine the degree to which the resources are utilised. Elaborating upon this, we may say that nature offers the essential raw materials for human use, but the extent to which the wide range of natural resources are used for man's benefit depends upon the human response to the environmental conditions and that this response depends, in turn, upon man's cultural development—the thought, the technical expertise, the organisation and the labour he can muster and use.

A country may provide its means of livelihood in a number of different ways:

(a) *By applying its labour force* to develop *its own natural resources* so that it can produce directly what it requires, *e.g.* Britain and coal, the United States and beef, China and rice.

(b) *By applying its labour force* to its own resources and *exporting its surplus production* in return for commodities which it cannot itself produce, *e.g.* Britain and iron and steel goods, Sweden and timber, Cuba and sugar.

(c) *By providing raw materials for some other country* to work up in return for foodstuffs and manufactured goods, *e.g.* Australia and wool, Malaya and tin, Sri Lanka and copra.

(d) *By providing labour to process and fabricate raw materials* not available at home and imported from other countries, *e.g.* Britain and cotton manufacturing, Switzerland and engineering products.

(e) *By providing labour and transport for the carriage of goods,* whether foodstuffs, raw materials or manufactured goods, from producing to consuming centres, *e.g.* British air lines, Norway's mercantile marine, Syria's oil pipelines.

ECONOMIC CONSIDERATIONS

2. The basic economic factors. The general economic conditions which largely determine a country's capacity to support its people are:

  (a) the possibilities for procuring *food*;
  (b) the available supplies of *raw materials*;
  (c) the available sources of *power*;
  (d) the facilities which exist for *transport.*

3. Food supplies. Except for a few small groups of primitive people, who live by collecting and hunting, *no large groupings of people can live purely and simply off the bounty of nature.* Some are largely dependent upon a single basic food resource, *e.g.* Icelanders who eat large quantities of fish, Bedouins who subsist mainly upon milk and milk products. In such cases a particular diet is dictated by the inability of the lands they dwell in to produce much in the way of food crops. *But where nature has provided favourable conditions of soil and climate man is able to grow varied crops and rear animals for food.* The kinds of crops and the kinds of animals raised depend in part upon the environmental conditions and in part upon the socio-economic conditions. Nature, however, sets certain limitations upon particular kinds of production and man ignores such limitations only at considerable risk; for example, many mid-western farmers in the United States flew into the very teeth of nature by planting wheat on *marginal land* (*i.e.* land which is barely worth cultivating) and ended up by creating a "dust-bowl" and bringing disaster upon themselves.

4. Raw materials. *All raw materials fall into three categories: animal, vegetable and mineral.* Animal and vegetable resources depend upon climate and soil. The geographical distribution of animal and vegetable species is often comparatively restricted; where they are widely spread it is often the result of human interference. Mineral resources depend upon geological structure.

The occurrence of specific minerals is frequently very restricted and most are very unevenly distributed. Water, which may be regarded as a mineral, is of prime importance and its quantity and quality are factors of major significance in influencing settlement, agriculture, grazing, manufacturing industry, power supplies and transportation. Animals, plants and minerals vary in their value and utility to man in his business of getting a living, but they supply his basic needs of food, clothing and shelter, and provide the bases for his industrial and commercial activities.

5. Power resources. At first man was dependent upon his own muscle power for fetching and carrying. In some areas man, or his animals, still provide most of the power. But in the more developed countries animate power has been replaced by *inanimate forms of energy*, such as *wind, running water, steam, oil, gas* and *electricity*. Modern scientific and technological development depends upon plentiful power resources and the demand for energy grows apace.

The increasing mechanisation of life—whether in agriculture, industry or transport—requires increasing amounts of energy. Since the Industrial Revolution, coal has been the most important basic source of power and the great industrial areas were, and to a great extent still are, tied to the coalfields. Lack of coal, for instance, has been one reason handicapping industrial development in South American countries.

6. Transport facilities. Facilities for communication and transport form a fourth determinant. *An efficient system of transport is necessary for the economy of any country.* An effective, low-cost transport system reduces distribution costs, and thereby permits wider markets and larger-scale production. An efficient transport system facilitates the movement of raw materials, of workers and of finished goods, and in this way allows firms a wider choice in the locations of their factories, so enabling them to choose sites which offer the greatest economic advantages. Again, the wider the distribution of commodities, the greater the choice available to buyers.

The great importance of transport facilities is amply demonstrated by the fact that national plans almost always include substantial provision for the extension and improvement of the transportation networks, *e.g.* Britain's current projects for new motorways, improved port developments.

HUMAN FACTORS

7. Social factors. The capacity of a country to support its people depends not only upon its quota of natural resources but on the human factor also. Natural resources lie in the potential stage until man finds a use for them and until man has the scientific and technical ability to use them. Among the more important social conditions are:

(a) physical health and well-being;
(b) standard of education;
(c) standard of living; and
(d) level of culture.

8. Physical health. *Physical health and well-being is an important factor influencing the energy and productiveness of peoples.* Some are more robust and energetic than others, but these characteristics are due rather to general health, food and climate than to any innate racial differences. The Hindus, Malays and South American Indians are often said to be lazy but this is probably the result of the environmental conditions in which they live and not to any inferiority in their physical make-up. Tropical environments tend to be enervating and energy-sapping diseases such as *bilharziasis* are rife. Cool temperate climates, with distinct seasonal, even daily, changes appear to offer the best conditions for a maximum output of energy. Such climatic change probably acts also as a mental stimulus: certainly the most notable advances in modern science, technology and the arts have come from peoples living in such environments.

9. Educational standards. *The leading countries at the present time are those with the best-educated peoples*; the most backward ones are, in general, those with the highest illiteracy rates. Education is a means of developing and directing natural intelligence. Intelligent enquiry and thought lie behind scientific discovery, mechanical invention, the application of power resources and the organisation of transport.

Educated peoples are better able to support themselves for they can apply their science and technology to the development of the natural resources and save man the drudgery of manual toil. Skill, foresight and organisation are essential qualities in economic development and these qualities are all manifestations of trained intelligence. Countries lacking adequate educational facilities are incapable of realising and organising their resources and are apt to squander and waste such resources as they have.

10. Standard of living. It is a truism that *countries which are most economical in the use of their resources are able to support the most people.* Such economical use can be interpreted in two ways:

> (*a*) it may involve everyone having less than he requires, which is a very undesirable form of it; *or*
> (*b*) it may involve getting the best results with the minimum of waste, which is a good form of it.

In general, countries possessing and demanding high living standards must be prepared to work hardest; the only alternative is for them to be content to support fewer people than those countries willing to tolerate a lower standard. Usually they are willing to work hardest. Usually, too, their people are well educated, possessing skill, foresight and organising ability which lead, in turn, to large-scale, highly-mechanised, well co-ordinated production. Better living standards, or the promise of them, are a great spur to increased economic effort.

11. Cultural level. *The level of culture*—using the term "culture" in its widest sense—*is an important factor in economic production.* Clearly, the primitive peoples of New Guinea who are still often in the Stone Age are incapable of competing with Europeans. Backward countries which have a limited technological development, *e.g.* many of the native African countries, are at a disadvantage compared with European countries. The higher the cultural level the better are people able to develop and use natural resources to support themselves.

Moreover, certain cultural traits, *e.g.* religion, social systems such as the Hindu caste system, may influence man's activities and these may affect economic production and the capacity of a country to support its population, *e.g.*:

> (*a*) *The Buddhist proscription of killing* includes animals and this, therefore, predisposes towards a vegetarian diet and a poorly developed animal industry.
> (*b*) *The Hindu reverence for cattle* has led to vast numbers of

virtually useless creatures lumbering the countryside and form-
ing a great drain on an already short food supply.

(c) *The Moslem attitude to certain economic activities* such as
mining, trading and money-lending, which are forbidden, acts
as a restrictive force.

(d) *Many African pastoralists* count their wealth in terms of
the number of cattle they possess; their quality, *i.e.* their
economic value, is a very secondary consideration.

(e) *The Roman Church's proscription of meat on Fridays*
formerly helped to stimulate the fishing industry and the trade
in fish.

(f) *Among many peoples*, though the actual preparation of the
ground is done by the menfolk, the tillage, planting, weeding
and harvesting is beneath their dignity and must be undertaken
by the womenfolk.

In these and many other ways culture features may be of great
social significance, exercising powerful influences on such
things as animal husbandry, food habits and human attitudes
with respect to work, progress and the like.

ECONOMIC SYSTEMS

12. Opposing systems. In this chapter we have been concerned with the economic and social factors which affect man's
capacity to make the best use he can of what nature offers and
to earn a livelihood for himself. Let us conclude by looking
briefly at the politico-economic systems that have developed
to achieve these ends.

Economic production and consumption vary widely between
people and people and country and country but, in a broad
way, there are two diametrically opposed systems which
regulate production and consumption:

(a) *The laissez-faire economy*, which held sway in the nineteenth century and continues to be followed in part at the
present day, which places a *minimum of restrictions* upon
economic activities.

(b) *The planned economy*, essentially a twentieth-century
development, which denies economic liberty and substitutes
for it a *rigidly controlled system* directed by some central
authority.

13. Capitalistic economies. Adam Smith, in his book *The Wealth of Nations* (1776), advocated a *laissez-faire* attitude in matters economic, believing that this was the best possible way of stimulating production. Economic freedom of this kind suited the nineteenth-century situation and both Britain and the United States reached high levels of economic productivity, progress and prosperity under economic *laissez-faire* in which capitalism held sway.

While many countries and many individuals prospered under such a system, the *laissez-faire* attitude implies that the weakest go to the wall and many people suffer from economic exploitation and social distress. The United States is the example, *par excellence*, of a free, largely uninhibited, capitalistic society, but it has given to the *majority* a standard of living unmatched anywhere else in the world. This arises out of its truly astonishing economic productivity. However, it should be emphasised that in this the United States has been blessed with a superlative natural endowment.

14. Planned economies. Karl Marx, the father of Communism, believed that if the greatest number were to benefit from economic production it should be taken out of the hands of individuals, whom he looked upon as ruthless, selfish capitalists, and be managed by some central authority for the benefit of the workers. Such authority would plan production and eliminate waste; it would ensure decent rewards and living conditions for all, preventing economic exploitation and social strife.

The Soviet Union was the first country to order itself upon communist principles and it can, after more than fifty years of endeavour, claim a fair degree of success. The communist pattern, however, inevitably leads to dictatorship by the central authority; and such "economic dictatorship" probably has as many faults and weaknesses as "capitalist economics."

15. Mixed economies. The failures of the capitalist system and the successes of communist planning, together with the economic disaster of the Second World War, led most of the so-called capitalist countries to adopt a measure of planning. While the United States, Britain, West Germany and Japan base their economies very largely upon private enterprise, they have all taken a leaf out of the communist book. For example, the most important single participant in economic activity in Britain at the present time is H.M. Government and the role of the government in planning and directing the national economy is, patently, going to increase. Even in the United States, the mightiest stronghold of the capitalist system, government interference is now well established.

Most of the underdeveloped countries are convinced that rapid economic advancement can be achieved only by a considerable measure of economic planning. On the other hand, and rather ironically, we see at the present day the Soviet Union flirting with the profit motive in an attempt to stimulate greater interest, efficiency and productivity in economic enterprises.

Thus, in practical terms, the economic systems of the countries of the world in most cases contain elements of both capitalistic enterprise and State planning, although this does not invalidate a broad division into those countries in which private enterprise is largely responsible for economic activity and those with predominantly planned economies.

PROGRESS TEST 3

1. Outline the five different ways in which a country may earn its livelihood. (1)

2. What are the basic economic factors which influence a country's ability to support its people? (2–6)

3. Give *four* examples to illustrate how cultural factors may influence human activities. (11)

4. Show how (a) physical health, and (b) the standard of education, may influence economic development. (7–9)

5. Explain the meaning of the following expressions: standard of living; *laissez-faire* economics; economic planning. (10, 12, 13, 14)

6. In what ways is an efficient system of transport necessary to the economy of a country? (6)

SUGGESTED PROJECTS

1. Using encyclopaedias and biographical dictionaries, find out as much as you can about Adam Smith and Karl Marx and write brief biographical essays on each.

2. Using reference books and encyclopaedias, write accounts of the economic and social conditions of:

(a) the Bedouins of Arabia; and
(b) the aborigines of New Guinea.

3. Since the end of the Second World War both India and China have made determined efforts to industrialise and modernise themselves. India has approached the problem through democratic planning and private enterprise, China by means of a rigorously controlled state planning system on communist lines. Find out as much as you can about these two countries and compare the results of these differing approaches to the same problem.

CHAPTER IV

THE EARTH'S RESOURCES

WEALTH AND RESOURCES

1. The meaning of wealth. To most people wealth means money. Although the terms "money" and "wealth" are loosely used to mean the same thing, to the economist they have very different meanings.

Money, in the economic sense, is merely *a medium for buying things, a token of exchange.*

Wealth, in the economic sense, means *land, goods, services* or, differently expressed, *natural resources.*

2. What are natural resources? Man lives in an environment, but in order to live—in the sense of to survive—in that environment he must derive from it certain basic items of human need: air, light, water, food, warmth, clothing, shelter. From these basic items he can sustain life. In the beginning, primitive man sustained life at the lowest level; he just managed to endure life. Today, most people desire to do something more than merely endure life; they want to enjoy it. Hence, in addition to procuring the basic necessities for existence, man wants some luxuries *e.g.* motor cars, gold watches, fine paintings.

All these human needs, however. no matter whether they be absolute necessities or frivolous luxuries, have to come from the earth's natural resources: air, sunlight, water, land, soil, vegetation, animal life and minerals. These he uses to satisfy his many needs. Basically, therefore, it is these natural resources which can be turned into useful products by the skill of man that constitute the real wealth of the world.

3. Kinds of natural resources. The natural resources which are available for man's use fall into two main groups:

(*a*) *Organic* or *living resources:* these include forests, natural pastures, wild-life, fish and other marine life.

(b) *Inorganic* or *non-living resources:* these inanimate resources include air, water, mineral fuels, metals, non-metallic minerals and building stones.

NOTE: Soil, which is composed of both organic and inorganic matter, falls between the two groups, but it is a resource of fundamental importance.

4. Latent resources. Before we proceed to look more closely at these various resources one point needs emphasising. Although nature has provided a wide range of resources for human use, *such resources do not become of significance or value to man until he has reached a particular stage of cultural development.* The resources are present, but they remain hidden or unused until man requires them, *i.e.* until he has a use for them. For example:

(a) *Metals* (*see* XIV). Primitive man used stones and flints for weapons. He could not begin to make his weapons and tools of metal until:

(i) he had learned how to distinguish metallic ores from ordinary rock;
(ii) he discovered techniques of smelting the ores to extract the metals.

(b) *Rubber* (*see* XIII). The latex of the rubber tree had long been known about, but rubber had little utility until certain developments in technology:

(i) until the method of vulcanisation was discovered which enabled the natural rubber to be hardened and which got rid of its stickiness;
(ii) until the invention of the pneumatic tyre and the advent of the motor vehicle which created the demand for rubber.

(c) *Petroleum* (*see* XV). Oil has been known (as bitumen) since biblical times but its potentialities as a fuel were not realised until about a century ago; but oil could not be used until:

(i) a use had been found for it as a fuel, with the invention of the internal combustion engine;
(ii) the process of distillation had been discovered by technologists;
(iii) the science of geology had become sufficiently advanced to be able to locate petroleum deposits.

Resources of this kind may be described as *latent resources*. Only when man finds a use for them and is capable of using them do they come to have any real meaning or value to him and only then are they realised. As a recent writer has said: "Resources are a function of culture."* Donald J. Volk

THE EARTH'S NATURAL RESOURCES

5. Soil. Soil is a fundamental natural resource and of tremendous importance to man and almost all living organisms, because the bulk of the world's food is grown in the earth's superficial covering of soil or comes from animals which feed on the vegetation growing in the soil. The soil is also the ultimate source of a wide range of industrial raw materials, *e.g.* timber, cotton, tobacco, vegetable oils.

(*a*) *Soil is composed of inorganic matter* (broken, pulverised rock) *and organic matter* (humus or decayed vegetable matter). It is important to plants, which cannot live without it, because:

    (i) it serves as a medium for seed germination;
    (ii) it acts as an anchorage for growing plants;
    (iii) it is a source of moisture and plant nutrients.

(*b*) Soil is a substance of *much greater complexity* than most people realise. It is not something dead, lifeless, immovable, inexhaustible; rather should we look upon it as being dynamic and destructible. Soil is slow to form (on average about 1 inch of it per century) but easily lost. Under certain conditions soil can be lost, a process known as *soil erosion*; this happens by:

    (i) the soil being washed away by torrential rain; and
    (ii) the soil being blown away by strong winds.

To allow soil to be lost in either of these ways is almost criminal for, in view of the world's rapidly growing population, we can ill afford to lose even one square yard of soil.

6. Vegetation. Cultivated crops apart, natural pastures and forests form important natural resources.

(*a*) *Grazing lands.* Many animals, especially the world's beef cattle and wool sheep, depend upon the natural pastures of the

* Donald J. Volk, "Natural Resource Use as a Focus for Geographic Education," *The Journal of Geography*, February 1967, p. 73.

prairies, pampas, steppes and savannas. Many wild grass-eating animals (herbivores) also depend on nature's grazing lands. The natural grasslands in themselves yield few commercial products—esparto grass is one of the most important—but they are essential for large-scale pastoral farming (*see* XII).

(*b*) *Forests.* The world's forests supply man with two groups of commodities (*see* XIII):

(i) timbers, both hardwoods and softwoods of various kinds, used for constructional work, furniture, woodpulp and, sometimes, fuel; and

(ii) forest products, such as vegetable oils and waxes, rubber, cork, gums, resins and fibres, which have uses as medicines, foods or industrial raw materials.

7. Animals. Man makes use of the animal world for a variety of reasons; he uses animals for:

(*a*) carrying and draughtage;
(*b*) foodstuffs, *e.g.* meat, milk, eggs;
(*c*) raw materials, *e.g.* wool, hides, horn.

In times gone by, many lived by herding animals, as a few peoples do even today; but nomadic pastoralism as a way of life is rapidly declining and disappearing from the scene. On the other hand, man is becoming more and more dependent upon certain types of animals for foodstuffs and industrial raw materials (*see* XII). Some species have become extinct, through ruthless extermination, while many others are gradually dying out.

Fish and other marine creatures are included among the animal resources and yield important supplies of fish-food, fish-oil, fertiliser and lesser commodities of a precious or semi-precious character, *e.g.* coral, pearls, fur, ivory.

8. Minerals. The earth's crust contains a variety of mineral resources of great use to man and which may be said to be indispensable in modern civilisation. These mineral resources may be divided into four main groups:

(*a*) Mineral fuels, such as coal and petroleum (*see* XV).
(*b*) Metals, such as iron, tin, copper and gold (*see* XIV).
(*c*) Non-metallic minerals, such as salt, sulphur and nitrate (*see* XIV).
(*d*) Constructional materials, such as sandstone, granite and clay.

The occurrence and distribution of minerals varies widely. Building stones, gravel and clay are widely spread and abundant except locally. Metals, which occur chiefly in the older rocks, vary greatly: some, like iron, are relatively plentiful; others, such as cobalt, are of limited occurrence. Some metals have been used for a long time and consumed in appreciable quantities whereas others are of recent discovery, of limited occurrence and fairly scarce. The mineral fuels are associated with sedimentary rocks and are concentrated in particular regions.

9. Water. Though so common, water is one of the most precious of all the natural resources. Water is indispensable for life but, quite apart from its crucial importance in this respect, it has numerous other uses, *e.g.*:

(*a*) *Domestic uses*—drinking, cooking, bathing, washing, sanitation, garden watering.

(*b*) *Municipal uses*—fire fighting, street cleansing, in hospitals, in schools.

(*c*) *Agriculture*—watering stock and crop growing, especially in arid and semi-arid regions where irrigation must be practised.

(*d*) *Industry*—for cleaning and processing commodities, for steam generation, for cooling purposes.

(*e*) *Power*—in earlier times running water turned waterwheels but nowadays the water is mostly used in the production of hydro-electric power.

(*f*) *Effluent disposal*—water is used to transport wastes from urban and industrial areas.

(*g*) *Transport*—waterways (rivers or canals) are utilised for the cheap carriage of commodities.

(*h*) *Food supplies*—water areas provide habitats for fish which in some areas may be significant as an article in the diet.

(*i*) *Recreation*—water may have an amenity value, providing opportunities for sporting activities or merely serving an aesthetic purpose.

The graph in Fig. 1 shows the increasing demand for water for these purposes in the United States.

10. Air. Air, along with water, is necessary for life. Without air neither man, nor animals, nor plants could breathe and live. The other planets in the solar system appear to be lifeless and one important contributing factor explaining this is that, unlike the earth, most of them have no atmosphere.

Air has uses to man besides merely providing him with the necessary oxygen to live: it helps to keep the earth's surface warm, it is a medium for carrying moisture around, it permits man to use air transport, and can be a source of nitrogen for the making of nitrates for fertilisers (although little, if any, is used for this purpose nowadays).

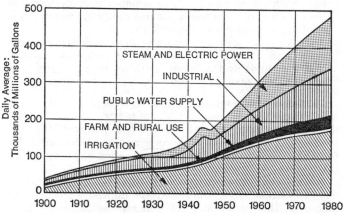

FIG. 1.—*Graph of water use in the United States*

Note (*a*) the large quantities of water required for the purposes of irrigation, industry and the generation of power; (*b*) the rapidly growing demand for water, particularly for industrial and power requirements: during the past 25 years the demand has more than doubled; (*c*) the estimated increase up to 1980.

THE CONSERVATION OF RESOURCES

11. The nature of resources. The earth's natural resources fall into two classes:

(*a*) *Inexhaustible resources*, *i.e.* those which will never run out and supplies of which will always be available.

(*b*) *Exhaustible resources*, *i.e.* those of which there is a limited supply and which, sooner or later, will be used up.

12. Inexhaustible resources. Air and water are the only two really inexhaustible resources.

(*a*) *Air*. Short of something catastrophic happening, the earth will always have its envelope of air around it. This does not mean that man cannot foul the air (for man has long liberated smoke and noxious gases into it) or contaminate it (by radioactive fall-out for instance) but, such things apart, there is no prospect of supplies of good, clean, fresh air running out.

(b) *Water.* Though there may be local shortages, there is no likelihood of overall water supplies ever running out. Unlike some of the earth's natural resources, water can be used and re-used but never used up.

(c) *Mineral resources.* Certain of these, such as most rocks, gravel and sand and clay, are present in such vast quantities that it is unlikely that there will ever be any shortage of them, except perhaps locally.

13. Exhaustible resources. The other resources—soil, vegetation, animal life and certain types of mineral wealth—are not inexhaustible. Soil, natural vegetation and animal life can be so managed that they could become nearly inexhaustible, but until very recent times little or no attention has been paid to this matter.

Mineral matter which is mined from the earth's crust is definitely exhaustible. Once used, the mineral wealth is gone. Moreover, the earth's store of mineral wealth, which is relatively limited, cannot be expected to meet indefinitely the great and constantly rising demand.

14. Conservation. Since some natural resources are of limited supply and are a decreasing asset, it becomes important to think about, and to practise, conservation of resources.

Conservation may be defined as *the careful and rational use of natural resources and their preservation from reckless exploitation and wanton destruction.* Conservation implies the careful control and management of resources so that they may continue to be of use and benefit to posterity. Conservation, as Monkhouse says, "is not so much a 'hold-back' as the maintenance of a favourable balance in the use of the environment."*

Let us now look briefly at the ways in which man can conserve the various natural resources.

15. Soil. Soil, as we have already noted, can be easily lost: it needs very careful use and management for its maintenance.

* *A Dictionary of Geography*, Arnold, 1965, p. 75.

If farmers neglect the soil it gradually becomes exhausted, useless, and may even be completely lost. Soil must be carefully tilled, continually replenished and periodically rested (not necessarily by allowing it to lie fallow), if it is to remain in good tilth, fertile and productive. Unfortunately, there are too many farmers the world over who are content to "mine" the soil, to rob it of its fertility, and who do not, or cannot, care for their soil properly.

Soil erosion, above all else, must be prevented. More soil is in fact, now being lost each year than nature makes; thus the soil is a shrinking asset. Obviously this cannot be allowed to go on indefinitely; only drastic action on the part of man can be really effective in reversing this trend. A great deal can be done to stop or hold in check soil erosion by following practices to combat it, such as:

(*a*) terracing sloping land to prevent soil being washed away;

(*b*) building walls across gullies to catch the soil being removed;

(*c*) contour ploughing, *i.e.* ploughing around instead of up and down hillsides;

(*d*) adopting, in heavy rain regions, the "basin" type of cultivation;

(*e*) rotating crops and growing "cover crops" between the main crops;

(*f*) replanting land denuded of vegetation with trees and grasses;

(*g*) erecting wind-breaks and shelter belts to lessen wind erosion;

(*h*) strictly limiting the number of animals to the bearing capacity of the pasture.

16. Natural vegetation: forests. Forests formerly covered a much larger area than they do today, but land was cleared because of:

(*a*) the need of land for cultivation;

(*b*) the demand for timber, for constructional purposes; fuel and charcoal making; and, more recently, for woodpulp and rayon.

NOTE: In spite of the growth of synthetic products and substitute materials, the demand for timber is greater than ever before and continues to increase. It becomes clear that a timber famine is likely in the future unless the wholesale depletion of forests is stopped and a programme of afforestation is vigorously adopted. Many countries, especially those that depend to a great extent upon their forest resources, such as Norway, Sweden and Finland, have adopted stringent forestry laws to conserve their timber resources but in many other countries progressive planting should be adopted. Moreover, man should be experimenting with alternative materials for the production of paper, for instance, since the paper industry is a greedy consumer of timber. In Ecuador experiments in the use of banana trash for the making of paper have been successfully undertaken; thus, alternative raw materials could be sought.

17. Natural vegetation: pastures. Many of the world's natural pastures are suffering, quite unnecessarily, from neglect and progressive deterioration.

(a) The causes of deterioration are:

    (i) the encroachment of the deserts along the margins; and

    (ii) overgrazing by stock which is reducing the carrying capacity.

(b) Man could do much to restore and improve these natural pastures by:

    (i) limiting the numbers of stock to the carrying capacity of the land;

    (ii) stopping ploughing up grassland in marginal areas; and

    (iii) attempting a certain amount of judicious reseeding.

18. Animal life. At the present time, as a result of breeding, man can very largely control the numbers of his domesticated animals. Wild life is in a much less happy state. Many useful and valuable species are becoming extinct owing to wanton killing or the destruction of their natural habitats.

(a) *The natural game of Africa* are being lost partly through the shrinkage of the area of their natural habitat and partly through illegal poaching, *e.g.* the elephant which is hunted by the natives for its tusks. Many of the animals of the African grasslands, if properly husbanded, could be made to yield valuable food supplies.

(b) *Marine creatures,* such as the whale, walrus, otter-seal, have been hunted almost to extinction; moreover, in certain areas, there has been over-fishing with the consequent depletion of the fisheries and the loss of important supplies of protein food.

Fortunately, man is now beginning to appreciate the importance of wild life and notable steps have already been taken to help preserve some of the declining animal population. But more needs to be done and there is an urgent need for closer international control of world fishery resources. An aspect, too, which man is only just beginning to be aware of is the fine state of balance which exists in nature; if he upsets this balance by killing off (through his use of chemical fertilisers, insecticides, etc.) insects, birds and other creatures, he may create even greater difficulties for himself in the future.

19. Minerals. Minerals differ from most of the other resources in that once mined they are lost to the earth's crust forever: in other words, minerals are essentially exhaustible resources and the earth's stock of mineral wealth is quickly being depleted. Already many deposits of certain minerals have been exhausted and there is a certain anxiety about some mineral wealth, more especially the fossil fuels. Since minerals are irreplaceable, it is important that they should be used sensibly, especially those that are in limited supply.

The conservation of minerals can be undertaken in various ways:

(a) care must be taken not to use them wastefully as often happened in the past;

(b) improved methods of extraction must be adopted whever this is feasible;

(c) the efficient recovery of minerals that have already been once used must be practised;

(d) substitute materials should be used wherever this is possible.

By adopting these methods great economies could be effected in the use of mineral wealth.

20. Water. Water, as we have already said, is not in any real sense short. But locally, or regionally, water supplies may be short. We are now reaching the stage where we are becoming water conscious and realising that there is a need for conservation of water supplies. It must be recognised that the provision of extra supplies of water often incurs great capital cost in the form of reservoirs, dams and pipes.

Water supplies, particularly in areas where pressure upon supplies is beginning to mount up and where many varying demands are put upon the available supplies, could be conserved by:

(a) metering water supplies and increasing the cost of water;

(b) limiting pollution through controlling the amount of effluent discharged into rivers;

(c) re-cycling water, particularly in some industries which are greedy users of water;

(d) making more efficient use of the water that is used;

(e) preventing waste through pipe leakages, evaporation, and so on;

(f) re-charging sub-surface supplies of water.

21. Conclusion. The welfare of the peoples of the future demands that we should adopt a more rational view with respect to the world's natural resources. But, as Volk says, a study of natural resources "should emphasise the possibilities inherent in substitutability and interdependence of resources rather than simply dwelling upon the need for 'conservation' of various resources considered in isolation."* The careful, rational, intelligent use of resources will entail the removal of human ignorance and carelessness and a measure of control and co-operation among the peoples and states of the world.

PROGRESS TEST 4

1. What is understood by the term "natural resources"? List the principal kinds of resources. (2, 3)

2. Elaborate the following statement: "natural resources fall into two main groups—organic and inorganic resources." (3, 5–10)

3. Explain carefully the meaning of the phrases: latent resources; exhaustible resources; inexhaustible resources. (4, 11–13)

4. In what different ways is water of use to man? (9)

5. What is soil erosion? In what ways may man combat soil erosion? (5, 15)

6. Explain the different ways in which the mineral wealth of the world may be conserved. (19)

* See **14** above.

7. What is meant by the conservation of natural resources? **(14)**

8. In what ways are natural pastures and forests of use to man? **(6)**

9. Explain briefly the meaning of the following: terracing; contour ploughing; humus; effluent; money. **(1, 5, 9, 15)**

SUGGESTED PROJECTS

1. Find out as much as you can about water and give a full account of its occurrence, uses, value and any relevant problems or developments.

2. Make a full study of soil under the following headings:

(a) the composition and character of soil;
(b) the importance and function of soil;
(c) the chief types of soil;
(d) soil erosion; and
(e) the protection and conservation of soil.

CHAPTER V

THE ECONOMIC ACTIVITIES OF MAN

ECONOMIC ACTIVITIES

1. Basic human needs. In order that man may live certain basic needs must be satisfied: these are water, food, clothing, shelter. Most of man's life and most of his energies are spent in supplying these needs. The ways and means he adopts to satisfy these essential wants are many and vary regionally.

In some environments the physical conditions of relief, soil, climate and vegetation make life extremely difficult; nature is niggardly and limits the available resources by which man can live. On the other hand, nature offers much less restrictive conditions in some areas and man finds it much easier to live; nature is more bountiful and offers a wider range of resources.

2. The use of the environment. While some peoples have learned little about using the resources which nature provides, others have learned much. The more man learns concerning the ways of using what his environment offers, the easier will his life become. If man merely lives off the land, *i.e.* merely collects the fruits of nature, his existence will be hazardous. Once he has learned the art of cultivation, however, his food supply becomes more assured. Food production, as distinct from food collecting, relieves him of the necessity of moving around constantly from place to place; it enables him to live a sedentary life: he can live and work in one spot.

3. The dawn of civilisation. The discovery of the art of growing crops was one of a number of developments (including the domestication of animals, the making of pottery and the weaving of cloth) which ushered in the New Stone Age or the Neolithic Revolution, somewhere about seven or eight thousand years ago. These inventions, which seem to have occurred in the Near and Middle East, had very important effects upon human life and may be said to have formed the basis of *civilised life*, as distinct from the barbarism and savagery which prevailed previously.

The art of cultivation made it possible for:

(*a*) man to live in one place permanently; and
(*b*) large groups of people to live together.

A sedentary and communal life allowed other things to follow:

(*c*) man could have a permanent dwelling and could acquire possessions;
(*d*) specialisation of labour, *i.e.* division of work, became possible;
(*e*) division of labour brought increased leisure which allowed artistic and literary developments to take place.

From this cultural revolution civilised life developed and a whole series of civilisations emerged, *e.g.* the Egyptian, Greek and Roman. Western civilisation as we understand it today is based upon, and has grown out of, these early cultures: it is merely the *culmination of cultural evolution*.

4. Cultural paradox. During several millenia of development man has come a long way, making many discoveries and inventing many things. The twentieth century, with its electronic devices, supersonic jets, nuclear power, is a far cry from the Neolithic Age. And yet, even at the present day, there are peoples in various parts of the world who live in much the same way as did the people of the Neolithic period. Here is one of the great paradoxes of our time: that side by side with the scientific and technologically advanced societies there are communities who base their existence upon the simple economies which prevailed in Neolithic times.

Let us now look at the different ways in which man, both in the past and at present, has lived and earned his livelihood. The world distribution of man's principal economies is shown in Fig. 2.

SIMPLE SOCIETIES

5. Collectors and hunters. In the very earliest stages of his cultural development, man was a food collector and petty hunter; he gathered wild fruits, nuts, roots, grubs, wild honey, and undertook fishing, the snaring of small fry and hunting. Living by such simple means, and entirely upon the bounty of nature, meant that man was compelled to live in small groups—perhaps limited to the family group—simply because the available food supplies in any area were incapable of

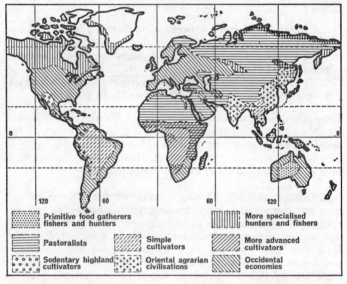

Primitive food gatherers fishers and hunters | More specialised hunters and fishers

Pastoralists | Simple cultivators | More advanced cultivators

Sedentary highland cultivators | Oriental agrarian civilisations | Occidental economies

FIG. 2.—*The principal economies of mankind*

This map, showing the principal modes of life, is of course generalised. Much of Asia is shown as being under pastoralism but there are many localities where cultivation takes place, as in the oasis settlements of Central Asia. Moreover, the map takes no account of mining or industrial activities which clearly are widespread in Europe and the United States and occur elsewhere in the world.

supporting more than a few people. *The size of the group, or in other words the density of the population, was limited by the productivity per square mile of land.*

Small groups of people still follow this mode of life; usually they live in the more remote and inaccessible areas.

Examples are:

(a) some of the *Eskimo and Indian tribes* of the arctic regions of North America:

(b) the *Yaghans* of Tierra del Fuego in the cold, bleak southern extremity of South America;

(c) the *Pygmies* of the hot, wet equatorial forests of the Congo basin in central Africa;

(d) the primitive but hardy *Bushmen* of the Kalahari Desert in South-west Africa;

(e) the *aborigines* or *Blackfellows* of Australia who dwell in the northern and semi-arid lands of that continent.

6. Herding and nomadism.

The domestication of animals meant that man instead of hunting animals began to herd them. Some wild animals, *e.g.* cattle, sheep, goats, horses, were amenable to domestication and these he tamed and herded. Such animals were especially useful to man for they provided food (milk and meat), raw materials (hides and hair), and could be used as pack- or draught-animals.

Such animals were herbivorous, *i.e.* grass-eating, and they wandered over the pasturelands in search of forage. In the beginning, man wandered with them, going whither they would; later he organised or systematised their movements so that *definite seasonal migrations from area to area* took place. Such wandering movement is called *nomadism*.

Formerly most pastoral people were nomadic; a few groups remain so still, though the numbers engaged in nomadic herding are rapidly declining.

(a) The *Bedouin* of Arabia continue to wander with their camels and horses from oasis to oasis. They breed camels and horses which they sell to the settled peoples living around the desert margins. In the past they also carried trade and were not averse to occasional raiding. They live very largely on milk and dates.

(b) The *Kirghiz* of the central Asian steppes were until quite recent times nomads rearing horses and sheep, but their migratory mode of life has been changed during the past generation or so by the Soviet Government which has "collectivised" animal herding.

(c) The *Fulani and Masai* of the African Sudan are traditionally pastoralists. These Negro tribes rear herds of cattle or, in the drier areas, flocks of goats. They count their wealth in the numbers of animals they possess. The Masai frequently drink the blood of their cattle.

(d) The *Lapps, Samoyeds and Tungus*, who live on the

northern tundra margins of Eurasia are rearers of reindeer. The reindeer provide milk, meat, hair and hide and are the basis of this nomadic existence.

NOTE: *Transhumance* is not to be confused with nomadism, although many nomadic herders practise transhumance. Transhumance may be defined as the vertical movement of flocks and herds up and down mountains according to the season in search of fresh pasture. It is essentially a response to (*i*) a shortage of arable land, and (*ii*) a shortage of pasture.

7. Primitive cultivators.

Many peoples are simple cultivators, growing crops upon which they subsist. Often the primitive cultivator is a food collector and hunter also. Even herders will sometimes grow crops if conditions are suitable and they sojourn a while in a given spot.

NOTE: This shows the inadequacy of trying to classify human activities too rigidly: and this is a matter constantly to be borne in mind, for people, particularly at the primitive level, are seldom exclusively food gatherers, fishers, hunters, herders or cultivators.

Simple cultivation is either of the shifting kind or the sedentary type:

(*a*) *Shifting cultivation*. This, widely practised in the tropical zone, involves the clearing of the vegetation cover, usually by the "slash and burn" technique, the planting of seeds, tubers or cuttings either by crude hoeing or simply by making holes in the ground with a digging-stick, and subsequently the harvesting of the crop. Such primitive tillage knows little or nothing of the plough, the rotation of crops or the use of fertilisers. After two or three years of cropping, the soil becomes exhausted and the cultivator clears a fresh patch of land. This practice is sometimes termed *milpa* cultivation. The Boro and other Indian tribes of the Amazon basin, some of the Negro peoples of West Africa and many of the hill tribes of South-east Asia carry on shifting cultivation.

(*b*) *Sedentary cultivation*. Settled cultivation is usually of a more developed kind. Simple cultivation of this kind varies widely, however, ranging from the backward methods pursued by many tropical cultivators to the skilled, highly intensive tillage practised by Oriental subsistence farmers. Peasant agriculturalists often have to work with simple, even crude, implements. Although manures may be used, chemical fertilisers are very seldom used, if only for the simple reason that the peasant cultivator cannot afford them. The peasants of Latin America, Africa and Monsoon Asia are commonly sedentary cultivators. Sometimes, as in the case of the Hausa of northern Nigeria, farming may be more diversified, the cultivators having flocks and herds.

COMPLEX SOCIETIES

8. Commercial fishing. The majority of people live in societies which are much more complex and earn their livelihoods by extractive or manufacturing industry or by performing services of some kind. The economies of complex societies are very largely based upon exchange; they produce primary products or manufactured goods for sale.

An example of an economy of this kind is commercial fishing (*see* XII, **10–16**). The production of fish and other marine products for sale, differs from primitive fishing, which is primarily for subsistence, in both its scale and organisation. Fishing on a commercial basis is normally a highly organised activity employing specialised craft and techniques. Examples are:

(*a*) the cod fisheries of Iceland and the Lofoten Islands of Norway which produce large quantities of cod;

(*b*) the herring fisheries of the north and west coasts of Britain; some of the catch is for home consumption, some is exported;

(*c*) the salmon fisheries of the British Columbian coast upon which is based a great canning industry;

(*d*) the recently developed Peruvian fishing industry whose catch is mainly processed for fish meal (used as a fertiliser).

Whaling, sealing, sponge fishing and pearling are commonly looked upon as branches of the fishing industry. The industry has given rise to many ancillary activities, *e.g.* barrel-making, canning, fish-oil extraction, the making of fertilisers and the manufacture of fishing nets.

9. Commercial grazing. Large-scale commercial grazing is the chief form of land use in the world's drier areas where tillage and forestry are not practicable, *i.e.* in continental interiors where the rainfall is light and occurs seasonally.

Commercial grazing is practically restricted to cattle and

sheep rearing, the two domesticated animals of greatest value, for the production of meat, dairy produce, wool and hides, primarily for export purposes (XII, 1–9).

(a) *Development.* It is an economic activity which has developed largely within the last one hundred years and has been closely related to:

(i) the industrialisation of Western Europe in particular, the growth in population, and higher living standards which have created the market; and

(ii) a series of scientific and technical inventions (*e.g.* the invention of barbed wire, the tin-can, refrigeration, modern machinery and transport) which have enabled supplies to reach the market.

(b) *Areas.* Commercial grazing is carried on in:

(i) *the drier temperate grassland areas, e.g.* the Great Plains of North America, the pampas of Argentina, the veld of South Africa and the interior lowlands of Australia; and

(ii) *the tropical grassland or savanna areas* of some tropical countries, *e.g.* the campos of Brazil, the llanos of Venezuela and Queensland, although the industry is not as well developed in these areas.

10. Commercial agriculture. Commercial farming differs from primitive subsistence agriculture in several respects:

(a) Some or all of the produce is for sale, either in the home market or abroad.

(b) Scientific practices, such as crop rotation, are consciously applied.

(c) Fertilisers, either natural or artificial, are usually much used.

(d) Farming practice is mechanised to a greater or lesser degree.

(e) Special strains and improved varieties of both plants and animals are raised.

As a human activity commercial farming is becoming increasingly specialised, *e.g.* market gardening, fruit-growing, dairying. Specialisation in one form is the concentration upon a particular crop, as in the case of plantation products: single-crop cultivation is known as *monoculture.* At the other extreme is mixed farming, as often practised in Britain, where not only is a variety of crops grown but a variety of animals may also be raised (*see* X and XI).

The application of science and mechanisation to agriculture is revolutionising the industry and reducing drastically, in many instances, the need for manpower.

11. Forestry. Some people—in total their numbers are comparatively small—earn a livelihood through forestry. In some cases forestry is associated with agriculture, as occasionally happens in Britain; and sometimes it is a seasonal occupation, as often happens in the Scandinavian countries.

The exploitable forests are:

(a) *The coniferous softwood forests* of Canada and northern Eurasia which yield constructional timber, wood-pulp, tar and other products.

(b) *The temperate hardwood forests*, now much depleted, of temperate latitudes, providing certain timbers for furniture making, *e.g.* oak, walnut, together with bark and nuts.

(c) *The monsoon deciduous forests*, chiefly of South-east Asia, yielding especially teak but also bamboo and rattan.

(d) *The equatorial forests* of Amazonia, west and central Africa, and the East Indian region, yielding prized cabinet woods, wild rubber and medicinal plants.

The demand for timber continues to increase and in order to replenish supplies many countries are now adopting forest conservation and afforestation programmes (*see* XIII).

12. Mining. The last of the extractive industries is mining. It is an activity going back thousands of years but becomes increasingly important as greater quantities of minerals are used and as more minerals are becoming useful to man (*see* XIV and XV).

(a) *Mineral resources are widely scattered* and often *highly localised*, therefore mining is a form of economic production which is often mixed with cropping, grazing and forestry. Because of the localised occurrence of minerals, there are often concentrations of population in areas which otherwise are unpopulated or very scantily peopled.

(b) *Mineral wealth is the basis of much of modern industry*, hence large numbers of people are engaged in mining either for fuels, such as coal and oil, for metals, such as iron and copper, for non-metallic minerals, such as salt and sulphur, or for building materials, such as sandstone and clay.

(c) *Mineral wealth is exhaustible*, hence mining is a "robber economy." Once used the resource is exhausted and, unlike animate resources, cannot be replenished.

NON-PRIMARY OCCUPATIONS

13. Manufacture. In contrast to all the foregoing types of activities and forms of production, manufacture is a secondary activity. Manufacture uses the primary raw materials from the sea, the land, field and forest to process them and convert them into commodities more useful to man.

In the widest sense manufacturing has a world-wide occurrence. Even the most primitive communities engage in some form of manufacture, *e.g.* the making of tools, pots, cloth. But such "domestic" or "cottage" industries stand contrasted with the highly complex manufacturing activities of modern communities.

More people are employed in manufacturing than any other activity save agriculture. In the more advanced countries, manufacturing is the whole-time occupation of the greater proportion of the population. This is true even of such countries as Denmark and the Netherlands which we tend to think of as being more particularly farming countries. (*See* Part Four, XVI–XX.)

14. Commerce. While the majority of mankind is engaged in primary production of one kind or another or in the secondary activity of manufacturing, a large, and increasing number of people, especially in the more advanced countries, are concerned with activities which do not add directly to the total volume of goods produced. Such people as, for instance, those engaged in buying and selling, in banking, financing and insurance, in transportation and commerce, are equally as necessary as "producers" in modern society.

Commercial activities, those organising, facilitating, and transacting exchange, fall into two groups:

(a) *Traders*, *i.e.* those who act as middlemen between the producer and the consumer, may be said to include in the broad sense, merchants, shippers, brokers, financiers and bankers: and

(b) *Transporters*, *i.e.* those who engineer the movement of goods and people from place to place (XXII and XXIII), *e.g.* lorry drivers, pilots, merchant seamen and those concerned with communications (XXIV), *e.g.* radio operators, telephonists.

Activities of this kind are usually termed *tertiary activities*.

15. Service occupations. A large and increasing number of people, especially in advanced societies, are employed in the professions or the servicing occupations. These people are not producers in the strict sense. To this group of human activities belong scientists, doctors, lawyers, teachers, ministers of religion, administrators, civil servants, policemen, artists, musicians, writers and many others. Service occupations of these kinds are often termed *quaternary activities*.

PROGRESS TEST 5

1. What inventions and developments ushered in the dawn of civilisation? (3)

2. Give *three* examples of peoples in the collecting or nomadic herding stage of culture; indicate briefly how they live and under what natural conditions they live. (5, 6)

3. Explain carefully the meaning of the following terms and quote an example of where each is found: nomadism; *milpa* agriculture; transhumance. (6, 7)

4. Distinguish between shifting cultivation and primitive sedentary cultivation. (7)

5. "Commercial fishing is a highly organised activity." What characteristics distinguish commercial fishing from "subsistence fishing"? (8)

6. Compare the features of primitive subsistence agriculture with commercial agriculture. (7, 10)

7. What are the chief types of forest that are exploited commercially? Give examples of the products yielded by each. (11)

8. What is meant by the term "primary occupation"? Describe, briefly, the chief primary occupations. (5–12)

9. Indicate how the development of commercial grazing in the southern hemisphere has been related to industrial, scientific and technical changes and developments. (9)

PART TWO

WORLD POPULATION, FOOD SUPPLY AND PROBLEMS

CHAPTER VI

THE POPULATION EXPLOSION

GROWTH OF POPULATION

1. The study of population. The study of population, or *demography*, includes the numbers, distribution and density of population, the growth and movements of population, and the age-group structure and literacy of population. The study of population is relevant to economic geography if only because people supply labour for economic activities and are consumers of goods. It is important for the economic geographer to know for any country or area he may be studying:

(*a*) the *size* of the population;
(*b*) the *density* of the population;
(*c*) its *growth* during recent times;
(*d*) the present-day *rate* of growth; and
(*e*) the balance between males and females and the age structure.

2. World population growth. Without doubt the most important fact about world population is the rapidity of its growth. This expansion has been so great during recent generations that we have come to speak of a "population explosion." Every hour sees the birth of some 13,000 babies. If we set against this the fact that some 4000 people die every hour we get a net increase of about 9000 per hour. This means the daily increase in world population is around 300,000 or, in other words, a population equivalent to that of Hull, Bradford or Leicester is added to the world total every day. Moreover, the proportion of deaths to births is gradually declining so that the net increase, irrespective of any acceleration in the birth-rate, will continue to rise—unless there are significant changes in birth control. Fig. 3 shows the accelerated increase in world population since the sixteenth century. The following table also shows this pattern of population growth during the past three hundred years by continents.

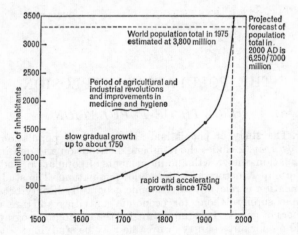

FIG. 3.—*Graph of world population growth*

Note how the population remained fairly stable during the sixteenth century, how it began to increase more during the period 1700 to 1850 (the time of the Agricultural and Industrial Revolutions) and how, since about 1850, population growth has accelerated.

Growth of Population by Continents (in millions)

	1650	1750	1850	1960	1975 (est)
Europe	100	140	266	588	649
Asia	330	479	749	1,556	2,100
Africa	100	95	95	225	353
Australasia	2	2	2	15·4	20
North America	1	1·3	26	190·5	220
Central and South America	12	11·1	33	200	280
Total	545	728·4	1,171	2,774·9	3,622

3. Estimated increase. The annual increase in population works out at about 55 millions, or roughly a million per week! Putting this in another way we can say that the world adds a population equal to that of the United Kingdom to its total annually. If the present trend continues, and there is little to suggest that it will be interrupted or changed, by the year A.D.

2000 (*i.e.* within the lifetimes of most of us) there will be twice as many people in the world as there are now. In case the year 2000 seems a long time ahead, let us remember that by 1975 the population was approaching 4000 million! By A.D. 2000 the figure is likely to be between 6000 and 7000 million.

It would be well to note that the population is not increasing at the same pace everywhere. While the world growth is at the rate of 1·9% per annum not all countries show such an increase: Eire, Norway, for example, show less; on the other hand, some countries, such as Mexico and Thailand, show rates of increase of over 3%. Again, we must beware of assuming that the countries with the largest populations, such as India, have the greatest rates of increase. This is not always the case; growth rates in Latin America (which has a total population of only about 280 million) are much higher, often twice as high, as those in Monsoon Asia (which has about 2100 million). However, it is true to say that the factor which is causing the greatest concern is the rapidly increasing population of the already numerically large countries of Monsoon Asia.

POPULATION DISTRIBUTION

4. Distribution of population. If we examine a world map showing the distribution of population, such as the simplified map in Fig. 4, we are immediately aware of the irregularity of this distribution: some areas are very densely peopled, others very thinly peopled. Even areas in close proximity, *e.g.* as in the Near East, the Indonesian islands, South Africa, show greatly differing densities.

The map, however, demonstrates quite clearly that *mankind is massed in four main regions of the earth*:

(*a*) In Western and Central Europe, especially in Britain, France, the Low Countries, Western Germany and Italy.

(*b*) In the east central part of North America, *i.e.* eastern United States and south-eastern Canada.

(*c*) In the Indian sub-continent comprising Pakistan, India, Bangladesh and Sri Lanka.

(*d*) In the far east of Asia, especially in eastern China, Korea, Japan and Taiwan.

Outside these four main areas of population concentration, mankind is much more thinly spread, though here and there are clusters of fairly dense or very dense population, *e.g.* in Egypt, Nigeria, Java, coastal New South Wales, the Plate estuary, south-eastern Brazil, California. There are many

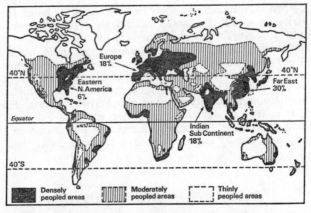

FIG. 4.—*World distribution of population*

The world's population is very unevenly distributed. Note the four areas of dense population, all of which are in the northern hemisphere and lie mostly in temperate or sub-tropical latitudes. Nearly three-quarters of the world's people live in these four areas. Note, also, the location of the thinly peopled areas, *i.e.* the ice-cap, tundra, forest, desert and high altitude areas.

areas, often of great size, *e.g.* the Amazon Basin, northern Canada, the Sahara, which are tenuously peopled and where the density is under 2 per square mile and often, indeed, under 1 per square mile.

5. Factors governing population distribution. *The population of any area is at once the cause and the result of its economic possibilities.* Man usually congregates where natural conditions most easily offer a supply of food or provide a means of earning a livelihood. Where conditions are difficult, *i.e.* where the chances of finding a food supply are limited or the opportunities of earning a living are closely restricted, man is not tempted to settle down and reproduce his kind.

The chief factors influencing the distribution of population are:

(a) accessibility;
(b) relief;
(c) climate;
(d) vegetation;
(e) soil;
(f) water supplies;
(g) mineral deposits.

Most of the world's population, some 70%, still live by agriculture, hence the conditions of climate and soil are of fundamental importance since they largely determine the food supply. The presence of mineral wealth is often an attractive force, especially in this technological age, and some of the greatest concentrations of population are to be found on some of the coalfields and other mineral fields: think, for instance, of the Ruhr Coalfield in Western Germany and the Appalachian Coalfield in the United States (see XVI, 9–11). In addition to the physical geographical factors, however, certain human factors, e.g. of an historical and political kind, have sometimes influenced settlement of areas and population densities within areas.

There remain large areas with sparse populations, chiefly cold desert regions, areas of aridity, rugged mountain regions and equatorial forest lands with their luxuriant, rank vegetation, marshy floodplains, and poor, leached soils. These may be called the "negative" areas (see Fig. 6 below).

CAUSES OF GROWTH

6. Causes of population growth. Let us come back to the problem of numbers. Why, the question naturally presents itself, should the world population, suddenly within the last two hundred years, have begun to expand at such an astonishing rate? In a general way it may be said that, until relatively recent times, the rate of population increase was limited by a variety of checks or "natural controls" as they are termed. The chief of these were:

(a) *Physical catastrophes* such as earthquakes, volcanic eruptions, droughts and floods.

(b) *Famine and starvation* caused by droughts, floods, locust plagues and other pests which ruined crops.

(c) *Plagues and diseases* which frequently in the past occurred on a large scale and decimated the population.

(d) *Wars, vendettas and social customs* such as head-hunting (once a common practice among some peoples).

All these *natural checks* have curbed population growth in the past.

Progress in medicine, in hygiene and in sanitation have been largely responsible for recent increases in population growth, since they have increased the chances of survival. But flood control, the introduction of irrigation techniques, the suppression of slavery and certain other social customs, have all helped. *Advancement in medical knowledge and improvements in public health have, without doubt, been the most important factors.*

One example will illustrate the importance of the struggle against disease. In Sri Lanka, in the past, malaria, carried by mosquitoes, led to the deaths of many people and this kept the population down. In recent years, malaria has been practically eliminated by using insecticides to kill the mosquitoes. As a result, the expectation of life has almost doubled within the short space of 25 years and the population of Sri Lanka is now increasing rapidly. In 1939 the population was about 5 million: today it is 13; while the numbers rose by 2·5 million between 1948–58, the increase during the succeeding decade was around 3·6.

NOTE: Social and political factors may predispose towards population growth. Such social customs as ancestor worship among the Chinese, polygamy among the Moslem peoples, and early marriage among the Hindus have encouraged population growth. Sometimes national policy aims deliberately at stimulating the increase in the population; for example, in the inter-war period, both Fascist Italy and Nazi Germany encouraged the procreation of children by offering state bounties and even medals to prolific mothers!

7. Solving the problem. If the current high birth rate and the recent trends in over-all growth continue, there is a very real threat of global over-population. There are two main problems with respect to the population dilemma: (a) the problem of local overcrowding, and (b) the problem of over-all growth.

Three main possible remedies may be adopted to ease, if not to solve, the problem of local overcrowding:

(a) *Pressure may be relieved by emigration.* In the past large numbers did migrate from over-populated countries, *e.g.* Italy, but the days of large-scale emigration appear to have gone for good and few countries will accept immigrants on any scale (the real exception here is between the countries of the British Commonwealth). Where immigration is allowed, it is usually reserved for scientists, technicians and people with specialist knowledge; impoverished, illiterate peasants, who have little to offer except their labour, are not welcomed.

(b) *Development of natural resources.* A more positive approach to the problem is to develop the country's natural resources so that it can support more people. Increased numbers could be supported by such measures as improving agricultural production, fishery development and exploitation of mineral wealth. Such developments usually need capital for their realisation and, all too often, it is the poor countries which are most overcrowded.

(c) *Industrialisation.* The development of manufacturing industry and the production of goods for export offers another possible alternative. Industrialisation is capable of absorbing surplus rural labour up to a point and the export of manufactures provides a source of income. Industrialisation, however, is at best merely a palliative and not a cure for overpopulation; nor is it always economically feasible or socially desirable. Again, countries lacking industrial raw materials, power resources and technological know-how are likely to find industrialisation difficult and of limited applicability.

From the point of view of over-all population growth, there is only one possible practical solution: birth control. This is not an easy matter, for it has to meet the challenge of religious, social and even economic and political factors. It is not likely to be easy to educate people to practise birth control, although there is a gleam of hope in that birth control is beginning to make headway in such over-crowded countries as Japan and India. However, it must be remembered that, in any event, birth control must be looked upon as a slow and a long-term method of slowing down population growth.

PROGRESS TEST 6

1. What is demography? What aspects of it are of importance to economic geographers? (1)

2. Explain what is meant by the phrase "population explosion." (2)

3. Outline the distribution of population over the earth's surface and indicate how geographical factors have affected this distribution. (4, 5)

4. Both Western Europe and China are areas of dense populations. What differing factors explain these two concentrations of population? (5, 6)

5. Suggest reasons for the phenomenal increase in the world's population during the past two hundred years. (6)

6. What possible remedies could be adopted to ease the present population problem? (7)

SUGGESTED PROJECTS AND DISCUSSION TOPICS

1. Draw bar graphs to show the population of the different continental areas in 1975. Use the figures provided in the table on p. 50.

2. The "man in the street" doesn't care about the population explosion. Discuss.

3. The earth could support three times its present population without any great difficulty. Discuss.

TEACHING AIDS

Film: "People by the Billions" (Freedom from Hunger Campaign).

Filmstrip: "World Population" (Picture Post, Hulton Press Publication).

CHAPTER VII

ECONOMIC ASPECTS OF THE POPULATION PROBLEM

SIZE OF POPULATION

1. Importance of size of population. The size of a country's population is of economic importance for two main reasons:

(*a*) *The factor of production* depends very much upon the amount, availability and quality of human labour, and the supply of this labour is itself closely related to the number, age composition and education of the population.

(*b*) People are consumers as well as producers, and the *standard of living* bears a close relationship to the numbers sharing the national income, that is the total of goods and services produced by the economically active population.

NOTE: Also of great importance is the size of a country's population in relation to other factors of production, such as the natural resources, physical handicaps, availability of capital. The total economic output of a country will fall far short of what it might be if there is insufficient manpower to make full and effective use of the non-human factors of production. On the other hand, if the population is too large in proportion to the non-human factors of production, then living standards, accordingly, will be much lower than they might be had a better balance between the two groups of factors been obtained.

2. Optimum population. Theoretically there is an optimum population for every country: this optimum is reached *when the labour force is just sufficient to make the best possible use of the available resources*.

But this fine balance is not necessarily constant; any increase in resources—an improvement in soil fertility, new mineral finds, realisation of power potential, stock of capital—will probably permit or require increased supplies of labour; it follows, therefore, that the level of the optimum population will be raised.

3. Over-populated and under-populated regions. Over-population does not depend merely upon the total number living in a country, nor upon the density of the population. For example, a population density of sixty persons to the square mile may mean over-population in one area but under-population in another.

(a) *Availability of resources.* Much depends upon the available resources, the capacity of the land to support the population, and the degree of cultural development.

(b) *Insufficiency of food.* A country is not necessarily over-populated simply because it is incapable of providing sufficient food to support its people.

Thus, Venezuela provides an illustration for, although its population is small, just over thirteen millions, and there is no shortage of cultivable land, it does not produce enough food to support its people and must import considerable quantities. Again, a country may be able, as in the case of Britain, to employ its labour force more effectively in manufacturing industry, exporting its surplus manufactured goods in exchange for foodstuffs.

(c) *Conditions vary widely throughout the world.* Some countries or areas are over-populated, others under-populated: in the first category fall the Netherlands and Italy in Europe, Japan and India in Asia, and the Republics of Haiti and El Salvador in America; in the second such countries as New Zealand, Canada, Paraguay and Nicaragua in America, and many parts of Africa.

4. Average density. The average density of population of a country is obtained *by dividing the total population by the land area.* This gives some interesting results, as the following table shows:

TABLE I. AVERAGE POPULATION DENSITY (1972)

Country	Population ('000s)	Area ('000 km²)	Density (per km²)
Australia	13,268	7,687	1·7
Belgium	9,756	31	319·7
Bermuda	55	0·053	1,037·7
Canada	22,207	9,221	2·4
France	52,360	547	95·7
W. Germany	61,967	249	249·3
Iceland	212	103	2·1
India	574,216	3,280	175·0
Rhodesia	5,900	391	15·1
United Kingdom	56,113	245	229·2
Soviet Union	249,749	22,402	11·1
Venezuela	11,293	912	12·4

The average density, which is frequently quoted in textbooks, is often practically meaningless. It fails to indicate the simple fact that many parts of a country (as in the case of Canada and Australia) are uninhabitable. One of the best illustrations one can give is Japan: the average density for Japan in the 1974 estimate was 295 per km^2, but in actual fact only about 16% of Japan's area is habitable, the rest, about 84%, is uninhabitable and almost devoid of any economic usefulness; hence the true density of population works out at over 2000 per km^2. One must beware, therefore, of accepting the average density at face value.

5. Some other aspects of population. In addition to the problem of numbers in relation to food supplies or the other factors of production, there are other questions which are often of major national importance: for example the rate of population growth or decline, the distribution between the various age groups, the balance between rural and urban populations, the proportion of males to females, and the degree to which the population is literate and educated.

(a) *Rate of growth.* The following examples illustrate the problems of changes in growth rate.

(i) *Britain.* Before the Second World War the rate of growth in Britain had declined and the population was not reproducing itself. It looked as if the population, which was then around 48 millions, would decline and some authorities estimated that by 1970 the population would have dropped to 30 million. For various reasons, the opposite happened and the population total now stands at 56 millions. This example serves to remind us that we must accept all estimates of future population numbers with a certain amount of reserve.

(ii) *Australia and others.* Some countries, such as Australia, whose populations were stagnant or nearly so, opened their doors to immigrants in the post-war years. Australia needed a larger population, partly for national security and partly to enable her to develop her economic potential. Immigration has enabled Australia to almost double its population in 25 years. Other countries such as New Zealand, South Africa, Rhodesia and Canada, all with relatively small population totals and all developing rapidly, have welcomed immigrants, more especially from the United Kingdom (*see* 6 below).

(b) *Age groups.* The age structure of the population is important from the economic point of view.

(i) *High proportion over 65.* Some countries, such as Britain and most West European countries, may have a considerable proportion of their population over 65 years of age (Britain, France and Belgium have over twelve per cent for instance). This age group is usually no longer economically active and becomes, to a greater or lesser extent, a burden to the state, for it has to be supported. Moreover, the economic activity of the population is only one aspect of the effects of ageing for, as J. I. Clarke says, "consumption also changes with ageing; requirements of foodstuffs, housing, schools, hospitals, transport, pensions and so on."*

(ii) *High fertility and high death rates.* On the other hand, there are some countries with high fertility and high death rates, such as India and Brazil, where the population is essentially youthful and where as many as 50% of the total numbers are under fifteen years of age. A large proportion of young people also brings its own problems. In many of the backward and underdeveloped countries birth rates may be very high but, unfortunately, large numbers of infants die through malnutrition and disease and in some cases only about half of them reach adulthood.

(c) *Literacy.* In many parts of the world, *e.g.* in Africa, Monsoon Asia and Latin America, illiteracy rates are high. Taking Latin America as a whole, for example, the latest census figure reveals that almost 40% of the population is illiterate.

National leaders have realised the importance of literacy and education (*see* IX, 12). It is necessary for:

(i) national cohesion;
(ii) economic development; and
(iii) social advancement.

Thus economic progress in agriculture, industry and commerce cannot proceed very far without an educated people; scientists, specialists, technologists and technicians are needed in large numbers if the plans and programmes of the governments of the underdeveloped countries are to be turned into practical achievements. Hence in many countries a substantial proportion of the national income is now being devoted to the provision of education at all levels.

* *Population Geography*, Pergamon Press, 1965, p. 68.

MOVEMENT OF POPULATION

6. Motives. An important aspect of population from the economic viewpoint is the movement of people from place to place. Sometimes movements have been slow, mere trickles of people, but at other times there have been mass movements.

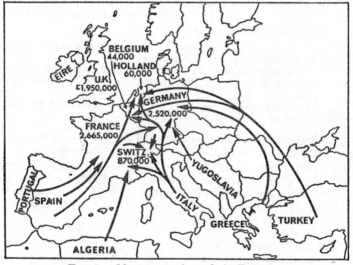

Fig. 5.—*Movements of people in Europe*

The map shows the recent movements of people between country and country in Europe, but especially to the Common Market countries. The figures indicate the total imported work-force, except for Britain, where they refer to the total number of immigrants.

At first man's movements were unconscious wanderings and, as a result of these driftings, he came to occupy most parts of the earth's surface. Later in history man moved consciously and mainly for two types or classes of reasons which we might term "attractive" and "repellent" reasons.

(a) *Attractive reasons.* Among the varied reasons which attracted man to move and settle elsewhere were:

    (i) more congenial climatic conditions;
    (ii) better economic opportunities (*see* Fig. 5);

(iii) higher standards of living;

(iv) adventure and the sheer attraction of "foreign parts."

Thus many Irishmen came to England and many Britishers have emigrated to the Dominions which promise (but do not always fulfil) better conditions of life and livelihood. (Note in this connection the "brain drain" to the United States.) Fig. 5 shows the movement of population in Europe since the Second World War.

(b) *Repellent reasons*. Some people quit their homelands voluntarily or involuntarily because of:

(i) harsh environmental conditions which make getting a living precarious, *e.g.* in Norway;

(ii) religious persecution, *e.g.* the Huguenots in sixteenth-century France and the Puritans in seventeenth-century England;

(iii) political persecution, *e.g.* the Jewish refugees from Nazi Germany.

These and other reasons conspired to urge people to move and from time to time mass movements of population have occurred. One can think of the great out-surge of the Vikings in the eighth and ninth centuries A.D., of the estimated 20 million Negro slaves who were forcibly carried to the Americas, and of the 60 million people who left Europe between 1820 and 1930 to try their luck in the "new lands" of the world.

7. Economic motives. These loom large in all human movements. Thus:

(a) *The Viking outpouring* was ascribed by H. A. L. Fisher to "common cupidity."

(b) *The early Portuguese and Spaniards* who went to the Americas were motivated by the promise of "get rich quick."

(c) *The Southern Chinese* who migrated into South-east Asia, and who now total more than 15 millions, were attracted thither by commercial opportunities.

(d) *The slave trade*. The presence of some 60 million Negroes in the Americas today is an outcome of the iniquitous slave trade of earlier times. A shortage of labour for the sugar, cotton and tobacco plantations set up by the Portuguese and Spaniards, and later the French and British, led to slaves being imported in vast numbers.

(e) *Malaya*. The present day multi-racial composition of Malaya stems from economic considerations. The native Malays showed little inclination for any work other than agriculture, hence when the tin mines and the rubber estates were opened up alien workers had to be brought into Malaya to provide an essential labour force. Today, there are some two and a half million Chinese and about 800,000 Indians in Malaya as against about four and a half million Malays.

8. Movements in Europe. Since the Second World War there has been a considerable movement of people between country and country in Europe. This has occurred on a much greater scale than most people realise. The movement has stemmed from the need for workers; the industrial boom of the past decade or so in the Common Market countries especially has led to the demand for a greater work-force. The figures in Fig. 5 indicate the total imported work-force in each country, except in Britain where the figure refers to the total number of immigrants.

(a) *France.* The total immigrant work-force is now nearly three million, consisting mainly of Algerians, Italians, Spaniards and Portuguese. They find work chiefly in building, metal works, domestic service and agriculture.

(b) *West Germany.* During the past decade 150,000 immigrants have entered West Germany annually. More than two million, chiefly Italians, Spaniards, Greeks, Turks and Yugoslavs, have found jobs in Germany.

(c) *Switzerland.* Switzerland, with 870,000 incomers, has the highest proportion of foreign workers—one in three. About 50,000 workers cross the borders daily.

These shifting populations are helping to make a united states of Europe a reality.

9. Internal migration. The migration of population takes place on an internal as well as an international scale.

(a) *In Britain,* for some time now, there has been a "drift to the South," particularly to London and the home counties, and this is causing many problems relating to land use, housing, communications and the like. The growing industrialisation of the south-east has been both the cause and the effect of this drift of population. The depopulation of the highland areas, not only in Scotland and Wales but in northern England and the West Country, has been proceeding steadily for many decades. Some attempts are now being made, as in the Scottish Highlands, to try and arrest this drift.

(b) *In Europe.* Similar internal movements can be traced in other countries, *e.g.* Norway is experiencing the same depopulation of its highland zone as Scotland; in France people are leaving the Central Massif and moving into the Paris Basin, the growth pole of the country; while in Italy there has been, throughout the present century, a constant movement of people from the south—the *Mezzogiorno*—to the north and since 1950 considerably more than 1 million have migrated to northern Italy.

(c) *In the United States.* For many decades the negroes of the South have been migrating into the big cities of the North-east. Since 1950 more than 6 million people have moved into California. While purely social reasons may explain some of these movements, at root they are mostly economic: higher wages, better opportunities, greater variety of work.

PROGRESS TEST 7

1. Why is (*a*) the size, and (*b*) the quality (*i.e.* age, sex, ability) of the population of a country important? (1, 5)

2. Write a short explanatory paragraph on each of the following: over-population; non-human factors of production; multi-racial countries. (1–3, 7)

3. "Theoretically, there is an optimum population for every country." Explain what this means. (2)

4. Explain why the term "average density" is of little value in describing the relationship between the total area and total population of a country. (4)

5. Why is literacy important in national development? Give, if you can, examples of six countries having a high illiteracy rate. (5)

6. Describe with the aid of examples, the relationship between poverty, hunger, disease and ignorance. (2–5)

7. "Man has migrated to other parts of the world for two main classes of reasons." Elaborate upon this statement. (6)

8. Explain what is meant by the phrase "a drift to the south" as applied to Britain. (9)

DISCUSSION TOPICS

1. Would-be emigrants to Canada, Australia and New Zealand look at these countries through rose-coloured spectacles.

2. The British Government should stop the "brain drain."

CHAPTER VIII

FEEDING THE WORLD'S PEOPLE

FOOD RESOURCES

1. Food and population. The study of population is inescapably linked with the complementary study of food production and resources. The world's population is growing at such an alarming rate that it has been termed an "explosion" and many thinking people believe that this very rapid growth is *the* most important and most pressing problem of our time. The problem which this growth presents resolves itself into two parts:

(a) Will there be enough living space for the population of the future?

(b) Will the world be able to feed all the additional mouths?

2. Living space. The problem of living space is the least troublesome of the two. From a purely quantitative point of view it has been calculated that the world's present population —all 3650 million of them—could be found standing room on the Isle of Wight! Clearly, then, there is still plenty of room on this planet of ours although, of course, mankind would not want to live like battery hens. Locally, where there is a shortage of living space, as in many of our big cities, man is now building vertically instead of horizontally.

We have been told recently that it is structurally feasible to build skyscrapers three miles high which will be capable of accommodating 30,000 people. And, if the worst happened, it is very likely that man would expand over the water, building vast rafts upon which he would permanently live, much as the floating populations of Canton live at the present time, or would even resort to building undersea cities in gigantic undersea "bubbles."

3. Food supply. The problem of food supply is much more serious. The threat of over-population and a shortage of food has been raised in the past, *e.g.* by Thomas Malthus over a century ago. In the nineteenth century the spectre was laid to rest through the opening up of the "new lands" of the world which supplied grain and meat in large quantities.

In recent years the threat has begun to loom large once again and there can be no denying that the possibility of an over-all world food shortage is very real indeed. The problem of finding sufficient food for the growing population of the future is aggravated, moreover, by the fact that already some *two-thirds of the present world population are underfed*, which means that they are suffering from either undernourishment or malnutrition.

The question thus arises: how can the world's food supplies be expanded to meet a growth in world population running at over 50 millions a year?

4. Limitations of the land surface. Only 29% of the earth's surface is dry land. Furthermore, only a very small proportion of this is fertile and capable of being used agriculturally. Fig. 6 shows the vast unproductive areas of the world. The

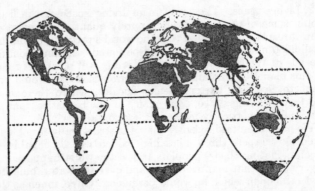

FIG. 6.—*The world's productive and unproductive areas*

Those parts of the earth's surface which through cold, aridity or mountainous character make close settlement and agricultural develop- ment well-nigh impossible are marked in black: these are the "negative" areas. The blank areas, totalling only about one-third of the land sur- face, may be termed the "positive" areas, *i.e.* those which are cultivated or are potentially cultivable.

conditions which limit the use of the earth's land surface for cultivation may be summarised as follows:

(a) approximately one-fifth of the total land area is *too cold*;
(b) approximately one-fifth of the total land area is *too dry*;
(c) approximately one-fifth of the total land area is *too mountainous*;
(d) approximately one-fifth of the total land area is *forested* or *marshy*.

Of the one-fifth (20%) of the earth's surface that is available for agricultural use, only about half of it (*i.e.* 10% of the total land area) is actually producing food at present.

In connection with this there are a number of points we might note: (i) the best land is already being used; (ii) much of the farming is below maximum efficiency; and (iii) some of the land which is not being used does offer possibilities for cultivation. A proportion, possibly as much as a quarter, of the 80% of the earth's surface that is too cold or arid or high or forested could be made suitable for farming purposes, but only through a large capital investment.

INCREASING SUPPLIES

5. The extension of food producing acreages. The problem of hunger could be alleviated, perhaps overcome, by the extension of food producing acreages and by increasing agricultural yields.

The world's food producing area could be increased by bringing more land into cultivation and this could be done by:

(a) *Terracing some of the steep slopes* in mountainous regions which have suitable climates for crop growing.

(b) *Extending and improving irrigation facilities* in some of the semi-arid and arid areas of the world.

(c) *Draining swamplands and improving flood-control measures* in certain wet and low-lying areas.

(d) *Clearing some forested areas*, especially tropical forest areas, for the cultivation of crops.

6. Increasing agricultural yields. Although the additional acreages resulting from the above measures would be valuable, in total they would increase the cultivable area by only a very small amount. Moreover, the effort would be costly in time and money. Making "two blades of grass grow where one grew before" seems to offer a better prospect for solving the problem; in other words, increasing yields rather than increased areas would appear to produce the more significant results.

Increased production along these lines could be achieved by:

(a) Increasing the output and use of fertilisers.
(b) Using better seeds and improving animal strains.
(c) Introducing and improving crop rotation practices.
(d) Extending the use of insecticides to control pests.
(e) Using more efficient farm tools and machinery.
(f) Controlling soil erosion and adopting soil conservation methods.
(g) Developing educational training aimed at farming improvement.
(h) Improving health and thereby labour efficiency.

7. The need for better farming. There is much room for better farming in the world. Over vast areas, especially in the tropical regions, farming continues to be carried on by backward and inefficient, and therefore wasteful, methods. The great majority of the world's farmers are subsistence farmers merely growing sufficient (but sometimes even less than enough) for their own needs and live almost entirely on what they produce.

Help, guidance, and practical aid are wanted for the farmers in a variety of ways:

(a) They need to learn how to use their land to the best advantage.
(b) They need instruction in new and better farming techniques.
(c) They need training in the use of fertilisers and green manures.
(d) They need guidance in animal husbandry.
(e) They need assistance in matters of food storage and marketing.
(f) They need better seeds, improved stock and more efficient agricultural implements.

Training for improvement is clearly necessary. Farm schools, demonstration farms, agricultural colleges, breeding centres, research establishments and pilot projects of all kinds are required in increased numbers. All of this, of course, costs money and since many of the more backward countries are too poor to finance projects of this kind, the richer countries must be prepared to play the role of the benevolent uncle.

8. Practical help. Already much help has been given by governments and international agencies—even individuals— to assist the underdeveloped countries. One could give a long list of institutions which have done much to help. Let us quote one or two examples.

(a) *The Food and Agricultural Organisation*, F.A.O. for short, a department of the United Nations, gives help in many ways but particularly in the field of technical assistance. F.A.O. experts are prepared to assist every government that is willing to co-operate and that assistance ranges from plant breeding to pasture management, from animal husbandry to fish culture, and from water control to locust control.

(b) *The Colombo Plan.* This organisation, set up by Britain in 1954, was designed to promote the development of the Commonwealth countries and the underdeveloped countries of Southeast Asia. Britain and the Dominions share most of the cost and provide most of the help which includes financial aid, the provision of equipment, technical training, and guidance from scientific, technical, agricultural, fishery and forestry experts.

(c) *The World Bank*, which is the shortened, popular term for the International Bank for Reconstruction and Development, was set up in 1944 for the purpose of granting loans to countries for the purpose of reconstruction or development when such countries found themselves unable to finance projects out of their own resources. The capital of the World Bank was subscribed by the members of the International Monetary Fund on a quota basis.

9. New sources and methods of food production. If the rapidly growing population of the world is to be adequately fed we must increase the total amount of food produced and increase the quantity of protein food. The main product of agriculture is carbohydrate; what is most urgently needed is protein food, for the conventional bulk foods (cereals, potatoes, yams) are deficient in protein content. More protein rich foods such as meat, milk, cheese, eggs and fish are required to remedy undernourishment and malnutrition.

The problem of increasing food supplies can be tackled in two main ways:

(a) by making much more effective use of the land and greater use of the sea and, also, of inland waters to produce more food; and

(b) by using new and different kinds of food, perhaps even synthetic foodstuffs.

Let us look briefly at a few of the ways and means by which man could increase the output of food and tap new sources of supply.

10. Fisheries. There are many ocean areas rich in fish that are not adequately exploited, *e.g.* the South African and Australian areas. Even so, a word of caution is necessary: the fish of the sea is not unlimited in quantity and it is probable that the total catch could be increased only twofold, or at most threefold, without serious danger of depleting stocks.

"Fish farming," *i.e.* the breeding of fish in ponds, lakes and canals, has long been practised in the Far East; this practice could be greatly extended and, in fact, certain developments along these lines are now taking place in Africa where the great natural and artificial lakes (Victoria Nyanza, Lake Kariba) have been stocked with fish. The time is fast approaching when we must stop hunting fish and begin to farm fish (*see* XII, **12** and **14**).

11. Cropping wild animals. Another possible source of food is cropping wild animals. The vast savanna lands of Africa are the haunt of large numbers of herbivorous creatures, *e.g.* antelope, gnu, zebra and the like, and a scheme is being studied whereby the more thorough protection of these animals could be combined with their provision of additional food supplies. There seems to be no reason why the conservation of wild life should not be linked with food production.

Several creatures, such as the capybara and the freshwater manatee, might provide unorthodox sources of meat, and since they feed on water weeds and swamp plants, they would not compete for food with the other land animals.

12. Processing of vegetable materials. Many plants are used as sources of vegetable oil; the seeds or fruits of the sunflower, cotton plant, groundnut and soya plants all yield valuable oil. The vegetable residue left after the oil has been expressed is used either for making animal feedstuffs or organic fertiliser or is simply discarded as waste. But this residue is rich in protein and is potentially valuable as a human foodstuff. At present this residue is frequently rendered unfit for human consumption through overheating during the oil expressing process or because it is contaminated. But if it could be made edible, it is estimated that this residual matter would yield twenty million tons of protein or roughly double the world's present estimated deficit of protein.

13. Hydroponics. This is a method of *growing plants by water-culture* or soil-less methods. Broadly, the method consists of growing crops in tanks filled with a soil substitute and water which is charged with dissolved plant nutrients. The plants use the inert seed-bed as an anchorage, growing upwards in the normal manner, and send their roots downwards to feed in the chemical solution. The success of hydroponics depends upon adequate sunshine, aeration of the roots, and the appropriate solution for the needs of the crop. Capital costs are high and the process is too expensive for general use but it can be of use in exceptional circumstances as in certain arid, rainless areas; for example, the method has been used on a small scale in the Persian Gulf State of Kuwait, and it has also been tried out in California and in Jersey in the Channel Islands.

PROGRESS TEST 8

1. Why is the problem of future food supplies a serious problem? (**3, 4**)

2. In what ways could food production be substantially increased? (**5, 6**)

3. Outline the problems of land use and explain why only a small fraction of the earth's surface is capable of being cultivated. (**4**)

4. Explain the meaning of the following terms: insecticides; soil conservation; crop rotation; malnutrition; hydroponics; fish farming. (**3, 6, 10, 13**)

5. Suggest new sources and methods of food production which could help solve the problem of world hunger. (**9–13**)

DISCUSSION TOPICS

1. Population will outrun food supplies.
2. There is no shortage of food; it is the distribution system that is at fault.
3. The increasing of agricultural yields is the surest way of solving the world's food problem.

TEACHING AIDS

Films:

"Food or Famine" (Petroleum Film Bureau).
"The Global Struggle for Food" (Concord Film Council).
"Can the Earth Provide?" (Concord Film Council).

CHAPTER IX

THE UNDERDEVELOPED COUNTRIES

MEANING OF UNDERDEVELOPMENT

1. The haves and the have-nots. Most people these days are aware, to a greater or lesser extent, of a simple, but undeniable, fact: that some countries are economically and technically well-developed and their peoples enjoy high standards of living while, on the other hand, there are other countries that are underdeveloped and backward by twentieth-century standards and whose peoples are poverty-stricken, often illiterate, and suffer low living standards. Before we proceed any further it will be useful to define exactly what is meant by the terms "underdevelopment" and "standards of living."

2. Underdevelopment. There is some difficulty in interpreting the term "underdevelopment" or, as it is applied to countries, "underdeveloped": clearly, underdeveloped is not the same as undeveloped, nor the same as developed. Perhaps the best and most intelligible interpretation of "underdeveloped" is to define it as the condition in which *per capita* real incomes in a country are low—low compared with the *per capita* real incomes in the "advanced" or "developed" countries such as the United States or most of the countries of Western Europe. Defined in this sense, underdeveloped is synonymous with "poor," and national poverty may be taken as best interpreting the condition of underdevelopment.

NOTE

(i) Some people advocate the use of the term "developing" as being more appropriate than "underdeveloped." This, it is true, is more acceptable to countries who are rather sensitive about being dubbed "underdeveloped"; but if we mean, as indeed we do, that the resources (human as well as natural) of these countries have been under or inadequately developed, then the term "underdeveloped" is more accurate and is a better term.

(ii) Some people have suggested that the term "pre-industrial-ised" might be a more adequate and less offensive description of the condition of underdevelopment; but this is scarcely, if any, better, for it suggests that industrialisation is tantamount to economic development and a necessary condition for development.

3. Living standards. In Britain we tend to measure living standards in terms of motor cars, automatic washing machines, colour television sets, and if people possess these material goods we say they enjoy a high standard of living. It cannot be denied that these things are *one* measure of living standards but the condition that *really* constitutes a high standard of living is one that ensures a sufficient and well-balanced diet, good housing, security of employment, and adequate social services (*i.e.* education, hospitals, water supplies, sanitation, old-age pensions). The have-not countries are the countries which *have not got* these essential things that constitute high standards of living. Fig. 7 shows the developed and under-developed regions of the world.

4. Characteristics of underdevelopment. A correlation exists between national poverty and many other features of the economic and social organisation of a country. Some of the more important characteristics of underdeveloped countries are listed below:

(*a*) A very high percentage (usually over 70%) of the population is engaged in agriculture.

(*b*) The primary industries of farming, forestry, fishing and mining dominate the economy.

(*c*) Agriculture employs large numbers of superfluous workers, *i.e.* a smaller labour force could produce the same total output.

(*d*) Farm holdings are small in size, agricultural techniques are primitive and the crop yields per acre are generally low.

(*e*) Incomes per head of the population are low and there is very little capital per head.

(*f*) Birth-rates and death-rates are both high, the expectation of life is short and the population is frequently greater than the country can adequately support.

(*g*) There is a relatively low output of protein foods and consequently the people suffer from inadequate nutrition and dietary deficiencies.

(*h*) There is over-crowding, bad housing and few public health

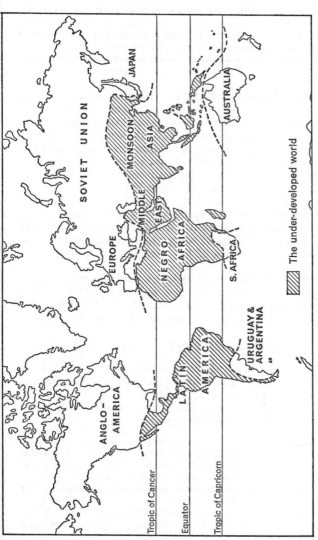

FIG. 7.—*The developed and underdeveloped regions*

Note that practically all the developed regions of the world are those settled by white or European peoples. The Latin American region, Negro Africa, most of the Middle East and most of Monsoon Asia fall into the category of underdeveloped regions. There are, however, considerable variations in the underdeveloped world and some countries are now developing quite rapidly.

services such as tapped water, proper sanitation, hospital services.

(i) Education services are poorly developed, usually at all levels, and there is a high degree of illiteracy.

(j) Women hold an inferior position in society and are not only denied equality but are frequently little more than chattels.

5. The underdeveloped countries. If we think of the underdeveloped countries as those which are poor and which are experiencing acute difficulties in raising their standards of living, then we can say that most of the countries of Africa, Southern and South-east Asia and Latin America fall into this category. Most, though not all, are located in the tropical belt and many of them were formerly colonies of the Western Powers. This distribution is shown in Fig. 7.

It is interesting to note that *the underdeveloped countries account for over two-thirds of the world's total population*. A measure of their backwardness is that between them they have only 10% of the total world energy consumption and account for a mere 7% by value of the world's total manufactured goods.

There is, of course, a wide variation in the degree of underdevelopment; some countries, such as Brazil and Taiwan, are undergoing quite rapid development, others, such as Somalia, Bangladesh and Paraguay, are making only very slow progress.

AGRICULTURE AND INDUSTRY

6. Agriculture. Most of the underdeveloped countries are basically dependent on agriculture and rely heavily upon one or a few crops, *e.g.* Egypt upon cotton, Sri Lanka upon tea, Nigeria upon vegetable oils, Cuba upon sugar. A number of common agricultural problems occur:

(a) *Soils,* especially in the humid tropics, are poor, leached and soon become exhausted; hence yields tend to be low. Moreover, in areas of heavy, torrential rainfall soil erosion is apt to occur and indeed large areas have suffered on this account.

(b) *Pests and diseases* are prone to attack plants and animals in all tropical lands and so create serious problems for the agriculturalist (II, **9**). For example, sigatoka disease completely destroyed the banana plantations on the Caribbean coastlands while the tsetse fly prevents cattle raising over large tracts of tropical Africa.

(c) *Primitive techniques* of cropping and grazing result in the spread of pests and diseases, low crop yields, and poor quality animals. There is a general lack of scientific farm management, use of fertilisers, and mechanical aids to cultivation.

(d) *Social customs,* such as the division of holdings, the mortgaging of land to moneylenders, religious taboos, the prestige value of mere numbers of animals, the prevalence of the large estate and absentee landowners (especially in Latin America), often militate against effective and efficient farming.

(e) *Subsistence agriculture* is characteristic over wide areas. This so-called self-sufficient type of farming is frequently self-*in*sufficient, for the cultivator often does not produce enough even adequately to maintain himself and his family, let alone produce a surplus for sale.

(f) *Crop specialisation,* or the dependence upon a single commodity, has been typical of many tropical countries. To put all one's eggs in one basket is risky to say the least, for a fall in the world market price or a crop failure resulting from climatic hazards or pestilence and disease may bring disaster.

(g) *Transport and markets*. Even where a farmer is able to produce a surplus he often finds great difficulty in marketing it, since there may be a lack of transport facilities to get it to the market or an absence of any marketing organisation.

7. Agricultural needs. The agricultural problems of the underdeveloped countries are manifold and complex. Changes in farming are likely to be slow, largely because farmers as a class tend to be conservative, but farmers will change their methods if it can be shown that they will benefit from doing so. It is important, however, that innovations and new methods should be geared to the local conditions: far too often in the past it has been assumed that the mere introduction of western ideas, techniques and management would bring an agricultural miracle. Sadly this has often proved not to be the case.

A number of changes in the present agricultural system would seem desirable however:

(a) *Agricultural education* would seem to be essential if farming is to become more efficient and productive; this means more agricultural advisors, schools, colleges, experimental farms—all of which, however, cost money.

(b) *Diversification of agriculture,* especially in those areas where there has been undue dependence upon a single staple; but it must be recognised that this is a fairly long-term business.

(c) *Improved seed and animal strains* would help enormously to increase agricultural output, but for these the underdeveloped

countries are largely dependent upon the agriculturally developed countries.

(d) _Fertilisers and insecticides_ are required in large quantities
to help fortify the inherently poor soils of the tropics and maintain soil fertility and to check the ravages of insect pests.

(e) _Agricultural machinery_ could be of great benefit in many
areas, enabling the peasant to cultivate more land and work it
more expeditiously as well as relieving him of much of the toil
and drudgery of farming.

(f) _Land tenure systems_ in many areas need changing. The
large estate, fragmentation of plots, indebtedness, all tend to
influence strongly the efficiency of farming, land care and
improvement. Co-operative organisation would help in many
areas.

8. Industry. Almost all the underdeveloped countries have a
strong desire to industrialise themselves: this is largely because they think industrialisation is a panacea for the condition
of underdevelopment and over-population.

Some countries are content to industrialise gradually and
slowly, paying due regard to their resources of power, minerals
and technological limitations; others are forging ahead at a
breakneck pace, determined upon industrialisation no matter
what the cost. Thailand and China may be said to represent
these two extremes.

However, apart from one or two countries, such as India,
Egypt and Brazil, which have achieved a considerable measure
of success, most of them still have only very modest industries.

9. Reasons for industrialisation. A number of reasons help to
explain this swing towards industrialism:

(a) It is recognised that no country can be powerful or politic-
ally secure without a well-developed industry, for industrialisation in the twentieth century is a primary determinant of
national power.

(b) The simple exchange of primary products for foreign
manufactured articles which, in general, was characteristic of the
underdeveloped countries prior to the Second World War
savoured too much of the "colonial" stage of development and
psychological motives of this kind have helped to further
industrialisation.

(c) Industrialisation offers one avenue of absorbing excess
population, a problem which faces many countries, especially in
Asia, and one which, if current rates of population growth are

maintained, is likely to face many more countries in the not too distant future.

(d) Industrialisation is seen to be a means of raising the low standard of living, an acute problem which confronts practically every one of the underdeveloped countries.

(e) Industrialisation is a means of diversifying grossly unbalanced economies and assisting national aims of greater self-sufficiency.

10. Problems of industrialisation.

Successful industrialisation implies not only the possession of adequate power, mineral and raw material resources but the acceptance of new values, an interested and mobile society, the availability of capital, industrial expertise, technological know-how and an educated labour force. Without these, which usually necessitate radical changes in the economic, social and institutional structures of a country, industrialisation may well create more problems than it solves.

Some of the problems facing the underdeveloped countries in their attempts to industrialise are:

(a) *Shortage of adequate power resources.* Since it is power potential above everything else which is a yardstick of a country's capacity for manufacture, it is essential that there should be adequate power resources available. Both Argentina and Brazil have made determined efforts to industrialise but time and again development has been handicapped by power shortages. Both have very little coal and what there is is poor in quality. Brazil has a shortage of oil and must import the bulk of her oil requirements; Argentina, with reasonable oil reserves, is more fortunate. Brazil has a vast hydro-electric power potential, but the demand for electric power has outrun the country's capacity to produce it.

(b) *Shortage of capital resources.* Not only the development of power resources and the exploitation of natural resources but the setting up of industrial plant, especially for heavy industry, require huge capital expenditure. Many of the underdeveloped countries simply have not got the capital to establish basic enterprises and are dependent upon financial aid from the developed countries. Most of India's iron and steel plants, for instance, have been established as a result of British, German and Russian financial and technical aid. Great schemes such as the Aswan High Dam, and the Volta Project have only been made possible through the help of international aid.

(c) *Education and training.* One of the greatest difficulties facing the underdeveloped countries is their shortage of trained manpower. They suffer acutely from a shortage of technologists and technicians and have often to rely upon foreigners to manage and run their enterprises. Again, the industrial worker is frequently capable of doing only the simplest repetitive job and is unreliable. India's textile industry, for example, is long-established and the most important of all the manufacturing industries but it has long suffered from a great turnover in its personnel. Without a consistent and reliable work force, manufacturing industry is bound to be inefficient. Not only is there a need for education and training at all levels but a need for a loyal and stable work force.

(d) *Political stability.* Political instability, which seems to be a malaise in many of the newly independent and underdeveloped countries, is a great handicap to economic development. The Latin American countries have long had a reputation for chronic political instability and to no small extent this has helped to keep them backward. Foreign investors are unwilling, naturally, to risk sinking their money into countries whose futures are uncertain or whose rulers show no scruples.

Internal unrest, constant changes of government, rioting, threats of expropriation and the like are not conducive either to investment or economic growth.

11. Need for industralisation. Notwithstanding the many difficulties and problems besetting industrialisation in the underdeveloped countries, it seems fairly clear that most of them would benefit from some measure of industrialisation. It would, in fact, be economic good sense to assist the under-developed countries in achieving this goal. Such help, granted, is likely to create new trade rivals in an already keenly competitive world, but it would at the same time lead to the development of new markets through the demands by the new wage-earners for consumer goods and by the states themselves for capital goods. Thus western standards of living would not necessarily suffer from the increasing industrialisation of the underprivileged countries. The strongest argument, however, for industrialisation is that it would help to promote better standards of living in countries where living standards are deplorably low. Higher standards of living would be likely to affect the social aspirations of the people which, as past experience shows, help to check population growth.

Summing up, it would be desirable for the underdeveloped

countries to adopt a measure of industrialisation where this is a feasible proposition. But these countries need the help, experience and financial assistance of the West to guide them in their efforts to industrialise, to promote their economic development, and to raise their living standards.

OTHER FACTORS

12. Social problems. Economic advancement in many of the underdeveloped countries is being held up by the social structures and social systems in those countries. Among numerous problems are:

(a) *Physical health.* Disease and inadequate feeding often undermine the energy and work capacity of the people. Indian agriculture is inefficient partly because the Indian peasant is often incapable of sustained hard work; he works slowly and rests frequently to conserve his energy. Until there are more doctors, hospitals and clinics as well as improvements in sanitation and water supply, not to mention adequate food supplies, many of these backward peoples will have to endure physical handicaps and poor health.

(b) *Culture traits.* Cultural features may influence man's activities and outlook and these may affect economic production and social advancement. Some examples were mentioned previously:

(i) Islam acts as a restrictive force from the economic point of view for such activities as mining, trading and money-lending are forbidden to members of the faith.

(ii) The Hindu reverence for the cow has burdened India with a vast and virtually unproductive cattle population which also forms a great drain on the food supply.

(iii) The Hindu caste system has in many ways militated against efficient economic development, *e.g.* by restricting particular jobs to particular castes.

(iv) Buddhism forbids the killing of animals and so predisposes towards a vegetarian diet and poorly developed animal husbandry.

(v) To many African cattle herders wealth is counted in terms of the numbers of animals they possess; their quality, *i.e.* their economic value, is a secondary consideration.

(vi) Among many communities womenfolk are denied adequate social status and may be regarded as little more than chattels.

Many of the social habits and customs will have to be broken down if these countries are to progress.

(c) *Literacy and education.* It is clear that economic and social advancement these days is close-geared to a literate and educated people. The leading nations at the present time are precisely those which are best educated. The better educated peoples are those who have made the greatest advances in science and technology; they are better able to support themselves for they can apply their science and technology to the development of their natural resources.

Skill, foresight and organisation are essential qualities in economic development and these usually are woefully lacking in the underdeveloped countries. Countries lacking adequate educational facilities are incapable of realising and organising their resources and are apt to squander and waste such resources as they have. Thus there is a telling need to raise education standards in these backward countries.

13. External aid. To conclude this chapter let us summarise the ways in which the developed countries can help the underprivileged. Basically, they can help in four main ways.

(a) *Financial aid.* The underdeveloped countries are, as we have already pointed out, chronically short of money. This could be provided by:

(i) *Gifts of money* from the wealthier countries or from voluntary organisations, *e.g.* Oxfam.

(ii) *Loans* from the World Bank, the International Development Fund and foreign governments.

(iii) *Sale of assets*, *e.g.* mineral rights, as in the case of oil in the countries of the Middle East.

(b) *Equipment.* Presents of equipment, in lieu of cash, are really another form of financial aid but items such as factory plant, agricultural machinery and transport equipment, are all of great value. Under the Colombo Plan, for example, many countries have been materially helped by gifts of equipment of various kinds.

(c) *Training schemes.* The developed countries can provide training at all levels to selected students from the underdeveloped countries; many thousands of students are already receiving scientific, technical, agricultural and medical training. Alternatively, skilled personnel can be loaned to the underdeveloped countries to assist them in development schemes and to teach them modern methods.

(d) *Economic help.* Practical help could be given by guaranteeing markets and economic prices for the agricultural commodities and industrial products which the underdeveloped produce. This would help them in an essentially practical way and would foster increased agricultural and industrial development, both of which are necessary for their future material prosperity.

PROGRESS TEST 9

1. Explain what is meant by the term "underdevelopment." Give some examples of underdeveloped countries. (2, 5)

2. What agricultural problems face the underdeveloped countries? (6, 7)

3. What can be done to help the underdeveloped countries improve their agriculture? (7)

4. Show how (a) animal pests, (b) social customs, may adversely affect agriculture in underdeveloped countries. (6, 7)

5. What reasons can be advanced for the desire of underdeveloped countries to embark upon a policy of industrialisation? (9)

6. What advantages are to be gained by the industrialisation of countries which, hitherto, have been producers of primary products? (11)

7. "Cultural features may influence man's activities and outlook." Justify this statement by quoting some examples. (4, 6, 12)

8. Show how (a) lack of power resources, and (b) political instability, may handicap the development of backward countries. (10)

SUGGESTED PROJECTS

1. Select *one* of the following underdeveloped countries and find out as much as you can about it, writing up your material in a well-ordered geographical survey: Peru; Mexico; Tanzania; Indonesia; Pakistan.

2. Find out as much as you can about *either* the Colombo Plan *or* the International Development Fund; in your final essay, indicate how effective the scheme has been.

DISCUSSION TOPICS

1. Is it desirable or possible for the "haves" to share with the "have-nots?"

2. No amount of external aid alone will solve the problem of the underdeveloped countries: only self-help will bring the solution.

PART THREE

THE PRODUCTION OF COMMODITIES

CHAPTER X

AGRICULTURAL PRODUCTION

IMPORTANCE

1. The importance of agricultural production. Agriculture is the most important occupation in the world as a whole for *something like 70% of the world's population are engaged in farming*, either the growing of crops or the rearing of animals.

The proportion of the employed population engaged in farming varies widely between countries, as the following table shows:

	(*approx. percentage*)
Gt. Britain	2
West Germany	8
Japan	15
Spain	27
India	58
Egypt	60
Colombia	72
Jordan	80
Guinea	95

The first seven of these figures are shown graphically in Fig. 8.

NOTE:

(i) Even in countries such as England and Belgium, which are predominantly industrial, farming is a major and important activity.

(ii) Even in Norway and Finland, where conditions are far from good for farming, agriculture is the single most important activity.

2. The role of agriculture. In a broad way agricultural production, whether it is concerned with the growing of crops or animal husbandry, produces commodities of two principal kinds:

(*a*) *foodstuffs*, *e.g.* cereals, fruits and beverages (XI), meat and dairy produce (XII); and

(*b*) *industrial raw materials*, *e.g.* cotton, rubber, vegetable oils, wool and hides (XIII).

Mostly farmers specialise, concentrating either upon food production or raw materials, but, sometimes, as in mixed farming, the farmer may produce both, as often happens in the United Kingdom. Sometimes a by-product of one type of farming may be a significant product in the other type of farming; for example, the cultivation of sugar-beet results in the production

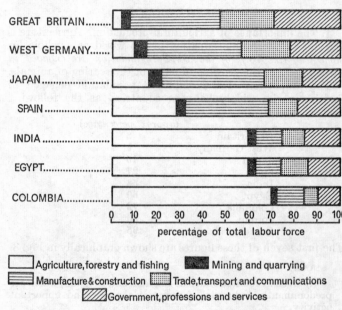

FIG. 8.—*Graph of economic activities*

The bar-chart graph shows the proportions of the employed population engaged in the main economic activities for a number of selected countries.

of sugar, a foodstuff, and the waste or by-product forms cattle-cake or fertiliser; likewise, the growing of cotton for its fibre yields cotton-seed, which is processed to give a vegetable oil used in the making of margarine.

3. The agricultural landscape. We are always impressed with the industrialised landscape with its chimneys, great factories, spoil heaps, communication lines. We readily re-cognise the industrial landscape and comment that man has left a heavy, and often ugly, imprint upon it.

When we turn to the agricultural landscape we tend to talk about the rural scene, the green fields, the countryside. What we often fail to do is to recognise that the hand of man upon the landscape is just as firm, though certainly less ugly; for the agricultural landscape is *a cultural, humanised landscape.* It is usually very different from the natural landscape.

In an agricultural landscape the most important features in it are those pertaining to man's farming activities, *e.g.* the field patterns, the walls and hedges, the farmsteads and barns, the signs of tillage, the growing crops, the domesticated ani-mals as well as, perhaps, ponds, ditches and wind-pumps.

TYPES OF AGRICULTURE

4. Types of landscape. The agricultural landscape differs widely from place to place: for example:

(a) In *England*: usually irregularly shaped fields, of varying size but usually fairly small, bounded by walls or hedges; the fields have a variegated colour in summer because a variety of crops are grown in the fields; the farmsteads usually lie amidst the fields and have an assortment of out-buildings; there will often be cattle and sheep and poultry as well as crops. In the hillier parts, farms will often run up the hillslope, having a portion of water meadow, arable and rough grazing land. There will be lanes and country roads linking the farms to the main highways.

(b) In the *Dutch polderlands*: here there will be a regular checkerboard of fields, bounded on every side by ditches for drainage purposes and numerous small bridges. The fields will be fairly small and the farm area small and the fields will be largely under grass for the damp polderlands are well suited to dairying. The farmhouses will be regularly spaced apart or will all be clustered together in one part of the polder. The land-scape will look trim, neat and well-organised; indeed, it will tend to look, as in truth it is, artificial. There will be field pumps and, perhaps in some of the older polders, windmills.

(c) In a *tropical plantation*: a similar orderliness to that in the Dutch polderlands is likely to be observed, although around the cultivated area there is likely to be forest. The trees or crops will be regularly laid out in rows and have a look of military smartness about them for they will be carefully tended and the soil beneath the trees hoed and clear of weeds. There will be, in all likelihood, a plantation nursery, processing sheds, plantation offices, perhaps a compound or even a village where the workers dwell and a light railway or road for transportation purposes.

(d) In the *Canadian prairies*: vast fields, laid out on a checkerboard fashion, usually without boundaries, stretch as far as the eye can see over flat or gently undulating terrain. This is a monotonous landscape broken only by an occasional farmhouse or a railside elevator. In winter the dark brown soil will be covered by a thin drift of snow; in summer it will be a sea of rippling golden grain. And in late summer and early autumn one is likely to be aware of a batch of great combine-harvesters carving their way through the ripened grain. Here is to be found mechanised farming at its most magnificent.

(e) In *Japan*: here, in direct contrast, are the smallest of fields, pocket-handkerchief fields, often formed out of steep hillslopes by dint of careful terracing. In summer many will be under water and many farmers will be seen working in the fields. Every square inch of land will be carefully cultivated and the bunds surrounding the fields will be growing bush crops. Everything will be vivid green. Few, if any, animals will be seen. Although most of the farmers will have their backs bent, toiling assiduously, every now and again one is likely to see a motorised hand plough or mechanical carrier, for the Japanese are gradually beginning to modernise and mechanise their farming.

5. Types of agriculture. There are many different types of agriculture. Some are backward, some are advanced; some are concerned with the production of food for small, local groups, some with the production of crops and animals for national or international markets.

(a) In some areas tillage is done in a primitive way with digging-stick, hoe and wooden plough; in others the agriculture is highly mechanised with tractors, combined harvester-threshers and the like.

(b) In some areas a wide variety of crops is grown, in others attention is devoted to a single main product.

(c) In some places the farmers own their own land, in others they rent their farmland or work it as share-croppers, *i.e.* in return for the land and perhaps seed and implements they hand over a proportion of the crop they grow, while in yet others the land may be owned by the state.

(d) Sometimes the farm plots are diminutive in size, sometimes hundreds of square miles in extent.

The diversity of methods, patterns and products is great.

6. Intensive and extensive agriculture. The land may be worked intensively or extensively.

(a) *Intensive farming*. Intensive methods involve much labour and/or capital per unit area cultivated. Such methods usually imply an absence of fallow, much use of fertiliser, carefully planned crop rotations, the use of specially selected seeds and the specialised and scientific breeding and feeding of animals, *e.g.*:

(i) In *Denmark* the most economical methods of farming are employed to get the maximum return from the land and the animals. There is relatively little land under grass; mostly the soil is cultivated intensively to produce grain, roots and other animal feedstuffs. Great attention is paid to breeding, feeding and milking. A successful co-operative system buys feeding stuffs, fertiliser, machinery, in bulk and, therefore, cheaply.

(ii) In *Japan* every patch of land is assiduously cultivated and slope land brought into tillage by terracing. Irrigation is practised and in southern Japan three crops of rice are harvested from the same field each year. *Catch crops*, sown either between the rows of main crops or in the short period between the harvest of the main crop and the sowing of a second, are grown. No land is left fallow and fertilisers (green manures, artificial fertilisers) are much used.

(b) *Extensive farming*. This kind of farming is practised where there is land in abundance. The criterion in this case is the output achieved per man, not per acre. Yields per acre are low, in contrast to the high yields per acre of the intensive system. For example:

(i) On the *prairies of the United States and Canada* wheat is grown under the extensive system (XI, 2–5). A highly mechanised type of farming is carried on because land is cheap and properties are large. The yields per acre are relatively low but the output per worker is large. Fertilisers are seldom used. Extensive farming is large-scale, mechanised and mainly concerned with one principal commercial crop.

(ii) In the temperate and semi-arid grasslands of *Australia* large-scale sheep farming is carried on: this is extensive grazing. The aim is the production of raw wool. Properties are often huge and the flocks run into tens of thousands, but the carrying capacity of the pastures is small. The ratio of animals to area is usually very low in extensive commercial livestock rearing and in parts of Australia, for instance, the sheep density works out at one sheep per five acres (*see* XIII, 7).

7. Monoculture. Where agriculture is given over almost exclusively to the production of a single commodity—crop or animal—the term *monoculture, i.e.* single-crop culture, is used.

(*a*) Various types of monoculture are:

(i) extensive cereal cultivation as on the North American prairies;

(ii) specialisation in a single plantation crop, such as sugar-cane or coffee;

(iii) the rearing of cattle for beef as on the tropical savannas of Brazil or Australia.

(*b*) The one-crop farmer is at a disadvantage in many respects:

(i) he is at the mercy of current world prices and if these fail he may suffer disaster;

(ii) a pest or plant disease may bring disaster: eradication is difficult because the host plant is never replaced by another;

(iii) natural disasters, *e.g.* winds, hail, drought, are likely to affect and spoil the whole of his crop.

8. Plantation agriculture. Plantation agriculture, occurring in selected tropical and sub-tropical areas, is mainly a development of the last one hundred years (although the system dates from the sixteenth century). It was made possible by:

(*a*) the capital resources and organisational capacity of Europeans;

(*b*) the labour supplied by native peoples or imported or indentured workers.

It is a system of farming suited to the production of *crops demanding processing and careful handling, e.g.* rubber, sugar-cane, tea, and to the production of *crops which do not give an immediate return.*

Certain features characterise tropical plantation agriculture:

(*a*) They are large-scale holdings, *e.g.*:

   (i) the *fazendas* or coffee plantations of Brazil;
   (ii) the rubber estates of Malaya.

(*b*) They often have to rely upon immigrant labour.

(*c*) They concentrate upon the production of a single crop.

(*d*) They commonly require heavy capital investment.

(*e*) They are often located in coastal areas for ease and economy of export.

LIMITING FACTORS

9. Factors controlling agricultural production. Agriculture in any area—the degree to which it is developed, the type of farming pursued, the crops that are cultivated—is dependent upon a combination of factors and conditions.

(*a*) *A market for the produce.* This is the most important factor for, clearly, there is no point in producing a commodity unless there is a market for it. The market may be provided by the farmer's own family, or a nearby market town, by a large city in the vicinity, by more distant parts of his own country, or by one or more foreign countries.

(*b*) *A remunerative price.* The producer must sell his produce at a profit otherwise he will eventually go bankrupt. World prices for most products vary considerably from year to year and the farmer may be badly hit if the prices are lower than he expects.

(*c*) *Adequate communications.* Unless the farmer is a subsistence cultivator producing solely for his own needs, he must have efficient and reasonably cheap means of transport, either by road, rail, water or air, to enable him to dispose of his commodities.

(*d*) *A labour supply* accustomed to farm work, except in the case of a holding worked by the farmer and his family. The organisation of labour, especially on large estates or communist collective farms, is a matter of great importance. Many undertakings, *e.g.* Ford's Amazonian rubber plantations, have partly foundered through inadequate supplies of labour.

(*e*) *A suitable climate.* Every crop has certain climatic requirements and the cultivation of a specific crop is largely determined by the climatic conditions. Upon the climate largely depends the kind of agriculture practised, *e.g.* whether cereal cultivation or grass and fodder crops will be predominant, whether beef-cattle or dairy-cattle will be reared, whether "wet" crops like rice or "dry" crops like millet will be grown.

(*f*) *A fertile soil.* Soils of most temperate lands which are not too wet are usually richer than those of cold areas and hot, wet tropical lands. Some soils are deep, some thin; some light, some heavy; some sandy, some clayey; some warm, some cold; some alkaline, some acid. The structure, texture, workability, and fertility will affect farming.

(*g*) *Social customs.* These, such as religious influences, may exercise a strong influence. For example, the practice among some peoples of sub-dividing land upon the death of the owner has led to excessive fragmentation. The social prestige of cattle in the African savanna lands, the Hindu veneration of cattle, and the Moslem attitude towards the pig illustrate the effect which social customs have upon animal husbandry.

(*h*) *Political factors.* Governments have sometimes introduced tariffs, bounties or subsidies, to persuade or compel farmers to produce commodities in accordance with national needs. During the years 1919–38 the growth of economic nationalism led many European countries to strive for agricultural self-sufficiency.

10. Limits of crop production. Certain conditions determine specific crop production in an area. It is possible to recognise three different limits of production:

(*a*) *the geographical limit;*
(*b*) *the economic limit;*
(*c*) *the actual limit.*

11. The geographical limit of production. Certain geographical conditions, the most important of which is climate, are necessary for the growth of any particular crop. For example, cotton cultivation in the United States is limited on the north by the two hundred consecutive frost-free days line and by the 77°F (25°C) isotherm for the three summer months, on the west by the 23-inch (584-millimetre) annual rainfall isohyet (unless irrigation is practised), and on the south and east by the 45-inch (1143-millimetre) rainfall line, for amounts in excess of this figure can ruin the crop. These may be termed the *absolute climatic limits* of the crop.

Sometimes crops require particular soil conditions and these may confine it to more limited areas within its possible climatic limits. The particular limits of crop production imposed by climate, soil or terrain form the *geographical limits of production*.

12. The economic limit of production. Sometimes, for economic reasons, it is not possible to grow a crop (or to rear animals) in an area which otherwise is geographically suitable. Among the economic reasons are that:

(a) the plant yield may be insufficiently great to justify its cultivation;

(b) the type of labour required may not be available in the area;

(c) adequate transport facilities may be lacking;

(d) competition from another crop, perhaps of greater value, may be a limiting factor;

(e) the likely occurrence of a plant or animal pest or disease may affect production.

NOTE: It is important to realise that the economic limits of production may change in response to changing economic conditions. Increased demand may lead to the expansion of the economic frontier, much as the exigencies of the Second World War led to much marginal land in England being brought into use. Economic factors, then, set the limits within which production becomes a feasible proposition at a particular time.

13. The actual limits of production. Although the geographical conditions may be suitable and though production may be economically feasible, the actual limits of production may be more narrowly demarcated. This may be illustrated by the Nigerian cacao industry. There is a wide belt of equatorial rain forest in southern Nigeria with high temperatures and plentiful rainfall which permit the cultivation of the cacao tree while economic production is feasible throughout much of this zone, yet the actual present-day limits of production are relatively small, the cacao-growing area being centred upon the city of Ibadan.

PROGRESS TEST 10

1. "Agriculture is the most important occupation in the world." Justify this assertion. (1)

2. What is meant by "a cultural or humanised landscape"? What features in the locality in which you live are the outcome of human action? (3)

3. Describe the features of the agricultural landscape in (a) the Dutch polderlands, and (b) the Canadian prairies. (4)

4. Compare and contrast the farming landscapes and farm activities in the Dutch polderlands and Japan. (4)

5. Draw distinctions between intensive and extensive forms of agriculture. (6)

6. Describe (a) the kind of region where plantation farming is usually carried on, quoting specific examples, and (b) the characteristic features of plantation agriculture. (8)

7. What are the principal factors affecting agricultural production in any area? (9)

8. Explain carefully the meaning of the following terms: monoculture; catch crops; by-products. (2, 6, 7)

CHAPTER XI

FOODSTUFFS FROM PLANTS

CEREALS

1. The cereals. Cereals are the chief food crops of man and are widely consumed as food staples. They are important because:

(*a*) they supply the greater part of his "calorie-intake";

(*b*) they yield highly per unit of land area cultivated.

The *principal cereals* are wheat, barley, oats and rye which are grown mostly in cool temperate lands; maize, which needs a warmer climate and is a sub-tropical crop; rice and various kinds of millet, which are mainly the products of tropical regions.

Wheat is the basis of bread, a staple of most white people, although so-called "black bread" is made from rye which is cultivated in central Europe and Russia. Barley, oats and maize, though sometimes consumed directly by human beings, *e.g.* in the form of barley bread, oats porridge, corn flour, are largely used nowadays as animal feedstuffs. Rice is the main dish of the peoples of eastern and south-eastern Asia. Some grains, notably barley, are also used in the making of alcoholic drinks, while all of them are sources of starch.

THE TEMPERATE CEREALS

2. Wheat. Like all the cereals, wheat is a species of cultivated grass. It is widely cultivated (*see* Fig. 9) and grows under many different conditions:

(*a*) in *cool temperature lands* where it is usually sown in *autumn*;

(*b*) in *continental interiors* with extreme climates where it is *spring* sown;

(*c*) in *hot tropical lands* where it is grown, often with irrigation, as a *winter* crop.

97

3. Essential requirements for wheat cultivation. Necessary conditions for wheat growing are:

(a) A fairly stiff, preferably loamy and non-acid soil.

(b) Mild, moist weather during germination and the early growing season.

(c) A temperature of at least 60°F (16°C) and sunshine for ripening.

(d) A frost-free growing period of approximately 100 days.

(e) Level or undulating land to facilitate mechanised operations if the wheat is grown under the large-scale extensive system.

Wheat is tolerant of considerable temperature and rainfall variation. It grows in the hot and fairly dry summers of the temperate grasslands and in the hot dry "Mediterranean" lands. Wheat grown under such conditions is called *hard wheat*; it is rich in protein and excellent for bread-making. Some of the wheat grown in the drier Mediterranean areas, such as southern Italy, produces a flinty grain suitable for making macaroni and spaghetti. Wheat may be grown with a mean annual rainfall of less than 15 inches (381 millimetres) and under *dry farming* methods with as little as 8 inches (203 millimetres) of rainfall a year. In western Europe, where the summers are moist, a *soft wheat* is produced: this is a starchy grain, not very good for breadmaking but suitable for cakes and biscuits.

4. Wheat production. Yields per acre are highest on the intensive farms of western Europe and in Denmark may be as high as 44 bushels per acre. Wheat, however, is a "robber crop" quickly exhausting the soil, hence under intensive farming systems it is normally part of a four-year rotation. In areas of extensive farming, as in the Canadian prairies or in Argentina and Australia, the yield per acre may be low, 15 to 20 bushels, but the output per man is high owing to the great use made of machinery. Yields in India and Pakistan are low but the reason here is mainly because of poor methods of farming.

The temperate grasslands of the Soviet Union grow nearly one-quarter of the total world production of wheat. North America accounts for roughly one-sixth, the United States growing slightly more than double that grown in Canada.

China is another major producer: she grows the same amount as the United States, about an eighth of the world total. India, France, Spain, Turkey, Italy, Argentina and Australia are all significant producers growing around ten million tons a year—about one-twenty-fifth apiece of total world production (*see* Table II).

5. International wheat trade. The big producers are not necessarily the exporters of wheat. The temperate grasslands of the United States and Canada, Argentina and Australia grow large amounts for export, since in the case of the last three their populations are small and they have a big surplus to spare. Most of their export goes to western Europe, especially the United Kingdom. At one time Russia was a major exporter, but during recent years the Soviet Union has frequently had to import wheat. Both China and India have begun to import wheat because of the rapid growth in their populations.

6. The other temperate cereals. Neither oats nor barley nor rye has anything like the importance in the world market of wheat, maize and rice. Fig. 9 shows the world distribution of these three cereals. They are mainly important because:

(*a*) they are more adaptable to climatic and soil conditions to which the leading cereals are unsuited;

(*b*) they are much used as animal feeding stuffs; and

(*c*) they are used for a variety of industrial purposes, *e.g.* in brewing and distilling and for the extraction of starch.

7. Barley. Originally the chief breadstuff, barley is now used principally as an animal feedstuff or in the making of alcoholic drinks, *e.g.* beer and whisky. Barley has the widest geographical range of all the cereals: since it will ripen at low temperatures, it will grow in higher latitudes than any other cereal and occasionally it is to be found beyond the Arctic circle while, since it is more tolerant of dry conditions than wheat, it will flourish in hot, semi-arid regions. Barley gives a higher yield per acre than any of the other temperate cereals.

World production of barley, around 150 million tons, is only about 40% that of wheat. Almost all of it is grown in the northern hemisphere, chiefly in the United States, Canada, the Soviet Union, the United Kingdom, France, West Germany,

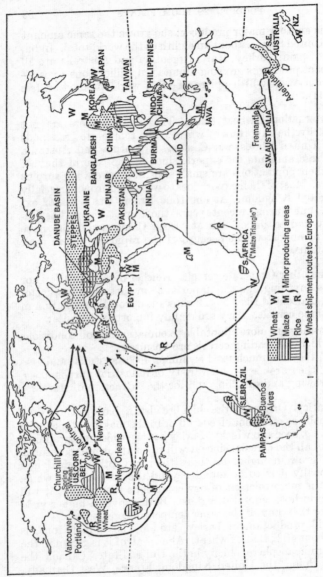

FIG. 9.—*World distribution of wheat, maize and rice*

These are the three cereals of greatest importance to man. Wheat and rice are essentially human foodstuffs, maize is primarily important as an animal feedstuff.

Denmark and Turkey. Very little (about one-twentieth of production) enters into international trade.

8. Oats. Oats thrive in the cooler, damper parts of those regions where wheat and barley are grown. Oats are grown both as a foodstuff and a feedstuff and are equally good for humans and animals. They form the cereal crop of such countries as Scotland, Norway and Newfoundland, where other cereals will not thrive. The great bulk of the oats grown, some 50 million tons in 1972, comes from the United States, Canada and the Soviet Union. As in the case of barley, very little oats —usually less than two million tons—enters into world trade.

9. Rye. Long known as the poor man's crop, it is eaten in the form of "black bread" by the people of central and eastern Europe. Rye bread is very nutritious, if not very appetising to look at. Rye is also much used in the making of beverages like whisky and vodka. It is a much hardier plant than wheat (although its optimum conditions coincide closely with those for wheat) and will grow in cool, damp climates and in poor soils. It is grown in the wheat belt, where either climate or soil is adverse to wheat, or, more usually, to the north of the wheat belt. Rye may be regarded essentially as a subsistence crop and about 90% of the total world output comes from central and eastern Europe. There is hardly any world trade in rye.

MAIZE

10. Maize. Maize or Indian corn, known by Americans simply as corn, is native to the western hemisphere. It is a species of grass of which there are several varieties.

(a) *Uses.* Maize does not make good bread, though it can be ground to produce corn flour which is used in bakery; nevertheless, it forms the staple foodstuff in many areas, notably in Mexico and Central America, in parts of southern Europe and in South Africa. Maize is most important, however, as an animal feeding stuff and the grain, corn meal and the growing plant are all used.

(b) *Conditions of growth:* Although maize grows under a considerable range of environmental conditions, for optimum growth and production the following conditions may be said to be necessary:

(i) a growing period of at least 140 days free from frost;
(ii) an average summer temperature of between 70° and 80°F (21° and 27°C);
(iii) warm nights with the temperature averaging about 58°F (14°C);
(iv) an annual rainfall of between 25 and 50 inches (635 and 1270 millimetres);
(v) frequent showers of light rain during the growing period;
(vi) plentiful sunshine during the ripening period;
(vii) a rich, well-drained, deep soil abundant in nitrogen.

11. World production of maize. Although production is widely distributed throughout the world, there are nine major growing areas (*see* Fig. 9):

(*a*) the Middle West, USA;
(*b*) the Central American Highlands;
(*c*) the south-eastern part of Brazil;
(*d*) the humid pampa of Argentina;
(*e*) the Danubian basin;
(*f*) the Caucasus–Black Sea borderlands of the USSR;
(*g*) the Punjab–Middle Ganges Lowland;
(*h*) central and northern China;
(*i*) South Africa.

Total world production in 1972 was 302 million tons, only a little less than that of wheat (*see* Table II). Present production is double that before the Second World War. This increase has been due largely to the development of high-yielding hybrid types of maize produced by selective cross-breeding. The United States is the predominant world producer accounting for almost half the total output.

12. Consumption and trade. The great bulk of the world's maize crop (some 80%) is consumed by animals, and some three-quarters of it never leaves the farm on which it is grown. World trade in maize is very small and is mainly due to the demands of countries which have intensive animal industries and rely largely upon imported feedstuffs. The United States is the world's leading exporter although a mere 3% of its output finds its way into the world market. The United Kingdom is the world's chief importer of maize.

TABLE II. OUTPUT OF SELECTED CROPS
(Figures in thousand metric tons for 1972)

Wheat		Rice		Maize	
U.S.S.R.	85,950	China	102,000	U.S.A.	141,053
U.S.A.	42,043	India	59,000	China	26,000
China	34,500	Indonesia	19,447	Brazil	14,892
India	26,477	Japan	15,281	U.S.S.R.	9,830
France	18,123	Bangladesh	14,387	Romania	9,817
Canada	14,514	Thailand	11,669	South Africa	9,630
Turkey	12,275	Burma	7,559	Mexico	9,400
Italy	9,423	Brazil	7,309	France	8,190
Argentina	7,900	S. Vietnam	6,348	Yugoslavia	7,940
World tota	347,703	World total	294,875	World total	302,854

Tea		Coffee		Cacao	
India	452	Brazil	1,500	Ghana	433
Sri Lanka	214	Colombia	680	Nigeria	244
China	200	Ivory Coast	270	Brazil	185
Japan	95	Mexico	220	Ivory Coast	185
Indonesia	72	Ethiopia	216	Cameroon	102
U.S.S.R.	71	Angola	215	Ecuador	68
Kenya	53	Uganda	200	Dominican Rep.	43
Turkey	39	Indonesia	185	Mexico	30
Taiwan	27	El Salvador	150	Papua New Guinea	26
World tota	1,374	World total	4,903	World total	1,477

Sugar Cane		Apples		Citrus Fruits	
India	115,378	France	2,829	U.S.A.	8,049
Brazil	84,000	U.S.A.	2,644	Japan	3,648
Cuba	45,000	Italy	8,873	Brazil	3,455
China	38,600	W. Germany	1,217	Spain	2,454
Mexico	34,000	Japan	1,000	Italy	1,819
U.S.A.	26,756	Turkey	850	Mexico	1,318
Pakistan	19,960	Spain	695	Israel	1,179
Australia	18,868	Hungary	600	Argentina	969
Colombia	17,860	Poland	560	China	890
Philippines	17,000	Argentina	512	India	870
World total	580,894	World total	19,505	World total	32,475

RICE AND MILLETS

13. Rice. Rice is essentially a tropical or sub-tropical crop and can only be grown where the climate is hot and moist, unless it is grown by irrigation. There are two chief types of rice:

(a) upland or "dry" rice; and
(b) paddy or "wet" rice.

Upland rice is relatively unimportant and most of the world's rice is paddy grown on flooded lowlands. Its high productivity, together with the great demands it makes on labour, make it a crop well-suited to the populous lands of eastern and southern Asia.

14. Geographical requirements. Although rice is grown under differing conditions, the primary requirements for successful cultivation are:

(a) *Level land with an impervious subsoil*, since the plant spends most of its life under water.

(b) *Abundant moisture;* this means 60 inches (1500 mm) or more of rain or compensating irrigation water.

(c) *Temperatures* of between 60° and 68°F (16° and 20°C) during the growing period and exceeding 75°F (24°C) for ripening.

(d) *Alluvial soils* are to be preferred, but rice is not a soil-exhausting crop like wheat.

(e) *A plentiful supply of cheap labour* since sowing, transplanting and harvesting is tedious, time-consuming work.

15. Methods of cultivation. Most rice is grown in the monsoon lands by traditional methods. More modern methods are used elsewhere.

(a) *In Monsoon Asia.* Almost all the coastal lowlands and wet alluvial valleys are devoted to paddy cultivation. In many areas its cultivation has been extended by terracing hill slopes. Oriental farmers divide up the land into small compartments or basins so that they can be easily filled either by the heavy monsoon rains or by irrigation water from ditches filled from rivers. The water is drained off when the rice plant reaches the ripening stage. In most Asiatic countries, apart from ploughing which is done by oxen or water-buffaloes, nearly all the farming operations are done by hand. Except in Japan, where there is much fertilisation, yields are generally low.

(b) *Outside the monsoon region.* The overwhelming bulk of the rice grown comes from the countries of Monsoon Asia but outside this region rice is cultivated in many other places. In some of these places as, for example, in Louisiana in the United States and in the Rhône delta in southern France, rice is grown by mechanised farming methods which contrast sharply with those traditionally practised by the oriental subsistence farmer. Yields are highest in Italy and fairly high in the United States, where improved seeds are often used.

16. Trade in rice. Of the world total production of some 295 million tons, which is approximately the same as wheat, about 95% is consumed in the country of its origin. Only a very small fraction of the output enters into international trade and most of this trade is carried on between the countries of Monsoon Asia, from rice-surplus to rice-deficit areas. China grows about a third of the world's production and India nearly a quarter but neither has any to spare. Burma, Thailand and the Khmer Republic are the chief exporters. Their surplus usually goes to Sri Lanka, Malaya and other lands which fail to grow enough for their needs or which, like China and India, may occasionally suffer from bad harvests. A recent trend has been the export to the Far East of rice from the western hemisphere. The appearance of the United States as an exporter (on a small scale) is a new feature of the world market (*see* Fig. 9 and Table II).

17. Millets. The term millet covers a variety of species of cultivated grasses; these form the humblest members of the grain crops, are a low-grade food, and their cultivation is an indication of a low standard of living. In sub-tropical and tropical regions of light rainfall, where water supplies are insufficient for wheat or rice, millet forms the chief grain crop. The main cultivated varieties are:

(*a*) *Sorghum* or Great Millet which is much grown in Africa and is variously called *durra* and *guinea-corn*; in India it is termed *jowar*.

(*b*) *Bajra*, a smaller spiked millet, which is important in India and Pakistan and occupies a considerable acreage in the drier parts of the two countries.

(*c*) *Kaoliang*, a giant millet, which is grown in northern China and Manchuria where it forms a valuable animal and human food.

VEGETABLES AND FRUITS

18. Vegetable foodstuffs. Apart from a few people who are basically flesh- or fish-eaters, various vegetable crops, after grain, form the chief article of diet; this is especially true of certain tropical areas. Vegetables, particularly the so-called green vegetables, are necessary for good health since they contain vitamins.

The chief vegetable foodstuffs consumed by man fall, broadly, into four categories:

(a) starchy tubers;
(b) root vegetables;
(c) pulses;
(d) green vegetables.

19. Starchy tubers. A number of starchy tubers, ripening underground, have become important food staples in some parts of the world. Less nutritious than grain, they have the merit of being easily cultivated. The most important tubers are as follows:

(a) *Potatoes.* The potato, a native of the Andes, now grown in practically every country in the world, is the most important of all the starchy tubers. It is particularly important in Europe and in the United States where it is well-suited to areas with summers that are apt to be cool and moist. Most of the potato crop is consumed as a vegetable but it is also fed to stock. Starch and industrial alcohol are also obtained from it.

(b) *Sweet potatoes.* Similar to the ordinary potato, it is chiefly cultivated in tropical regions, generally in primitive fashion by sedentary and shifting peasant subsistence farmers. In the Pacific Islands it forms, along with coconuts and fish, the basic diet of the people.

(c) *Manioc.* This grows in most tropical regions but is especially important in South America, notably in Brazil; it is also cultivated in wet, tropical Africa and in equatorial Asia. The flour, made from the ground-up, dried tuber, is known as cassava. The plant is also the source of tapioca, a foodstuff eaten in temperate lands.

(d) *Yams.* There are more than two hundred species of yam. Yams vary greatly in size. They are usually grown by primitive cultivators in the humid tropics.

20. Root vegetables. Similar to the starchy tubers in that they are root swellings and grow partially underground are carrots, turnips, swedes, parsnips, mangolds. All are essentially crops of the cool temperate lands. Root crops play an integral part in the crop rotation systems of modern scientific farming. Carrots and parsnips excepted, root crops are mainly grown as fodder crops.

21. Pulses. This is a general term for leguminous plants including peas, beans, soya-beans, ground-nuts, lentils, etc.

Beans, of which there are many varieties, are widely grown as they flourish under a great range of climatic conditions. The soya-bean, which in the Far East is a multi-purpose crop, has recently come to be cultivated on a large scale in the United States as a source of vegetable oil.

22. Green vegetables. A variety of green vegetables, *e.g.* cabbages, cauliflowers, Brussel sprouts are grown as subsistence crops, often in gardens and allotments, as well as field crops.

23. Market gardening. Many vegetables, and often also salad crops, such as lettuces and tomatoes, are intensively cultivated on small specialised plots, known as market gardens or, in North America, as truck-farms. The emphasis is on the commercial cultivation of carefully graded, meticulously packed garden-crops which have a ready sale in urban areas where the people enjoy high living standards (*see* X, **9**).

Earlies or *les primeurs* are grown in areas which are favourably placed climatically, *e.g.* the Scilly Isles, the south Cornish coast, the Channel Islands, Brittany, Florida, Cuba; these are dispatched, often by air, to city markets where they command high prices (thus offsetting the extra cost of carriage) because of their "out of season" availability.

24. Fruits. Like vegetables, fruits are grown on a small scale round farmsteads in most parts of the world. Again, as with vegetables, they may provide the whole of the commercial farmer's income, and they may be marketed in the fresh, preserved or canned condition. With the introduction of cold storage, the speeding up of shipping services, and the rise in living standards in many countries, certain fruits, *e.g.* apples, oranges, bananas, have entered much more widely into international trade.

Fruits fall into three principal classes:

(*a*) *tropical fruits:* bananas, pineapples, dates, coconuts, Brazil nuts;

(*b*) *sub-tropical fruits:* citrus fruits, figs, grapes, almonds, walnuts;

(*c*) *temperate deciduous fruits:* apples, pears, plums and other stone fruits and various "soft" fruits.

Output figures for one fruit of each type are shown in Table II.

25. Apples. These are the most important cool temperate fruit. They are widely grown in Europe, in the north-western and north-eastern parts of the United States and the adjoining parts of Canada, in south-eastern Australia and New Zealand. In France, Germany and Britain a portion of the crop is converted into cider. Pears, a similar hard deciduous fruit, have a slightly wider range than apples, but both production and exports are much smaller.

26. Citrus fruits. Two of the citrus fruits, oranges and lemons, are grown mainly in lands having a Mediterranean type of climate, but oranges may also thrive in warm lands with wetter summers such as Florida, southern Japan and south-eastern Brazil. Lemons are more restricted in their distribution coming mostly from southern Italy and Sicily and southern California. Ninety per cent of the world's grapefruits are grown in the United States, especially in Florida and Texas; some come from the West Indies and British Honduras and South Africa. Limes, cultivated mainly for limejuice, come chiefly from the West Indies, *e.g.* Dominica.

27. Bananas. They are the principal tropical fruit entering into international trade. Characteristically produced on plantations situated on tropical coastlands, bananas are transported green in air-conditioned ships to Europe and North America, where large quantities are consumed.

Commercial production is most significant in the West Indies, Central America, Colombia, Ecuador and Brazil. A small but sweet variety, of less importance than formerly, is grown on the rich volcanic soils of the Canary Islands. Banana production in the West Indies and the Central American Republics has in the past suffered from disease, which sometimes wipes out whole plantations, and hurricane damage.

28. Pineapples. Grown in tropical regions, especially in areas near the sea, pineapples require a moist but light soil. Most of the pineapple entering international trade is in the canned form, either fruit or juice. Half of the world's commercial production is accounted for by Hawaii, but considerable quantities are also produced in Mexico, Cuba, Brazil, Malaya, the Philippines, Taiwan, Queensland in Australia and Natal in South Africa.

29. Dates. Dates are peculiar among the world's crops in that their chief habitats are the hot desert oases, especially those of Afro-Asia. Dates like great heat but require water around their roots. Most date-palms yield 100–200 lb of fruit a year and, like bananas, form a staple article in the diet of some native peoples. Most of the export dates come from the palmeries of Iraq, Algeria, Morocco and Tunis. There are also date groves in southern Spain and southern California. Iraq is *the* outstanding producer and exports about two-thirds of its total output chiefly to the United Kingdom and the United States.

30. Grapes. The vine, a deciduous fruit most commonly identified with "Mediterranean" lands but not confined to them is especially valuable because, besides providing grapes as table dessert, it also yields currants and raisins (dried grapes), and wine (*see* Fig. 10). Outside the lands of Mediterranean climate, *viticulture* is carried on in parts of central Europe (in areas warm enough to provide late summer and

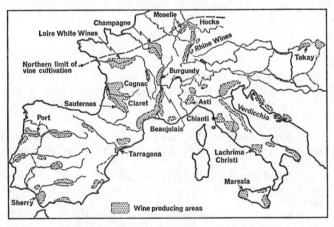

Fig. 10.—*Wine-producing areas in Europe*

Italy, France and Spain are the world's leading producers of grapes; France, Italy, Spain and Algeria the chief producers of wine. The lands around the Mediterranean Sea account for some 75% of the total world production of wine. The map shows the chief wine-producing areas and the more important types of wine.

early autumn temperatures of 60°F (16°C), southern Russia, the southern shores of Lakes Erie and Ontario in the United States, and, with irrigation, in the Murray Darling Basin in Australia and in the "oasis" towns of north-western Argentina.

31. Wine. The main end-product of viticulture is wine, whose character varies with the variety of the plant, the soil, the climate and the manner of preparation. Some wines, such as the *vin ordinaire* of France and Algeria, are cheap and un-distinguished, but others are of quality and often command high prices: such, for example, are champagne, claret and burgundy, all from France, the hocks of the Rhineland, the port of the Douro valley in Portugal, the sherry of Xeres in Spain, the asti and chianti of Italy and the tokay of Hungary. Some wine is produced in the grape-growing areas of Australia, South Africa and Argentina.

The lands around the Mediterranean Sea are *the* great wine producers, accounting for 75% of total world production. France, Italy and Spain are the greatest producers and France the leading exporter. Fig. 10 shows the different wines produced in the European countries.

SUGAR

32. Sugar-producing crops. Sugar, used not only for sweetening food and drink but in the preparation of jams, canned fruits and confectionery, comes from the juices of many plants but the three main sources are:

(*a*) *Trees* such as the sugar-maple, the date-palm and several other palms, but these form the least important source.

(*b*) *Sugar-cane*, a tall, tropical, thick-stemmed perennial grass cultivated mainly on plantations by monocultural methods.

(*c*) *Sugar-beet*, a root plant, belonging to the beet family, grown in cool temperate lands.

The vast bulk of the world's sugar supply comes from cane (about three-fifths) and beet (two-fifths). Cane provides some 95% of the total exportable supplies. Molasses and rum are by-products of cane-sugar production.

33. Growing conditions compared. The following table compares the different conditions of climate, soil and labour for sugar-cane and sugar-beet.

	Cane	Beet
Temperatures:	70°–80°F (21°–27°C)	60°–73°F (16°–23°C)
Rainfall:	Minimum of about 50 in. (1270 mm) unless irrigated.	About 25 in. (635 mm) mainly in growing period.
Soil:	Deep, fertile, well-drained soil.	Well-drained, fertile, loamy, stone-free, limey soil.
Labour:	Abundant cheap labour necessary.	Makes fairly heavy demands on labour.

34. World production. The principal cane-producing regions are the West Indies (especially Cuba), Indonesia (especially Java), India, the Philippines, Taiwan and southern China. Other areas of note are the tropical coastlands of Queensland, Mauritius, Hawaii, Natal, the Gulf Coast of the United States, and Brazil. The world's leading exporter of cane-sugar is Cuba.

Nearly all the world's supply of beet comes from either the large sugar-consuming countries which share the more fertile soils (*e.g.* loess soils) of the Great North European Plain, especially Russia, France, West Germany, Poland and Czechoslovakia, or from the United States, particularly California, Colorado and Utah, where it is grown under irrigation. Scarcely any beet-sugar enters into international trade.

THE BEVERAGES

35. Tea. A native of south-eastern Asia, tea requires *considerable warmth, plentiful moisture, a deep, fertile, well-drained soil and makes heavy demands upon labour*. It is typically grown on hill slopes. Frequent pickings are made throughout the year. The bushes are pruned to a height of about 4 feet to produce a flat "top" to facilitate picking. The collected leaf is taken to the processing plants on the estates or plantations where withering, rolling, fermentation, drying, sorting and packing (in foil-lined chests to preserve the flavour and prevent deterioration in carriage) is undertaken.

The chief producing areas are Assam and the Nilgiri Hills in

India, the hill country of central Sri Lanka, western Java, central and southern China and southern Japan. Plantations also occur in Uganda, Kenya, Tanzania, Malawi and Natal, in Taiwan, Pakistan and in the Soviet Union. India, Sri Lanka and China are the three major producers. India and Sri Lanka almost dominate between them the world export trade (Table II). More than half of the world's exports are consumed in the United Kingdom.

36. Coffee. In origin an Old World plant, the bulk of world production now takes place in Latin America. Plantations occur in tropical regions, usually on sloping land, where there are *long, hot and moist seasons followed by a short, dry and cool season, where frost is absent, and where the soils are rich and deep and well-drained*.

The chief producers are listed below (Table II gives the output figures for 1972):

(a) *South-eastern Brazil*, where nearly one-third of the world's total output is produced; here coffee is cultivated on large plantations or *fazendas*, especially in the areas of terra rossa soil, red earth rich in iron and potash which is derived from weathered igneous rock.

(b) *The hill country of Colombia*, up to altitudes of around 6000 feet, where small farmers specialise in the production of a finer, milder variety known as *café suave*. Colombia produces about one-tenth of the world output.

(c) *The republics of Central America* and some of the West Indian Islands which tend to specialise in coffee of a very high quality; the coffee is cultivated on the western slopes of the Cordillera and on the western sides of hills in the islands where there is a dry season.

(d) *In Africa*, three countries, in order of production Ivory Coast, Angola and Uganda, have a substantial output but the combined production is only about 15% of the world total.

Brazil continues to dominate the world export trade in coffee, most of which goes to the United States and the countries of northern and central Europe.

37. Cacao. Cacao, in its native home and distribution, is almost the reverse of coffee. The cacao tree is native to Latin America, but about two-thirds of the world's total production (over 1 million metric tons) of cacao comes from the countries of West Africa, where it is mainly grown as a cash crop on peasant farms. Latin America (Brazil, Ecuador, Venezuela, Dominican Republic) produces most of the rest (*see* Table II).

The cacao tree is essentially an equatorial plant requiring *uniformly high* (80°F 27°C) *temperatures, an abundant and evenly distributed rainfall, deep, rich, moist, but not saturated, soils and shelter from direct sunlight and strong winds.* Optimum conditions are usually found in equatorial coastal lowlands which are a little removed from the littoral.

The fruit, borne on the trunk and main branches, consists of large, oval-shaped, purplish pods from which the individual beans, encased in pulp, have to be extracted and dried before being bagged for export.

In the importing countries (mainly the United Kingdom, the countries of Western Europe, and the United States), the beans are processed: if cocoa is the desired product the beans are ground up, the fatty content (butter) extracted, and the residue powdered; if chocolate is to be made, the powdered cocoa is mixed with a proportion of cocoa-butter and sugar, along with milk if "milk" chocolate is desired.

PROGRESS TEST 11

1. Choose *one* of the following cereals and (*a*) give the essential geographical requirements for its successful cultivation, and (*b*) describe the international trade in the commodity: wheat; maize; rice. (2–5, 10–16)

2. Compare the methods of rice cultivation in Monsoon Asia with those in Europe and the United States. (15)

3. (*a*) What are millets? (*b*) Name the chief varieties grown. (*c*) Indicate the chief growing areas. (17)

4. Write brief accounts of (*a*) market gardening; (*b*) viticulture. (23, 30)

5. Compare the conditions of production of citrus fruits with those of bananas. (26, 27)

6. Contrast the geographical conditions under which cane-sugar and sugar-beet are grown. (33)

7. Describe the cultivation of grapes and the production of wine. (30)

8. Choose *one* of the hot beverages and (*a*) give its geographical requirements; (*b*) name the chief producers and exporters. (35–37)

9. "Wheat is grown under many differing climatic conditions." Describe the conditions required. (2, 3)

10. Briefly outline the meaning of the following terms: robber crop; black bread; manioc; animal feedstuff; *les primeurs*; leguminous plants; *vin ordinaire*. (1, 4, 12, 19, 21, 23, 31)

PRACTICAL WORK

1. Draw a map of either France or Spain and locate accurately upon it the areas where wine is produced.

2. Using the production figures in Table II, draw bar graphs to illustrate the production by various countries of wheat, maize and rice.

3. Using the production figures in Table II, draw pie graphs (divided circles) to illustrate the production by various countries of tea, coffee and cacao.

CHAPTER XII

FOOD FROM ANIMALS

ECONOMIC IMPORTANCE AND DISTRIBUTION OF ANIMALS

1. Economic importance of animals. Animals contribute much to the world's economy: in fact, the annual value of their contribution is greater than that provided by all the minerals. Animal life as a whole is contributing more each year to the world's economy. Animals, chiefly domestic animals, are used for several purposes:

(*a*) for carriage or as draught animals;
(*b*) for food, chiefly meat and milk;
(*c*) for wool, hair and silk; and
(*d*) for hides, skins and other raw materials.

In this chapter we are concerned only with animals as producers of foodstuffs, *i.e.* with the production of *meat, milk* and *dairy produce*. Some account of the *fishing* industry will be included.

2. Cattle rearing. Cattle are reared for three reasons:

(*a*) as draught or work animals;
(*b*) for beef production; and
(*c*) for dairy products.

It is unusual for cattle to be reared for a dual purpose. Cattle for draught purposes are reared mainly in south-eastern Asia and such beasts yield poor milk and meat. Elsewhere cattle are raised mostly for beef or milk and they are, in fact, the world's chief providers of meat and dairy produce.

The demands of beef and dairy cattle in respect of feedstuffs, stalling, attention and labour differ greatly and usually there is specialisation in one or the other. In areas of mixed farming economy, as in Western Europe, it is not uncommon for both beef and dairy cattle to be raised on the same farm.

3. Distribution of cattle. Cattle are widely spread throughout the world but are chiefly to be found in three environments:

(a) *In the temperate grasslands, e.g.* the prairies of North America, the pampas of Argentina and Uruguay (Fig. 11), and the grassy plains of Hungary and southern Russia.

(b) *In the tropical grasslands, e.g.* the campos of Brazil, the llanos of Venezuela (Fig. 11), the Sudan of Africa, and in the Northern Territory and Queensland in Australia (*see* Fig. 14, below).

(c) *In cool, moist, temperate lands* which have been *cleared* of their natural forest cover and developed as man-made pasture lands, *e.g.* in Western and Central Europe, in the north-eastern part of the United States and coastal New South Wales and Victoria, Australia (*see* Fig. 14).

4. The special case of India. India has more cattle than any other country in the world: some 176 million. Why, since it is not a country of either natural or artificial grasslands, has it such a large cattle population? Why, especially, when the peoples of India eat little meat or dairy produce? The reason is that cattle have a ritualistic status; they are sacred and cannot be killed. The result is that India is plagued with large numbers of cattle—poor, undernourished creatures of little economic value. They yield little milk and are inefficient as work animals. On the other hand, they consume large quantities of food that can ill be spared.

5. Beef production. The finest beef cattle are raised in the cool temperate lands of Europe and North America, but these areas are incapable of meeting the great demand for beef, hence the meat deficiency must be imported from elsewhere. In the case of north-western Europe beef is supplied mainly by the southern hemisphere producers. Fig. 11 shows the distribution of cattle in S. America, as outlined below. (For sheep, *see* XIII, 7.)

(a) *Argentina and Uruguay.* Large beef herds are reared on the pampas or temperate grasslands of these countries. Argentina has 55 million head of cattle, Uruguay 7 million. Argentina produces more than 2 million tons of beef a year. Cattle ranching for beef production was stimulated by a series of inventions and developments:

(i) the enclosing of the range lands by barbed wire fences;

FIG. 11.—*Cattle and sheep in South America*

Note how most of the cattle are to be found in the warmer and wetter areas, and most of the sheep in the drier areas, approximately where the rainfall is under 20 inches (510 millimetres). Argentina and Uruguay are the most important countries for pastoralism and are the chief exporters of meat and wool.

(ii) the introduction of alfalfa, a nutritious plant of the clover family;

(iii) the invention of beef extracts, *e.g.* "Bovril," "Oxo," and of canning;

(iv) the development of the refrigeration process.

The beef is prepared in *frigoríficos* (slaughter-houses and freezing plants) and *saladeros* (canning factories) and the frozen, chilled and tinned meat is exported to European markets, especially England. As Argentina's own population grows and as the standard of living rises, she finds she has less and less meat to spare for export.

(*b*) *Brazil and Venezuela.* The tropical grasslands of these two countries, *i.e.* the Brazilian Plateau and the Orinoco Basin, hold out great possibilities for beef production. Some cattle are already raised, but the export trade is still small. Although improvements and developments are taking place, a number of factors hinder the beef industry:

(i) the inferior breeds reared do not produce good quality meat;

(ii) the tropical grasslands are not particularly nutritious and generally the grazing is poor;

(iii) insect pests are often a nuisance, *e.g.* the cattle-tick;

(iv) there are inadequate communications and packing plant.

(v) there are seasonal water shortages.

Attempts are being made to improve beef production by up-grading the cattle (through breeding with imported stock), by using insecticides, by improving communications, by building processing plants, and by sinking wells.

(*c*) *Australia.* Substantial numbers of beef cattle are herded on large ranches in the tropical parts of Australia and frozen beef from the Northern Territory and Queensland is shipped to Britain. The beef cattle industry here suffers from most of the difficulties suffered by Brazil and Venezuela. Perhaps even more serious here is the problem of drought and watering points (using artesian supplies) have had to be provided on ranges and along the stock routes. (Australian cattle-raising areas are shown in Fig. 14, p. 129.)

6. Dairy produce. Dairying demands more intensive farming than does beef production; hence the dairying areas are much more restricted. Dairying tends to occur:

(*a*) *in cool, moist climates* of equable character which are not favourable for cereal cultivation; and

(b) *near large urban concentrations of population* who enjoy high living standards and demand fresh milk.

Milk, in its liquid state, has an economic limit of distribution of about 200 miles (382 kilometres), but in its processed form of butter and cheese there is, under modern methods of transport, no limit to the distance carried. Considerable quantities of milk nowadays are processed, *e.g.* condensed and powdered milk. The dairying industry has tended to become highly specialised, each dairying area concentrating upon either fresh milk or butter or cheese production.

7. Dairying areas. The principal dairying areas are:

(a) *North-western Europe.* Dairying is very highly developed in many parts of the Atlantic fringe, especially in Denmark, Holland and Britain, and to lesser extent in Eire, northern France, the North Sea coastlands of West Germany and in parts of Norway and central Sweden. It is also significant in the Alpine region. The large industrial urban populations of the United Kingdom and West Germany provide big markets. Denmark tends to specialise in butter production, Holland and Switzerland in cheese.

(b) *North-eastern United States and the St Lawrence lowlands of Canada.* In North America, cattle grazed on the cool, moist northern Atlantic coastlands produce milk for the big cities, *e.g.* Boston, New York, Baltimore and Philadelphia. States farther west, such as Michigan, Minnesota and Wisconsin, have a smaller milk sale and tend to concentrate upon butter and cheese. In this part of the United States and in the St Lawrence lowlands of Canada dairying is handicapped by the cold winters which necessitate winter shedding and stall feeding.

(c) *New Zealand.* The well-watered plains of the North Island, New Zealand, have become an important dairying area in the southern hemisphere. This dairy industry has been made possible only with the introduction of the refrigeration process. The United Kingdom imports large quantities of butter from New Zealand. The equable climate of New Zealand means that animals can be kept out-of-doors all the year round and there is little need of accessory feeding-stuffs.

8. Pig products. Pig rearing is often associated with the dairying industry since the waste skimmed milk provides a good pig food. The classic example of the integration of dairying and pig-rearing is provided by Denmark, which is an important producer of bacon and canned meats.

The chief pig-rearing areas of the world are:

(a) *Western and central Europe* (about 80 million), where they are chiefly reared on potatoes and skimmed milk.

(b) *The United States and southern Canada;* in the former, they are mostly found in the Corn Belt and are fed on maize.

(c) *Brazil and Argentina*, where they are also largely fed on maize.

(d) *China* (about 200 million) where they forage on whatever domestic or field left-overs there are.

NOTE: To the Moslems, Jews and Hindus the pig is regarded as an unclean animal and they will not eat pig meat. Because of this cultural prejudice, pig-keeping is largely absent through much of Africa, the Near and Middle East and in the Indian subcontinent.

In addition to the production of pork and the cured forms of pig meat, *i.e.* bacon and ham, pigs yield lard. The bulk of the pig meat entering into international trade is in the form of bacon, ham and canned pig meat. Denmark, Poland, Eire and Canada are important exporters. Britain is a substantial importer of processed pig meat from Denmark and Poland.

9. Mutton. Sheep are not often reared for a dual purpose; usually they are reared either for their wool or their meat, although there are now many dual-purpose crossbreeds. Whereas sheep raised for wool yield better quality wool under drier conditions, sheep reared for their flesh require better pasture and so are found in the wetter areas.

Mutton and lamb are much less important than beef. Apart from the United Kingdom, Australia and New Zealand and the countries of the arid zone of the Old World, there is very little market for mutton and lamb as a foodstuff.

Most of the world's mutton and lamb comes from the sheep-rearing countries of the southern hemisphere and New Zealand dominates the world market. New Zealand's production has been geared to the British market, for the United Kingdom is the world's largest consumer. The cool, equable, moist lowlands of New Zealand are well suited to the rearing of sheep for meat and in this respect New Zealand contrasts with Australia which is predominantly concerned with the production of wool (*see* XIII, **7**). Other significant producers of mutton and lamb are Argentina, Uruguay and Chile.

THE FISHING INDUSTRY

10. Fish as food. Fish are eaten chiefly by people living fairly close to the sea, but the practicability of transporting processed fish, *i.e.* in its dried, cured, frozen or canned form, over long distances makes it possible for people living far removed from the sea to eat fish, which is a valuable protein food. The quantity of fish consumed by peoples differs very widely; to some, such as the Icelanders, it is a staple foodstuff and the *per capita* consumption is large. The coastal dwellers of the Far East are lovers of fish and it is an important item in their diet.

11. Factors affecting fishing. The major fishing grounds of the world are found in temperate latitudes and the chief reasons for this are:

(*a*) Fish food is more abundant in *cooler waters* than in warmer waters and so fish tend to be much more plentiful in temperate latitudes.

(*b*) *The continental shelves* with their shallow waters are better developed in mid-latitudes than elsewhere; especially is this the case in the northern hemisphere.

(*c*) *The coastal regions in higher latitudes* are either infertile or overcrowded, hence people have turned to the sea to augment their food supplies.

(*d*) *It is easier to keep fish fresh* and therefore to trade in fish in cooler climates than in warm regions.

12. The world's principal fishing grounds. The major fishing grounds lie approximately between 30 and $66\frac{1}{2}$ degrees N bordering the continental areas of the northern hemisphere (*see* Fig. 12). There are four chief fishing grounds:

(*a*) *The marginal seas off north-western Europe* with which may be included the Icelandic area.

(*b*) *The shelves and banks of north-eastern North America* between Cape Cod and Newfoundland.

(*c*) *The north-western Pacific coast region of North America* between Oregon and the Bering Strait.

(d) *The marginal seas of eastern Asia* around Japan, Korea, and off the coast of China.

In the southern hemisphere neither the fishing grounds nor the fishing industry, with one remarkable exception, are so well developed although potentialities exist off northern Chile and Peru (which has been developed), off the western coast of South Africa, and off the western coast of Western Australia (Fig. 12). Within the last decade the Peruvian fishing industry

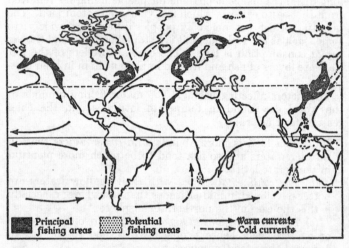

FIG. 12.—*The world's major fishing grounds*

The chief fishing grounds are to be found on the continental shelves, where the sun-lit, aerated waters are favourable for plankton upon which fish feed.

has developed with truly astonishing speed: in 1950 Peru's catch totalled a mere 84,000 tons, in 1970 it was in excess of 12 million tons, although by 1973 it had dropped back to 4·5 million tons. The Peruvian catch, however, is largely processed into fish-meal which is used as a fertiliser.

13. The chief fishing countries. The East Asian countries account for a substantial part of the world catch for Japan nets 10 million tons and China 5·3. The USSR ranks second in the world with 7·7 million tons. The West European countries especially Britain, Norway, France, West Germany and Iceland, land about 12% of the world catch. North America, particularly the Maritime Provinces of Canada and Newfoundland and the coasts of California, British Columbia and Alaska, accounts for about 5%. In South America, apart from the Peruvian catch, there is little development. Some commercial fishermen also work off the coasts of Morocco, South Africa and southern Australia. Tropical waters are not very productive though some Indians, Malays and Filipinos are fishers, but their markets are very restricted.

14. Fish farming. Although new techniques of fishing have been introduced, man, for the most part, still hunts his prey. In the Far East the practice of "farming" fish has long been undertaken and this old idea has been adopted by other peoples and fish farming of one kind or another is becoming of increasing importance.

Fish farming, or *pisciculture*, may be defined as the rearing of fish in freshwater ponds under more or less controlled conditions. For example, fertilisers can be used to increase the supplies of plants and phytoplankton on which the fish feed and particular species of fish, such as carp, can be raised. Farming of fish in the sea, however, is a difficult matter but by no means an impossibility in the future. But in many of the new man-made lakes, *e.g.* Lakes Kariba and Volta, fish have been introduced and new inland fisheries created. Fish farming schemes have been introduced in many of the underdeveloped countries.

15. Whaling. Commercially, the whale is the chief marine mammal. Few whales are to be found in Arctic waters as a result of too intensive catching in the past and nowadays the whales are chiefly hunted in Antarctic waters. International conventions have been drawn up to limit the annual catch and the length of the hunting season. Such regulations have been introduced to avert the threat of extinction but there are reasons for believing that these rules are not stringent enough.

Prior to the Second World War, Norway was the chief whaling country and had the largest whaling fleet, but vessels from the United Kingdom, the Soviet Union, France, the Netherlands, Japan and South Africa also participated in the seasonal whale hunt. Today, the United Kingdom no longer has a whaling fleet and even Norway has sold her ships. The industry, a declining one, is now dominated by Japan and the Soviet Union.

The chief commercial product is whale oil, which is largely used in the manufacture of margarine, soap and lubricants. Attempts to market whale meat have not been very successful. Some whale hide is used nowadays in the manufacture of shoes.

16. Industries associated with fishing. Only about 40% of the world fish catch is marketed fresh. About an equal amount is processed in some way for human consumption: large quantities of sardine and salmon are canned, haddock and herring are frequently cured, cod is often dried (dried cod finds a market in the Caribbean region and in central Africa), and large quantities are frozen.

Much of the catch which is unsold (this applies to a large proportion of the Norwegian herring catch) is converted into fish-meal which forms a valuable fertiliser. As mentioned earlier, almost the whole of the Peruvian catch is turned into fertiliser. Valuable by-products are fish-glue and liver-oils, *e.g.* halibut and cod-liver oil.

The fishing industry also supports many ancillary industries which include boat-building, box-making, the making of cans and the manufacture of nets.

PROGRESS TEST 12

1. Outline the economic importance of animals. **(1)**

2. Outline the distribution in the world (*a*) of cattle and (*b*) of sheep. **(3, 9)**

3. Give a brief account of cattle raising in the pampas of Argentina and Uruguay. **(5)**

4. Explain why the tropical grasslands have no major areas of beef production. **(5)**

5. What factors favour the dairying industry? Do these apply in the case of Denmark? **(6, 7)**

6. (*a*) Describe the location of the chief pig-rearing areas of the world, and (*b*) indicate the chief products of the pig-rearing industry. **(8)**

7. Account for the importance of the seas of north-western Europe as a fishing area. **(11, 12)**

8. Write brief explanatory notes on the following: fish-farming; alfalfa; cattle tick. **(5, 14)**

CHAPTER XIII

INDUSTRIAL RAW MATERIALS

1. Importance. Although some animal and vegetable food-stuffs yield by-products which may have industrial uses, many commodities are grown for specific manufacturing processes. Textiles may be of vegetable, animal or chemical origin but the vegetable fibres are the most important of all the different kinds of fibres used in textile manufacture. Edible oils, again, may be of animal or vegetable origin; in the past the former were the most important, but during the past one hundred years the vegetable oils have far surpassed oils and fats obtained from animals. Rubber can now be made synthetically, but until quite recently all the world's rubber came from plants.

It is important to emphasise two things:

(a) *The use of a particular commodity may change* as a result of:

(i) the finding or the invention of a substitute;
(ii) changes in fashion or usefulness.

(b) *New uses may be found for commodities* and this may lead to greatly increased production.

The chief industrial raw materials (other than minerals which will be dealt with separately later) are: fibres, vegetable oils, tobacco, rubber, hides and skins, bone and horn and timber, along with various other forest products.

Countries seldom are fortunate enough to be able to produce all, or even most, of the industrial raw materials they require, and even if they produce some it rarely happens they produce enough for their needs. This has meant that there is considerable international trade in industrial raw materials. This trade is linked with the revolutions in industry and communications which have characterised the past two hundred years and their concomitant, a rising standard of living which has made for a greater volume of manufactured goods and more sophisticated products.

TEXTILE FIBRES

2. Types of fibres. With the notable exception of wool and silk, the chief textile fibres are of vegetable origin. The chief one is cotton, followed by rayon (made from cellulose). Among the others are flax, jute and hemp. The newest fibres, *e.g.* nylon, Terylene, are made synthetically: nylon is derived from coal, Terylene from petroleum (*see* XIX, **10, 11**). Certain other fibres, such as glass fibre and asbestos fibre, are made from minerals.

3. Cotton. Cotton fibre is derived from the bolls (opened seed pods) of a tropical or sub-tropical perennial shrub generally grown as an annual. Cotton is sometimes cultivated for local use, but primarily it is a cash crop. There are numerous varieties, and these days new ones are bred to suit the particular conditions occurring in specific producing areas. The quality of cotton is largely determined by the length of the fibre, but other qualities such as fineness and lustre are taken into consideration. It is usual to classify cotton into two main types: *short*-stapled cotton, and *long*-stapled cotton.

Ideal conditions for good cotton production are:

(*a*) *Equable, warm conditions* in the growing period with temperatures reaching 77°F (25°C) in summer.

(*b*) *A minimum growing period* of at least 200 frost-free days, since cotton is killed by frost.

(*c*) *25–40 inches (635–916 millimetres) of rain* during the growing period or the equivalent supply of water by irrigation.

(*d*) *Dry, sunny conditions* during the maturing period since rain at this time is apt to spoil the bolls.

(*e*) *A deep, rich, well-drained soil* but one with a high moisture-holding capacity.

(*f*) *A large supply of labour* to meet the heavy demands of ploughing, sowing, weeding and picking.

The *United States* is the world's foremost producer, accounting for nearly a quarter of the total production. Most of it comes from the cotton belt in "the South" where the cotton is of medium grade; higher grade cotton is produced under irrigation in California and Texas. Fig. 13 shows the United States Cotton Belt. *China, the Soviet Union* and *India* are the next most important producers, followed by Brazil, Egypt, Mexico and Pakistan. Table III gives their output figures for 1972. Most of the world's high-grade cotton is grown under irrigation, notably in Egypt, Sudan (the Gezira), Peru and the Imperial Valley of the United States.

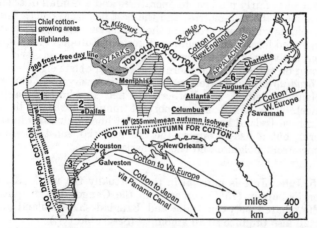

FIG. 13.—*The United States cotton belt*

Note the climatic controls: the 200 frost-free day line, which also corresponds closely with the summer isotherms of 77°F (25°C), marking the northern limit; the 20-in. (510-millimetre) isohyet which marks the western limit; and the occurrence of heavy autumn rains in the south which have prevented the extension of the cotton belt to the Gulf Coast. The chief producing areas are: 1. the High Plains of north-west Texas; 2. the Black Waxy Prairies; 3. the coastal plain of southern Texas; 4. the Mississippi floodplain; 5. the Middle Tennessee Valley; 6. the Piedmont plateau; and 7. the Atlantic coastal plain.

Rather less than half of the world's cotton crop enters into international trade. The chief exporters, roughly in order of importance, are the United States, Egypt, Mexico, Brazil and Pakistan. The bulk of the exported cotton goes to the important cotton textile manufacturing countries of Europe—the United Kingdom, France, Belgium, West Germany and Italy —and to Japan.

4. Flax. The flax plant, a member of the nettle family, has been used for the making of linen cloth from very early times and may well be the oldest of all the textile fibres. Linen is made from the fibrous material of the stalks of the flax plant, a plant which is also grown for its seed (linseed). Flax grows most successfully in well-drained clay loams. It is planted in spring, and harvested three or four months later. The flax plant likes fairly uniform temperatures and a rainfall of about 30 inches (765 millimetres) and the best flax fibre comes from the plants which are grown in the extensive forest clearings of the mixed forests and deciduous forests of Europe. Flax, however, is a very exhausting crop and, because of this, it is seldom grown on the same land more than once in about eight years.

Leading producers are European Russia (easily first), France, Poland, Belgium, the Netherlands and Czechoslovakia (in order). The USSR has important manufactures of linen. Northern Ireland has one of the largest linen industries in the world, but it has to import the raw material, most of which comes from Belgium and the Netherlands.

5. Jute. Jute is unusual in that virtually the whole of the world's supply (75%) comes from the Ganges–Brahmaputra delta, shared between India and Bangladesh. Thailand and Brazil also produce small amounts. (*See* Table III.)

Jute is a tall, reed-like plant, grown under very hot and wet conditions, hence it competes with rice for space. Like flax, jute has to be retted (*i.e.* rotted in water) following the harvest, and the fibre beaten out of the stalk. It is exported from Calcutta in India, Chittagong and other Bangladeshi ports, to Dundee, in Scotland, and to West Germany, France and Belgium. Some of the largest jute mills in the world, however, are located in Calcutta and other neighbouring cities. Jute is the fibre used in the manufacture of sacking or gunny-cloth as it is called in India. It is "the brown paper of the wholesale trade" and is used as the foundation of carpets and linoleum and in the making of upholstery and twine.

6. Hemp. Many different kinds of hemp are grown in different parts of the world. All are used for making ropes, string and the like. There are three chief kinds:

(a) *True hemp*, from which soft cords are made, grown principally in western Russia, Poland, Rumania and Italy.

(b) *Manila hemp*, or *abaca*, the basis of a harder fibre, suitable for ships' hawsers since it is tough, strong and water-resistant.

(c) *Sisal*, suitable for binder twine and sometimes used for matting, which is grown in Yucatan, Mexico (where it is called *henequen*), and on plantations in East Africa.

7. Wool. Wool sheep, as has already been indicated (*see* XII, 9), are generally to be found in fairly dry, temperate grassland areas. Such animals require little attention apart from dipping to discourage pests and the annual round-up for shearing,

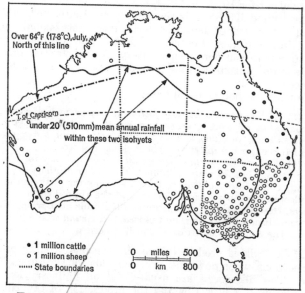

Fig. 14.—*Distribution of sheep and cattle in Australia*

Australia is the greatest sheep-rearing country in the world. She has about 145 million head of sheep, over 70% of them merinos. She produces about one-third of the world's total wool production, nearly half of the world's wool exports. By their nature sheep are unsuited to tropical heat, hence most of them are found south of the Tropic of Capricorn. Most of the wool sheep (chiefly of the merino breed) are grazed on the drier pastures of the interior in the south-eastern part of the continent, mostly in the areas between the 10–30-in. (255–765-millimetre) rainfall isohyets.

hence they may be grazed successfully in areas of low population density. Fig. 14 shows the distribution of sheep in
Australia, the world's leading producer.

The world's leading producers of wool are also, with the
exception of the Soviet Union, the chief exporters. The world
export trade in raw wool is dominated by four countries:
Australia which accounts for about 40% of the total trade,
New Zealand about 14%, Argentina about 10% (see Fig. 11)
and South Africa about 9%. All are southern hemisphere
countries with large acreages under grass and with no important wool textile industries of their own. Table III shows
their output for 1972.

The United Kingdom is the leading wool importer, taking
about one-quarter of the wool entering into international trade.
The United States, France, Belgium, West Germany and
Japan import considerable quantities. The substantial import
by Japan of Australian wool has been a notable development
in recent years.

Two further points are of note:

(a) *Wool is used in the manufacture of carpets*, as well as in the
production of wool textiles and some countries, *e.g.* India,
Iran, China, produce a coarser type of wool of lower grade
which is exported for the carpet-making industry.

(b) *Wool textile manufacturers may also use*, mostly for blend-
ing certain *special wools* obtained from other animals, *e.g.* the
long, silky fibres obtained from the Angora goat (*mohair*),
collected in South Africa, Turkey and the United States, *cash-
mere*, the soft downy wool from the Kashmir goat which lives
in the Himalayan region, and *alpaca* and *vicuna* wool obtained
from the Andean countries of South America.

8. Silk. Silk is produced from the cocoons of silk-worms.
The cocoons, when unwound, produce a lustrous gossamer-like
fibre. The silk-worms are usually fed on mulberry leaves.
The rearing of silk-worms and the production of raw silk is
almost entirely a domestic industry mainly undertaken by the
wives of peasant farmers. This is certainly the case in China
and Japan which are the chief producers of silk. The Soviet
Union ranks third in raw silk production. Korea, India and
Italy are producers of lesser note (*see* Table III). The Rhône
valley, formerly of some importance as a producer, is no longer
important for sericulture, although the silk-weaving industry
of the Lyons district is still of note. Japan is the largest ex-

porter of raw silk; most of it goes to the United States, France and the United Kingdom, which have silk manufactures.

TABLE III. OUTPUT OF SELECTED RAW MATERIALS
(Figures in thousand metric tons for 1972)

Cotton		Wool (clean)		Jute & Kenaf	
U.S.A.	2,995	Australia	455	Bangladesh	1,213
U.S.S.R.	2,450	U.S.S.R.	251	India	1,066
China	1,410	New Zealand	228	China	513
India	1,127	Argentina	84	Thailand	382
Pakistan	702	South Africa	58	Burma	66
Brazil	673	U.S.A.	37	Brazil	63
Egypt	520	China	36	Nepal	50
Turkey	516	Uruguay	35	U.S.S.R.	50
Mexico	379	U.K.	32		
		Turkey	26		
World total	13,031	World total	1,527	World total	3,488

Silk (tonnes)		Rubber		Tobacco	
Japan	19,137	Malaysia	1,325	China	803
China	15,020	Indonesia	845	U.S.A.	793
S. Korea	3,602	Thailand	337	India	409
U.S.S.R.	3,000	Sri Lanka	140	U.S.S.R.	300
India	2,145	India	109	Brazil	255
N. Korea	1,350	Liberia	64	Turkey	173
		Nigeria	62	Japan	142
				Bulgaria	142
World total	45,360	World total	3,060	World total	4,768

Groundnuts (in shell)		Soya Beans		Palm Oil	
India	3,924	U.S.A.	34,916	Malaysia	730
China	2,500	China	11,750	Nigeria	650
U.S.A.	1,485	Brazil	3,500	Indonesia	270
Nigeria	1,233	Indonesia	515	Zaire	180
Brazil	920	U.S.S.R.	500	Ivory Coast	80
Senegal	600	Mexico	364	Angola	70
Burma	486	Canada	320	Sierra Leone	62
		S. Korea	224	Ghana	60
World total	16,100	World total	53,804	World total	2,400

VEGETABLE OILS

9. Use of vegetable oils. The greatly increased use of vegetable oils, which increased fourfold between 1850 and 1950, resulted from three main factors:

(a) The production of animal fats lagged behind the increasing world demand for fats.

(b) The continually extending uses to which vegetable oils can be put.

(c) Technological improvements in the extraction and processing of vegetable oils.

The introduction of margarine as a substitute for butter and the growth of the soap-making industry were the two main factors stimulating the development of vegetable oil production, but more recently vegetable oils have found an increasingly wide range of uses, *e.g.* in paints, varnishes, lubricants, plastics.

The increasing demand for vegetable oils led to a great expansion of tropical plantation agriculture.

10. The chief vegetable oils. There are seven main sources of vegetable oils.

(*a*) *Groundnut oil.* More commonly known as peanuts or "monkey nuts," groundnuts yield a valuable edible oil which is much used in the making of margarine but which is also used in the manufacture of soap and plastics. Groundnuts are widely grown in the tropical regions, notably in West Africa, India, China and Central America. Considerable quantities are now grown in the United States. Table III lists the groundnut output of the leading producers.

(*b*) *Palm oil.* The oil palm is a native of West Africa whence comes one-quarter of the total world production. Nigeria is the foremost producer. In West Africa the palm grows wild. Oil is expressed both from the fruits and from the kernel. Palm-kernel oil is a valuable ingredient in margarine production; the ordinary palm oil is mostly used for soap and candles and in the manufacture of tin-plate. In the East Indian region the oil palm is grown under the plantation system. (*See* Table III.)

(*c*) *Coconut oil.* This is the oil obtained from *copra*, the dried flesh of the fruits or coconuts of the coconut palm, a tree characteristic of the sandy coastlands of tropical regions, especially in and around the Indian and Pacific Oceans. Coconut oil is highly valued and usually forms the basis of high-grade margarine and quality toilet soaps. The largest producers of copra are the Philippines, Indonesia, India and Sri Lanka, listed in Table III.

(*d*) *Olive oil.* In the lands around the Mediterranean Sea olive oil, derived from the fruit of the olive tree, has long been used as a foodstuff, taking the place of animal fats in human consumption. Once an olive tree has become established, it will continue to yield several hundreds of pounds of fruit each year for as long as a century. Olive oil is used largely as a cooking oil and in soap-making. The chief producers are Spain, Italy, Greece, Turkey, Portugal and Tunisia.

(*e*) *Soya-bean oil.* The soya-bean is a plant of warm temperate areas and is native to the Far East. Soya-beans are an important crop in Manchuria, China proper, Korea and Japan. During recent decades the United States has become a major grower of soya-beans and producer of soya-bean oil. In addition to its use in the preparation of foodstuffs, soya-bean oil has been put to many industrial uses, *e.g.* in the making of paints, varnish and printing ink.

(*f*) *Linseed oil*. This is obtained from the crushed seed of the flax plant. When flax is grown for its oil, it is usually cultivated under warmer conditions than are desirable for fibre. Argentina and the United States are the leading producers of linseed, but India and Canada are not far behind. Linseed oil is much used in the preparation of paints and varnishes since it is especially valuable as a "drying oil."

(*g*) *Cottonseed oil*. The seeds of the cotton plant, which are left behind after the ginning of cotton and which at one time were thrown away as waste, contain an oil which is now extracted and used for a variety of purposes, *e.g.* as a lubricant, in soap-making, in the manufacture of margarine. Most of the cotton growing countries export either the seed or the extracted oil.

TOBACCO AND RUBBER

11. Plantation crops. A large number of commodities are grown under the plantation system but perhaps the two most important industrial crops are tobacco and rubber. Tobacco was one of the early plantation crops, but plantation rubber production is a growth of the present century. Plantation agriculture is a specialised form of large-scale production, more particularly concerned with tropical and sub-tropical crops. The system requires large capital outlay and hence is normally undertaken by large companies or corporations. Usually plantation crops require some immediate processing and so factories of one kind or another are commonly associated with the plantations. It is a type of agriculture which may be very successful and highly profitable; at the same time, because it is a monocultural system, it is highly susceptible to fluctuations in market prices and the rubber industry in the past has suffered disastrously on this account (*see* X, **8**).

12. Tobacco. The different species of the tobacco plant are all native to the Americas. Since its introduction into Europe towards the end of the sixteenth century, the habit of smoking has waxed and waned but the present century has seen its almost world-wide adoption and consumption continues to increase. Tobacco is grown in many countries, both tropical and temperate, but it thrives best under sub-tropical conditions.

The most favourable conditions for tobacco plants are fairly constant temperatures of 70°–80°F (21°–27°C), absence of frost, regular water supply, a humid atmosphere, and well-drained soils which are rich in plant foods and not too acid. The flavour and quality of tobacco depends upon the plant type, the climatic conditions under which it is grown, the soil and the processing of the leaf. Table III lists the output figures for 1972.

(a) *The United States* dominates world production and is also the greatest exporter, accounting for over 75% of all tobacco entering world trade. The state of Virginia specialises in cigarette tobaccos, Kentucky in pipe tobaccos. It is an economic crop for the small farmer. The United Kingdom takes about half of the United States' export.

(b) *Europe.* Tobacco is widely grown in Europe but Bulgaria, Greece and Turkey are the main growers. Greece grows "Turkish" tobacco from which "Turkish" cigarettes are made.

(c) *Africa.* Tobacco growing has become an important activity in Rhodesia, Zambia and Malawi where the sandy soils, warm summers (around 20–25°C) and cheap Negro labour favour production.

(d) *Many other countries*, notably China, India, Japan, Brazil and the Soviet Union, grow large amounts of tobacco, but most of it is consumed internally.

13. Rubber. The tremendous growth in the world's output of rubber during the last one hundred years or so is attributable to three inventions:

(a) The discovery of *the vulcanisation process* in about 1840.

(b) The invention by Dunlop in 1890 of *the pneumatic tyre.*

(c) The invention of *the motor-car* shortly before 1900.

Most of the rubber which is produced goes into the making of vehicle tyres, but rubber finds many other uses, *e.g.* as insulating material, floor coverings, hose-pipes, footwear.

Approximately half the world's supply of rubber consists of *natural rubber* which is obtained from the latex exuded by a number of equatorial forest trees, the most important of which is the *Hevea brasiliensis*, a native of the Amazon basin. The other half of the world's supply is obtained synthetically;

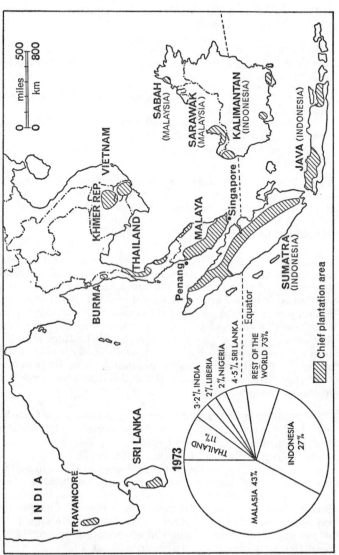

FIG. 15.—*Rubber plantations in South-east Asia*

More than three-quarters of the world's natural rubber comes from South-east Asia where it is cultivated on plantations. Nowadays, as much rubber is made synthetically as is grown naturally.

synthetic rubber is made by the chemical treatment of petroleum, coal and limestone.

14. Conditions of growth. The principal requirements for the growth of the rubber tree are those characteristic of equatorial lowland areas:

    (a) *High temperatures* averaging 80°F (27°C) and not falling below 70°F (21°C).

    (b) *Heavy rainfall*, at least 60 inches (1524 millimetres), evenly distributed throughout the year.

    (c) *Undulating land or gentle hill slopes* allowing good drainage.

A rich, deep soil is desirable but the rubber tree will grow on a variety of soils. Much labour is entailed in rubber production and so much cheap and reliable labour is required. In Malaya, where there was a labour problem, Indians had to be imported to man the plantations.

15. Rubber in Malaya. Malaya is the world's greatest producer of natural rubber, accounting for one-third of the total production. The rubber growing areas are mostly along the western coastlands between sea level and the 750-ft contour. Some 3½ million acres are planted to rubber. The trees grow on a variety of soils: in clays and alluvium and in quartzite and shale soils. Only the peaty soils are avoided. More recently newer plantations have been set up on the eastern side of the peninsula, but the only really important area so far is in the north-east in Kelantan. Some 500,000 Indians are employed on the rubber estates.

16. Production and trade in rubber. The countries of southeast Asia (particularly Malaya and Indonesia), which are the principal producers of natural rubber, are also the chief exporters. Output for 1972 is shown in Table III.

Fig. 15 shows the distribution of rubber plantations in southeast Asia, as well as a pie chart of world production. The collection of wild rubber from Amazonia, which was important during the period 1890–1910, is now insignificant. The leading importers are the United States, accounting for about 40% of the total production, the United Kingdom about 13%, West Germany about 8%, and France about 7%.

FOREST PRODUCTS

17. The world's forests. Over one quarter of the earth's land surface is covered with forest. Formerly the forests were more widely spread, but the need of land for cultivation and the use of wood for constructional purposes, fuel and other products led to large areas being cleared. Lands long settled, such as the Mediterranean lands, Western Europe, China and much of India, have very little natural forest left.

There are three principal types of forest:

(a) The *coniferous forests*, nearly all found in the northern hemisphere, occurring roughly between 50 and 70 degrees N.

(b) The *temperate deciduous forests*, found between approximately 30 and 50 degrees N on the western and eastern sides of the continents.

(c) The *tropical forests* found in the Amazon and Congo Basins and in the East Indian region.

18. Wealth from trees. Trees are a source of wood, most of which can be burnt as a fuel or converted into charcoal which has special uses and about 40% of the total wood production is used as firewood. The remaining 60% is used by industry. Timber is used mainly:

(a) *For constructional purposes, e.g.* in house building, furniture making, pitprops, telegraph poles, tools.

(b) *For the production of wood-pulp* used in:

(i) the production of newsprint and paper generally;

(ii) the making of the artificial fibre rayon.

Trees, however, have various other uses and a wide variety of useful commodities are obtained from them. Pine-trees may be tapped for resin, which may be distilled into turpentine; certain trees, notably the sugar-maple and some palms, yield sugar; the rubber tree gives latex and several tropical trees grown in central America exude chicle, the basis of chewing-gum; the thick bark of certain Mediterranean oak-trees growing in Portugal and Spain provides cork, while tannin, used in processing leather, is obtained from the barks of certain oak-trees, from wattle-bark, and from the quebracho tree and mangrove. A variety of medicines and drugs are also obtained from certain trees, *e.g.* Canada balsam, eucalyptus oil, cocaine, while camphor is got by distilling the leaves and wood of the camphor plant.

19. Kinds of timber. Timbers are commonly divided into:

    (*a*) *Softwoods* which come mainly from the coniferous forests.

    (*b*) *Hardwoods* which are classified as:

      (i) temperate hardwoods;
      (ii) tropical hardwoods.

Commercially, *softwoods* are easily first in importance. Supplies are chiefly obtained from the *taiga* of northern Eurasia and North America, and from the Pacific forests of western Canada and the United States. Some is also derived from the coniferous forests which clothe the upland massifs of central Europe. Softwoods are used for many constructional purposes as they are strong but easily worked and are often available in long lengths since many of the trees grow tall and straight. Vast quantities, however, are used for pulping.

    Hardwoods are chiefly used in the making of furniture or for special purposes where very hard, tough, resistant timbers are needed, *e.g.* in the making of dock gates, railway sleepers, sports gear. In contrast to the softwoods which usually grow in great stands or colonies composed of a single species, the tropical hardwoods are dispersed throughout the forest and their extraction is more difficult. Moreover, lumbering is impeded by the climate, which is too hot for comfort, and by the wet terrain which hinders transport.

20. Production of timber and wood-pulp. The Soviet Union possesses half the world's coniferous forests, but her Siberian forests are largely undeveloped; she produces large quantities of white-wood timber and wood-pulp. Norway, Sweden and Finland are important producers. Both Sweden and Finland mill much timber and produce considerable quantities of wood-pulp; Norway has fewer mills and concentrates upon pulp. The United States and Canada between them account for some 60% of the world's total production of wood-pulp and newsprint. Japan is a smaller, but notable, supplier of pulp and West Germany and the United Kingdom produce small amounts of newsprint.

In spite of the United States' enormous production of wood-pulp, its appetite for newsprint is insatiable and it is compelled to import large quantities from Canada. The United Kingdom, which has very little forest cover, has to import large quantities of timber, pulp and newsprint chiefly from Canada, Norway and the Baltic Lands.

Certain tropical hardwoods, notably teak and mahogany, are highly prized in commerce. Teak, a tree of the monsoon deciduous forests, comes from South-east Asia, principally from Burma, Thailand and Indonesia. These countries are responsible for about 45% of the world production of tropical hardwoods. Other producing areas are West Africa and Central America. British Honduras is a notable producer of mahogany. Brazil produces ebony and greenheart.

PROGRESS TEST 13

1. What are the chief animal and vegetable raw materials used in industry? Indicate the importance of (a) rubber; (b) vegetable oils; (c) timber; from the point of view of industry. (1, 9, 13, 18)

2. Cotton is the most important of the vegetable fibres. Describe (a) the geographical conditions needed for the production of raw cotton, and (b) outline the international trade in raw cotton. (3)

3. Compare the conditions under which flax and jute are grown. (4, 5)

4. Distinguish between the different kinds of hemp. Name the chief uses of hemp. (6)

5. Under what kind of geographical conditions are wool sheep reared? Name the chief producers and exporters of raw wool. (7)

6. Write a few lines on each of the following, explaining what it is and where it is produced: henequen; mohair; soya-bean; copra; chicle. (6, 7, 10, 18)

7. Account for the rapid increase in the production of vegetable oils during the past one hundred years. (9)

8. Give a brief survey of the production of vegetable oils, noting (a) the chief sources of oils, (b) the particular uses of each of the different oils. (10)

9. What are the chief distinguishing features of plantation agriculture? Name the principal plantation crops. (11, and X, 8)

10. Give an account of the world distribution of forests. What important products are derived from forests? (17–19)

11. What are the principal geographical requirements for the growth of the rubber tree? Name the chief producers and importers of rubber. (14, 16, Table III)

12. Give an account of *either* cotton growing in the United States *or* rubber cultivation in Malaya. (3, 15)

SUGGESTED PROJECTS

1. Using the figures of world rubber production in Table III, draw a pie graph to illustrate the world's output of rubber.

2. From your own reading and research, write a full account of the different methods of producing wood-pulp and describe the various uses to which wood-pulp is put.

3. Using a dictionary or other work of reference, find out what are the following and whence they come: karri; quebracho; purpleheart; abaca; jarrah; logwood; gutta percha; kapok; tree-cotton; tung nuts; vegetable ivory; coir.

4. The coconut palm has many uses and is of very great importance to the peoples of tropical regions; find out all you can about its usefulness, writing up your findings under a planned series of headings.

CHAPTER XIV

METALS AND MINERALS

MINERAL RESOURCES

1. The nature of mining. Mining differs from the other primary occupations of agriculture, fishing and forestry, in that the product of the industry is a wasting one. While with due care and proper organisation it is possible to obtain crops, fish and timber from field, sea and forest indefinitely, this is not the case with mineral wealth. Once it has been extracted from the earth it has gone for good, hence we sometimes call mining a "robber industry."

Because of this, mining settlements are essentially ephemeral; they flourish for a time until the mineral is exhausted and then, unless they change their character, decline. One can see this in many of the former lead-mining villages in the Yorkshire dales; once the lead-mining industry declined, these settlements lost most of their population and are today small rural communities largely composed of "week-end cottagers." In some parts of the world the former flourishing mining centres have become "ghost towns" such as the aptly named Tombstone in Arizona.

2. The occurrence of minerals. Although mineral resources are widely spread throughout the earth's crust—indeed the whole of the crust is composed of mineral matter—comparatively few minerals are found in sufficiently concentrated quantities to justify their commercial exploitation and, for this reason, the mining of minerals is usually confined to localised areas.

Minerals occur in three main ways depending upon the geological conditions under which they were formed:

(a) *In lodes or veins.* When igneous rocks were intruded into the crust various liquids and gases found their way into cracks and fissures, eventually cooling and congealing to form metallic lodes and veins. A number of these metals often occur in association with each other, *e.g.* copper with nickel, silver with lead and zinc, iron with manganese.

141

(b) *In sedimentary beds.* Some minerals are laid down in horizontal sheets or layers which are said to form beds. Minerals laid down in beds include coal (originally derived from accumulated organic matter), many iron ores, such as those of eastern England, salt, anhydrite and potash which may originate as precipitates or evaporites.

(c) *In alluvial deposits.* Many minerals are found in alluvial deposits at the bases of hills or in valley bottoms. Usually originating in the veins and lodes of nearby hills, the minerals, exposed by erosion, have been carried downslope and dumped in the debris accumulating at lower levels. Alluvial deposits often bear minerals which resist corrosion by water, *e.g.* the tin of Malaya, the "placer" gold of Yukon in Canada, the diamonds of Namaqualand, South West Africa.

3. Distribution of mineralised regions. Whereas coal is chiefly associated with carboniferous basins, and petroleum with folded structures in zones of sedimentary rocks, metallic minerals are usually found either in ancient "shield" areas and old plateaus which have often suffered metamorphism or in regions of young fold mountains which have experienced more geologically recent earth movements and intrusions. The Baltic and Canadian Shields and the Plateaus of Brazil, Africa, India and Australia provide examples of the former, the Andes and the Rockies examples of the latter.

NOTE: Many areas which are rich in mineral wealth are poor agriculturally; for example, the Canadian Shield is cold and barren, the Plateau of Western Australia is hot, dry and lacking in surface water, while the Andes are often difficult of access, windswept and covered with thin, stony soil.

4. The exploitation of mineral resources. The utilisation of mineral resources is dependent upon a variety of factors:

(a) *The size of the deposit* and the percentage of metal content in the ore. Ores are often termed high-grade or low-grade according to the abundance of metal in the ore.

(b) *The depth at which the ore occurs.* If it is near the surface it may be worked by open-cast methods. Deep mines are costly to establish and work.

(c) *The distance of the ore body from the consuming market* and the transport facilities available for the shipment of the ore.

(d) *The existence of a satisfactory labour supply* which may be difficult to recruit in remote, inaccessible and unattractive areas.

(e) *The availability of capital* which may be required in large quantities for large-scale enterprises involving expensive mining plant and perhaps transport facilities.

(*f*) *The presence or absence of fuel and power resources* required in processing the ore, *e.g.* for concentration, smelting and perhaps final refining.

(*g*) *The international demand for the metal.* If the demand is great enough, mining will often be undertaken in the most unattractive environments *e.g.* Port Radium (for uranium) in arctic Canada.

IMPORTANT MINERALS

5. Iron ore. Iron ore is the raw material from which pig iron and its derivatives, cast iron, wrought iron and steel are made (*see* XVIII). Iron occurs very widely in nature and accounts for an estimated 5% of the earth's crust. To be commercially important, however, the ore must contain a high proportion of iron, or, if the percentage of the metal content is low (but normally not less than 20%), the deposit must be very large and readily accessible. In some areas where iron ore is plentiful it remains unexploited because there is little demand for it, owing to the absence of industrial development.

6. Iron-ore production. Some of the former large producers are mining far less and some of the developing countries are substantial producers.

(*a*) *Europe.* Europe is no longer as important as it once was in world production and increasingly it is having to depend upon extra-European supplies.

(i) *Britain's* iron ores are now almost entirely exhausted except for the low-grade Jurassic ores of which about 2·5 million tons are mined, mostly by open-cast methods, annually.

(ii) *Sweden* is the largest producer with about 21 million tons annually. She has large reserves of high-grade ore in Norrland at Kiruna, Gällivare–Malmberget and Koskullskulle; also, rich haematite at Dannemora and magnetite at Grangesberg.

(iii) *France* ranks second as a producer with an annual output of around 16 million tons. The ores of the great Lorraine field are low-grade but easily worked. Smaller deposits occur in Normandy and in the Pyrenees.

(iv) *Spain* has valuable high-grade ores in the north near Bilbao and Santander; production is around 3·5 million tons a year.

(v) *Luxembourg* has a small production (about 5 million tons) of *minette* ores similar to those of Lorraine.

(b) *North America.* This continent has numerous important deposits of iron ore. Fig. 16 shows the movements of iron ore between mining and producing centres in N. America.

(i) *Canada* produces about 25 million tons. The chief producing regions are Steep Rock near Lake Superior, and the recently discovered rich deposits at Schefferville in western Labrador. Production in Bell Island ceased in 1966.

(ii) *United States* output is around 46 million tons. The very rich deposits of high-grade ore near the western and southern shores of Lake Superior are fast dwindling. Other deposits are worked in the Birmingham area of Alabama.

(iii) *In Mexico* important deposits occur in the vicinity of Durango (Cerro de Mercado, the iron mountain), at Colima and in the State of Chihuahua but total output is only about 3 million tons annually.

(iv) *Cuba* has fairly large deposits of high-grade ores in Oriente province; these have hardly been exploited as yet.

(c) *The Soviet Union.* Replacing the United States in 1958 as the world's foremost producer, her output is now around 110 million tons annually. She has rich deposits in:

(i) *Southern Ukraine,* at Krivoi Rog.
(ii) *The Ural Mountains,* at Magnitogorsk.
(iii) *The Kuznetsk basin* in Central Asia.

(d) *Other areas.* The remaining significant producers of iron ore in the world are:

(i) *China,* now producing an estimated 25 million tons annually, chiefly from southern Manchuria.

(ii) *India,* producing some 20 million tons from scattered deposits in the Singhbhum district of Bihar-Orissa, in eastern Madhya Pradesh, and in the Bombay region.

(iii) *Australia* produces some 40 million tons, chiefly from Iron Knob in Southern Australia and from Yampi Sound in the north-west coastal region.

(iv) *North and West Africa,* chiefly from Algeria, Mauretania and Sierra Leone.

(v) *South America.* Important deposits occur in Brazil, Venezuela and Chile. Venezuela's production comes from the northern margin of the Guiana Highlands (Cerro Bolivar and El Pao), Brazil's production of 28 million tons comes mainly from the Itabira area.

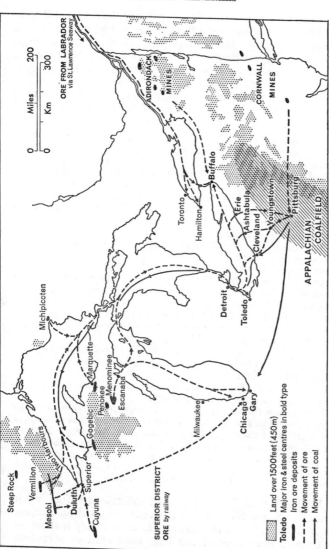

FIG. 16.—*Coal and iron ore movements in North America*

Iron ore from the Superior and Labrador ironfields is shipped through the Great Lakes to the lakeside iron and steel centres. Some is also carried to Pittsburg region. Coal is taken from the Pennsylvania coalfield in the Appalachians to the lakeside centres.

7. Copper. Along with gold, copper was the first metal to be used by man, but after the Bronze Age it had only a limited usefulness. Today, thanks largely to the electrical industry, it is one of the most important metals. Copper is the principal metal used in the electrical industry because of its high conductivity, its ductility (which allows it to be drawn out into thin wire), and its resistance to corrosion. Copper is also used as an alloy metal in the making of bronze and brass and cupronickel.

(a) *Production.* The bulk of the world's supply of copper (over 80%) comes from seven major producers: United States, Chile, Soviet Union, Zambia, Canada, Zaire and Peru (*see* Fig. 17). The *United States* ranks an easy first with about one-quarter of the total world output. The chief deposits occur in the Western Cordillera, in Utah, Arizona and Montana. The USSR is the second largest producer, drawing most of its copper from the Urals and the Lake Balkash area. Chile ranks third, with Zambia in fourth place.

The mines of the *Zambian* "*copperbelt*" adjoin those of Katanga Province in Zaire, which is the sixth largest producer. Railways to Beira (Mozambique) and to Lobito Bay (Angola) have made these rich Central African deposits accessible. Chile's ore comes chiefly from mines high up in the Andes (at Chuquicamata and Potrerillos) and at El Teniente in the central part of the country. Most of Canada's copper comes from the gold- and nickel-bearing rocks of Ontario. Output figures for the major producers are shown in Table IV.

(b) *Trade and consumers.* None of the world's main copper-producing areas is located in a major industrial region, hence after smelting, or, at least, concentration, the metal has to be moved over considerable distances. Zambia, Zaire, Chile and Canada export most of their output.

The United States, in spite of its large production, imports copper from Canada, Chile and Mexico. Britain (a century ago the world's greatest producer—mainly in Angelsey) imports from Zambia, Canada and Chile. Japan does not produce sufficient from her own mines to meet her needs and must import some copper. Other important importers are West Germany and France.

8. Lead and zinc. The ores of lead and zinc are often found in association (*see* Fig. 17). Both occur in mixed ore bodies, as at Boliden in northern Sweden. Lead is a very soft metal which resists corrosion; it has long been used as a roofing material, for making pipes and in the production of paint.

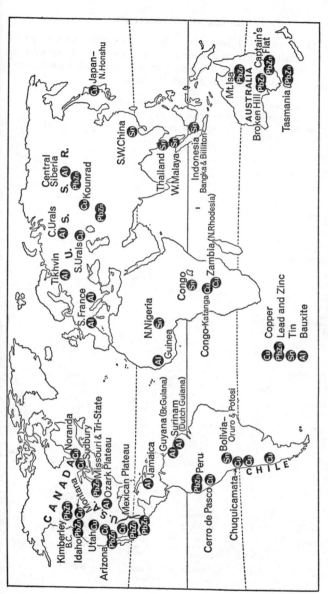

FIG. 17.—*Distribution of minerals*

This map shows the world's main deposits of copper, lead, zinc, tin and bauxite.

Zinc is a protective metal which resists corrosion and so is used for galvanising iron and steel products; it is also used in the making of plates for the printing industry, in the making of batteries, and in the production of brass.

TABLE IV. OUTPUT OF IMPORTANT MINERALS
(Figures in thousands of metric tons for 1972)

Iron Ore		Copper Ore (Cu content)		Bauxite	
U.S.S.R.	113,467	U.S.A.	1,510	Australia	13,697
U.S.A.	45,798	U.S.S.R.	1,050	Jamaica	12,989
Australia	39,254	Chile	724	Surinam	6,777
Brazil	28,628	Zambia	718	U.S.S.R.	4,700
China	25,300	Canada	709	Guyana	3,707
Canada	24,387	Zaire	413	France	3,258
Liberia	22,543	Peru	217	Guinea	2,650
India	22,126	Philippines	214	Greece	2,435
Sweden	21,317	Australia	172	Hungary	2,358
France	16,525	South Africa	155	U.S.A.	2,235
Venezuela	11,089	Japan	112	Yugoslavia	2,197
World total	433,800	World total	6,780	World total	65,800

Lead (Pb content)		Zinc (Zn content)		Tin (Sn content) (metric tons)	
U.S.A.	562	Canada	1,280	Malaysia	76,830
U.S.S.R.	460	U.S.S.R.	650	Bolivia	32,405
Australia	421	Australia	498	U.S.S.R.	28,000
Canada	377	U.S.A.	434	Indonesia	21,766
Peru	189	Peru	354	Thailand	22,072
Mexico	161	Japan	281	China	20,000
Yugoslavia	120	Mexico	272	Australia	12,080
China	108	Poland	193	Nigeria	6,730
World total	3,410	World total	5,650	World total	197,900

Manganese		Gold (Kilogrammes)		Silver (metric tons)	
U.S.S.R.	2,682	South Africa	908,300	Canada	1,508
Brazil	1,180	U.S.S.R.	215,000	Peru	1,250
South Africa	1,362	Canada	63,214	U.S.S.R.	1,244
Gabon	988	U.S.A.	49,859	Mexico	1,165
India	612	Japan	26,319	U.S.A.	1,158
Australia	562	Australia	23,483	Australia	700
China	330	Ghana	22,521	Japan	312
Ghana	244	Philippines	18,871		
Zaire	196				
World total	8,570	World total	1,411,550	World total	9,060

Salt		Phosphate rock		Potash (K₂O content)	
U.S.A.	40,843	U.S.A.	38,465	U.S.S.R.	5,498
China	17,820	Morocco	15,105	Canada	3,747
U.S.S.R.	12,228	U.S.S.R.	10,500	W. Germany	2,845
U.K.	9,400	Tunisia	3,387	E. Germany	2,458
W. Germany	8,282	China	2,170	U.S.A.	2,412
India	6,521	South Africa	1,966	France	1,760
France	5,237	Nauru	1,906		
World total	144,100	World total	80,000	World total	20,490

(a) *Production*. Both ores are mined in substantial amounts in Canada (Kimberley, British Columbia), in the United States (especially in the Ozark Highlands), in Mexico, in Peru, in the Soviet Union (particularly in Central Asia) and in Australia (notably at Broken Hill, New South Wales). In Europe some lead is produced in West Germany, Yugoslavia, France, Belgium and Spain, while zinc is produced in West Germany, Belgium, France and Poland. The United States and the Soviet Union are leading producers of both lead and zinc. (*See* Table IV.)

(b) *Demand and trade*. Considerably more zinc is produced and used than lead. World output of zinc has increased by about 25% since before the Second World War, whereas lead production has increased only slightly. Growing exhaustion of the ore bodies of lead has created something of a world shortage, has resulted in an increase in its price, and in the use of substitute materials. The United Kingdom has to import most of its lead and zinc which come mainly from Canada and Australia.

9. Tin. Until about one hundred years ago tin was mainly used as an alloy in the making of bronze, pewter and gun-metal and was chiefly worked in Cornwall where it had been mined for over two thousand years. The development of the tin-plate industry, resulting from the growth of the canned food industry, led to a spectacular increase in the use of tin.

(a) *Production*. The chief producers are Malaya, Bolivia, USSR, China, Indonesia, Thailand, Nigeria and Bolivia (*see* Fig. 17 and Table IV). In Malaya and the Indonesian islands of Bangka and Billiton the main workings are alluvial and the tin is obtained by dredging. In Bolivia the ore is obtained from lodes by deep-mining at heights of 12,000 feet (3657 metres) or so. Mining in Bolivia is costly and the industry has experienced great difficulties in recent years; the output has declined.

(b) *Trade*. All the above-named producing countries, save China, export the processed ore which goes to the United States, the United Kingdom and the other advanced industrial countries, where it is mostly used in the manufacture of tin-plate and "tin-cans."

10. Bauxite. After steel, aluminium is the most commonly used metal. During the present century its use has grown rapidly and today more than five times as much is used as before the Second World War. It is one of the most useful and versatile of metals.

The main source of aluminium is bauxite (an impure

aluminium hydroxide), a tropical reddish clay which has a wide distribution. High temperatures are required for its smelting and hydro-electric power is used.

(a) *Production of bauxite.* The foremost producing area is in and around the Caribbean Sea. For many years British Guiana (now Guyana) and Dutch Guiana (Surinam) were the leading producers, but during the past few years Jamaica has taken the lead. They all export their production, mainly to North America. There are also important deposits in France (around Les Baux which gave its name to the ore), and in Hungary, Yugoslavia and Greece. There are scattered deposits in the Soviet Union and supplies in West Africa, chiefly in Ghana and Guinea. Australia is beginning to develop fairly extensive deposits recently found in Cape York peninsula and in Arnhem Land. The main producing centres are shown in Fig. 17. Table IV gives output figures for 1972.

(b) *Uses of aluminium.* The smelting of bauxite and the production of aluminium is dealt with in Chapter XVIII (22–24). Magnesium excepted, aluminium is the lightest of the metals. A wide range of light but strong alloys, *e.g.* duralumin, magnalium, are now made and are used in aircraft, railway and motor-car construction. Aluminium is also used in the manufacture of domestic utensils, wire and foil.

11. Gold. Gold is one of the "precious" metals along with silver and platinum. Mainly used as a standard of value and as a durable source of wealth, it is also used in jewellery. South Africa is the chief source of gold and accounts for two-thirds of the total world output. The principal mining area is the Witwatersrand, or Rand for short, in the Transvaal, but there are other important mines in the Orange Free State. The other important producers are the Soviet Union (Lena Valley Fields), Canada (the Shield), the United States (the Western Cordillera), Australia (Western Plateau), Ghana and Rhodesia. Table IV shows the output of gold and silver in 1972.

12. The ferro-alloy metals. A number of metals, notably manganese, nickel, cobalt, chromium and tungsten, are alloyed with steel to impart special properties to it such as hardness, strength, durability and resistance to rusting and high temperatures. For example:

(a) *Manganese-steel* gives a hard tough steel used in making rock-crushing machinery.

(b) *Nickel-steel* gives a strong, tough and ductile steel and non-magnetic steel.

(c) *Chrome-steel* produces a stainless steel used in the manufacture of cutlery.

(d) *Cobalt-steel* has anti-corrosive and magnetic properties and is much used for high-speed cutting tools.

(e) *Tungsten-steel* is used for high-speed cutting tools and, because of its toughness, for armour-plating.

(f) *Vanadium-steel* gives a metal which is less liable to fatigue or fracture under great stress or sudden shock.

The engineering, armaments, aircraft and motor vehicle industries are the chief users of alloy steels. Table IV shows output of nickel and manganese.

NON-METALLIC MINERALS

13. Classes. The non-metallic minerals can be usefully divided into:

(a) *Industrial minerals*, such as asbestos, mica, graphite, sulphur and salt, which are used in various industrial undertakings and very often in the chemical industry.

(b) *Mineral fertilisers*, such as nitrates, phosphates, potash and guano, which are much used in agriculture.

14. Industrial minerals. These five minerals have various uses.

(a) *Asbestos*, a fibrous mineral which does not burn or melt and is very resistant to electricity, forms an ideal fireproof material. It is used for fireproof clothing, safety curtains, lagging and the making of tiles and "asbestos-cement" sheets. Canada and the Soviet Union are the major producers of asbestos.

(b) *Mica* also has resistance to heat and electricity and hence has important electrical uses. 1t is used for the "windows" in stoves and furnaces. The United States and India are the largest producers.

(c) *Graphite*, a finely crystalline form of carbon, is used for the "lead" in pencils, in the making of crucibles for metal smelting, as carbon brushes in electric motors, and as a "moderator" in atomic reactors. Small quantities come from Sri Lanka and Malagasy Republic, but most graphite is made synthetically these days.

(d) *Sulphur* is an essential raw material in the chemical industry. It is obtained from three sources: either native from areas of vulcanism *e.g.* in Sicily, or from the mineral iron pyrites

(FeS_2), or as a by-product from natural gas. The United States, Mexico and France are the major producers (*see* Table IV).

(*e*) *Salt*, like sulphur, is a basic raw material of the chemical industry but it is also used for pickling and salting foodstuffs and is a very necessary constituent of the human diet. Salt may occur as a natural brine or as a crystalline solid (rock salt). Over 140 million tons are produced annually. The chief producers are the United States, China, the Soviet Union, the United Kingdom, West Germany and India (*see* Table IV).

15. Mineral fertilisers. A number of mineral products are important as chemical fertilisers:

(*a*) *Nitrates* (sodium nitrate or Chile saltpetre and potassium nitrate or saltpetre) are of infrequent occurrence in their natural state. The chief deposits are found in the Atacama Desert of northern Chile. The Chilean nitrate trade declined when synthetic nitrates began to be made. Nowadays most of the nitrogenous fertilisers are manufactured chemically.

(*b*) *Phosphates*. Sources of phosphate are phosphatic rock (quarried in Morocco and Florida), the mineral apatite (worked in the Soviet Union and Sweden), and guano (bird droppings), found principally on the islands off the Peruvian and South-west African coasts and on Nauru and Ocean Island in the Pacific. Basic slag, which contains phosphates, is much used nowadays as a fertiliser.

(*c*) *Potash*, like rock salt, occurs in beds which were laid down when former inland seas dried up. The best known and richest deposits occur at Stassfurt in East Germany but there are deposits in Alsace in France, at Suria in Spain, in Utah and California in the United States, in the Solikamsk region of the Soviet Union, while both Israel and Jordan procure it from the Dead Sea (by evaporation).

16. Other important minerals. Finally, let us not forget the more humdrum, but none the less very important, sand, clay and limestone as well as building stones. Sand, clay, and limestone are all used in the making of manufactured products.

(*a*) *Sand* is an important ingredient in the manufacture of concrete and glass, and is used in the making of moulds for iron foundries.

(*b*) *Clay* finds its greatest use in brick-making and cement manufacture; the special white clay, kaolin (mined in Cornwall) is much used in the pottery industry.

(*c*) *Limestone* has many uses: it supplies lime for cement and concrete manufacture, is used as a flux in iron ore smelting, is used as an antidote for "sour" soils, and finds a role in many industrial processes including sugar-refining and glass manufacture.

PROGRESS TEST 14

1. Give an account of the different ways in which minerals may occur. (2)

2. What factors influence the exploitation of mineral resources? (4)

3. Describe the difficulties of mining in (a) the Canadian Shield, (b) Western Australia, (c) Central Africa. (3, 4)

4. Give an account of the distribution of iron ores in *either* Europe *or* North America. (6)

5. Describe the production of and world trade in copper. (7)

6. Name the chief tin producing areas in the world. Compare the occurrence of and methods of working tin in Malaya and Bolivia. (2, 9)

7. Describe the principal uses of the following minerals: copper; zinc; tin; aluminium; graphite; salt. (7, 8, 9, 10, 14)

8. Give a general outline of the ferro-alloy metals and their uses. (12)

9. Locate the principal sources of (a) sulphur; (b) phosphate; (c) potash. Indicate the chief uses of each. (14, 15)

10. (a) What is bauxite? (b) Locate the chief deposits. (c) What are the chief uses of aluminium? (10)

11. Describe and locate the main deposits of iron ore in the southern hemisphere. (6)

12. Write explanatory notes on the following: kaolin; asbestos; guano; graphite. (14, 15, 16)

CHAPTER XV

FUEL AND POWER RESOURCES

RESOURCES

1. Difference between fuel and power. The terms *fuel* and *power* are often loosely and inaccurately used. Coal, for instance, is commonly said to be a major source of energy but, strictly speaking, it is merely a fuel which is burned to produce power—steam power or electric power. Falling water, through its motion or propelling power, provides energy. Alternatively, it may have its inherent energy harnessed to drive a turbine which, in turn, provides a source of power—hydro-electric power.

Thus, we can draw a distinction between fuels and sources of energy.

(*a*) *Fuels:*

    (i) Wood and associated vegetable matter.
    (ii) Coal and lignite (brown coal).
    (iii) Peat.
    (iv) Alcohol.
    (v) Petroleum oils.
    (vi) Natural gas.
    (vii) Nuclear fuels.

(*b*) *Sources of energy:*

    (i) Man power.
    (ii) Animal power.
    (iii) Wind.
    (iv) Running or falling water.
    (v) Tidal power.
    (vi) Geothermal energy.
    (vii) Solar energy.
    (viii) Steam power.

2. Energy income and energy capital. Scientists look at the problem of fuel and energy in a different way and class the fuels as forms of energy since, in an indirect way, they provide energy.

To the scientist the forms of energy available on earth can be divided broadly into two main groups:

(*a*) *Energy income, e.g.* human and animal power, wind and water power, and direct solar radiation.

(*b*) *Energy capital, e.g.* the "fossil fuels" (wood, peat, coal, lignite, petroleum, natural gas), atomic energy and, little used yet, terrestrial heat energy.

3. Reserves of energy. There are enormous untapped reserves of energy capital and energy income. These are able to meet any foreseeable needs of the world for many centuries, perhaps millennia, to come. Indeed, there is enough for all time, *provided that man is able to harness these reserves in a suitable form at the places where the energy is needed and at a reasonable cost in labour and materials.*

With our present knowledge and techniques it is not economically practicable to utilise many of these sources of energy. Unfortunately, those that are capable of being harnessed at reasonable cost are not evenly distributed over the earth, especially in relation to the distribution of population and the needs of people and herein lies one of the big problems of the present time.

4. The significance of energy. From the very earliest times man has sought ways and means to conserve his own muscle-power. He succeeded in doing this in a number of ways:

(*a*) by using animals to do carrying and hauling;

(*b*) by making use of the wind, *e.g.* sails, windmills;

(*c*) by using running water to turn wheels.

In more recent times he has used fuels to provide steam-power, electrical energy, and so on.

Today, life in all technically advanced countries would be impossible were it not for the abundant supplies of power that are available. We are all familiar with the effects of power cuts: the rhythm in homes, factories, transport and communications grinds to a halt when power supplies run out. It is only when there is a breakdown that we realise how essential energy is to modern life. Like water supplies, we tend to take it for granted.

Power is especially important to industry, for industrial manufacture is geared to powered machinery and transport. Some of the newer industrial countries, such as Brazil, have suffered chronically through power shortages.

Even aspects of the modern world economy such as agriculture are requiring increased quantities of energy. The modern farm, for instance, needs fuel for its tractors, harvesters and vehicles, and electricity for its pumps, milking-machines and other equipment.

The demands upon energy are almost unlimited and growing apace.

5. Consumption of energy. In 1973 the rate of consumption of energy in the world was approximately equal to 10,000 million tons of coal a year. The main sources of this energy were:

    (a) *Coal*, representing about 32%.
    (b) *Petroleum*, representing 42%.
    (c) *Natural gas*, accounting for about 16%.
    (d) *Hydro-electric power*, for about 3%.
    (e) *Wood*, accounting for 4%.
    (f) *Nuclear power*, accounting for 3%.

Since the 1930s coal has lost much ground as a source of energy. Both petroleum and natural gas have forged ahead, and the consumption of these two forms of energy continues to increase rapidly. In spite of the spectacular character of the hydro-electric power schemes, water power is gradually declining *in its relative importance* to the other power resources.

It is not easy to apportion this use of energy but roughly one-half is used in industry, one-fifth in transport, one-fifth for domestic purposes, the rest for miscellaneous purposes.

6. Future consumption. It is estimated that the current annual rate of increase of energy consumption is about 5%. The general opinion, based on recent trends, is that *the demand for energy will double itself during the next generation* and that by around A.D. 1980 the world will be using something of the order of 15,000 million tons of coal equivalent.

COAL

7. Origin of coal. Coal is mineral matter found in layers or beds in sedimentary rocks. Technically it is called a *hydrocarbon*, but it is essentially fossilised vegetation. It originated

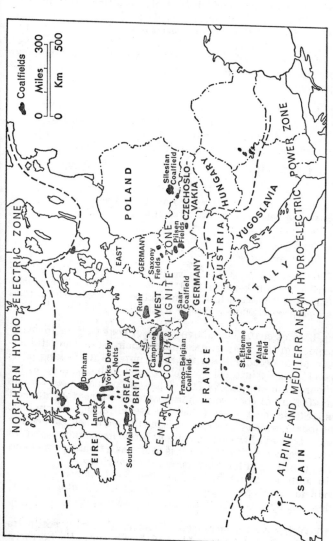

FIG. 18.—*The coalfields of Europe*

The major coalfields of Europe lie on the northern flanks of the Hercynian Highlands of Central Europe; they form a discontinuous belt stretching from Britain to southern Poland. This "coal trough" is the seat of the great industrial belt of Europe. Note also which countries depend very much on hydro-electricity.

from the great forests which formerly grew over wide areas of the earth's surface in earlier periods of the earth's geological history. Most of the coal deposits were laid down during the Carboniferous Period—so named because the rocks of this age are coal-bearing—of some 250 million years ago. Unlike most other mineral products coal is combustible and herein lies its importance.

8. Varieties of coal. Coal, originally of organic origin, is composed of varying amounts of carbon, oxygen, hydrogen and nitrogen together with some impurities. Coal can be classified into various types according to its carbon content:

(a) *Anthracite.* A hard, shiny, clean coal, containing over 90% of carbon, which burns hotly but with little flame and smoke.

(b) *Bituminous coal.* Coals of this group contain 70–90% of carbon; they may be shiny or dull, burn freely, are smoky and leave ash behind; they are often sub-divided into:

(i) coking coals;
(ii) gas coals;
(iii) steam coals.

(c) *Lignite or brown coal.* Usually brown in colour, it has a low carbon content between 45–65%; it burns with a long, smoky flame and leaves much ashy material behind because it contains a high proportion of vegetable matter.

9. Uses of coal. The above types of coal vary in their occurrence, in their importance and in their uses. The bituminous coals are economically the most important. Coking coals convert readily into coke which is used in blast furnaces for reducing iron ore (*see* XVIII). The gas coals are used for the manufacture of coal gas; when heated in retorts they give off gas. Steam coal is suitable for steam-raising in engines. Anthracite, which burns slowly, is much used in central-heating plant. Lignite's low carbon content limits its usefulness, but in those areas where it is found it is useful as a domestic fuel and is frequently used for conversion into electricity.

In addition to its fuel value, coal yields many synthetic products: ammonia, dyes, perfumes, disinfectants, plastics, nylon, are by-products of the carbonisation of coal.

10. Distribution of coalfields. The world's coal deposits are very unevenly distributed. Most of them occur in the northern

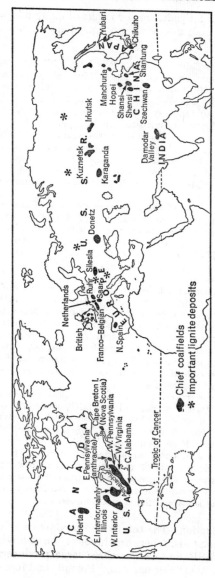

Fig. 19.—*Chief coalfields of the northern hemisphere*

Compare this map with the distribution of industry shown in Fig. 21. Where are there important coalfields in the Southern Hemisphere?

hemisphere in mid-latitudes on the flanks of highlands belonging to the Hercynian mountain system. This distribution is shown in Fig. 19.

(a) *Europe.* In Europe a great "coal trough" extends from Britain, across northern France and Belgium, through Germany to southern Poland. Outside these main deposits are the small fields of Spain, the coal pockets of the Central Plateau of France, the Saar Basin, and the small fields of Czechoslovakia. Fig. 18 shows the distribution of coalfields in Europe.

(b) *The Soviet Union.* There is a great coal basin, the Donetz field in the Ukraine, and fields on the flanks of the Ural Mountains, while in the Asiatic territories there are great coal deposits in the Karaganda, Kuznetsk, Irkutsk and Siberian fields. The Siberian coal and lignite basins are only partly explored.

(c) *South-east Asia.* China has large reserves of coal widely scattered throughout the country; the fields in southern Manchuria are especially rich and productive. Japan has small coalfields in Kyushu and Hokkaido. India has scattered deposits but the main fields lie to the west of Calcutta; most of the Indian output comes from the Jherria and Raniganj fields.

(d) *North America.* A very large proportion of the world's coal deposits, perhaps a third of the total reserves, are to be found in North America, especially in the United States (*see* Fig. 16 above). The most important deposits occur on the western flanks of the Appalachians and account for about 70% of the United States output. The fields of the interior, notably that in Illinois, also have an appreciable output, accounting for roughly a quarter of the total. There are small pockets of coal in the Western Cordillera. Canada has significant deposits in Nova Scotia and the Prairies.

(e) *Southern hemisphere.* In general the coalfields are small and very widely scattered. Australia has a fairly large field in New South Wales and small fields in Queensland and Western Australia. The Republic of South Africa has coalfields in Transvaal, Orange Free State and Natal. In Rhodesia the Wankie Coalfield is of note. Small deposits occur at Enugu in Nigeria. South America is particularly poorly endowed; there are small deposits of low grade coal in the extreme south of Argentina and in south-eastern Brazil, a small field in central Chile and several scattered fields in Colombia.

11. World production. The total world production of coal is around 2000 million tons. There are three very large producers: the USA, the USSR and China; three large producers: the United Kingdom, West Germany and Poland: and four fairly substantial producers: India, Japan, France and South Africa. Five other countries (Czechoslovakia, Australia, Belgium, Spain and the Netherlands) produce over 10 million tons a year (*see* Fig. 19).

Coal Production (in thousand metric tons)

	1966	1968	1972
United States	492,548	500,665	535,242
Soviet Union	439,170	416,224	451,119
China	250,000	300,000	400,000
United Kingdom	177,388	166,713	119,500
Poland	117,354	128,634	150,697
West Germany	126,290	112,165	102,707

OIL AND NATURAL GAS

12. Origin of petroleum. Mineral oil or petroleum is, like coal, a hydrocarbon. It is derived from plant and animal remains which became sealed in sedimentary rocks. Oil occurs in geological "traps" and is found at varying depths; some oil wells penetrate to depths of 10,000 feet (3048 metres). Natural gas is usually, though by no means always, associated with petroleum deposits. Although nowadays it is possible to predict, with a considerable measure of accuracy, the reserves of oil present in any field, the life of an oil well is still largely unpredictable; there are some which flow for long periods while others dry up after a few months.

13. The refining of oil. Petroleum cannot be used in its crude state; it must be refined. This is done by the process of distillation. The crude oil is broken down into its "fractions" (light, medium and heavy oils) by vaporising it in a fractionating tower or cracking plant. From this process heavy fuel oils, lubricating oils, diesel oil, paraffin and petrol are produced.

Before the Second World War most of the petroleum refining was undertaken on, or near to, the oilfields but in recent years refining has moved from the sources of oil to the consuming areas, hence the great new refining centres as at Fawley near Southampton, at Rotterdam and Marseilles.

14. Producing areas. Like most mineral deposits, oil appears to be irrationally distributed over the earth's surface.

There are, however, six main areas where oil is present in large quantities:

    (a) In the interior plains of North America.
    (b) In the Caribbean area of the Americas.
    (c) In the north Saharan region.
    (d) In the Ural–Caucasus region of the Soviet Union.
    (e) In the Tigris–Euphrates–Persian Gulf depression.
    (f) In the region of South-eastern Asia.

15. Oil production. Slightly more than 2500 million tons of crude petroleum are now being produced annually; this is *roughly five times as much as in 1950*. The USA continues to be the premier producer (as she has always been) with an output of 467 million tons—almost one-sixth of the world total. Second is the USSR with about 400 million tons; her output continues to expand rapidly. Third is Saudi Arabia with 285 million tons; fourth Iran with 248 million tons; and fifth is Venezuela with 168 million tons. The Middle Eastern countries of Kuwait, Iraq and the United Arab Emirates are also important producers; Kuwait is by far the most important with rather more than 150 million tons. Libya, in north Africa, is a relative newcomer as an oil producer and its output, until very recently, has gone up by leaps and bounds; in 1972 its output was 106 million tons. Canada, 75 million tons, and Nigeria, 90 million tons, are also relative newcomers. Indonesia is a fairly substantial producer, some 50 million tons; before 1939 she made an important contribution to world supplies, but her output has remained stagnant and she contributes a decreasing proportion to world trade.

16. World trade. Petroleum is the most important commodity entering into world trade at the present time. This is due to three factors:

    (a) It has become a *vital source of energy* to the advanced countries.
    (b) *The demand for it* by these countries is much greater than their home supplies (often very meagre) can meet.
    (c) *Most of the major producers have a large surplus*, over and above their own requirements, for export.

The greatest proportion of the international trade is between the countries of Western Europe, with their negligible home supplies and their enormous demand, and those of the Middle East. Britain alone in 1975 imported 150 million tons and two-

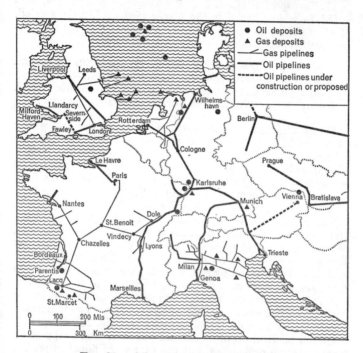

Fig. 20.—*Oil and gas pipelines in Europe*

Note the great oil pipelines running inland from the oil importing ports such as Rotterdam, Marseilles, Genoa and Trieste. The line to Berlin comes from the Ural-Volga oilfield. The gas pipelines are a newer development. Natural gas is found in northern Italy, Aquitaine and the Netherlands; and, more recently, it has been found in the North Sea. Britain's natural gas supplies from the North Sea will be equivalent to the production of 30 million tons of coal a year.

thirds of it came from the Middle East. The second great movement of oil is from the Caribbean area to the United States since, despite her huge output, she is a net importer to the tune of over 50 million tons a year. A third flow, becoming increasingly important, is that from the Soviet Union to the countries of eastern Europe.

17. Transport of oil. Oil, as the foregoing account has indicated, is seldom found in the places where it is most needed. Most of the oil produced has to be transported to the consuming centres and it is moved in two main ways:

(a) *By pipelines* (*see* Fig. 20) which often run for several hundred miles across deserts, forests and mountains.

(b) *By tankers*, now some of the largest vessels afloat which account for nearly half the world's mercantile tonnage.

18. Natural gas. The importance of natural gas as a source of energy has grown very rapidly since 1945. Until that time natural gas was little used outside the United States. Now it provides about 16% of the world's energy. The United States is the leading producer and user, accounting for about 50% of world total output. The United States has, incidentally, more miles of gas pipeline than she has miles of railway track.

The other main producers are the USSR, Canada and the Netherlands. Smaller producers are the UK, Romania, Mexico, Iran, West Germany and Italy. Italy was the first European country to make use of natural gas on any scale and her post-war industrial growth owed much to her gas resources which, however, are now beginning to run out. The rich finds in northern Netherlands and the discoveries in the North Sea off the eastern coast of England have had important consequences for both these countries (*see* Fig. 20).

In the past, imports of natural gas were handicapped by transportation difficulties, but the process of liquefaction has largely solved the problem.

HYDRO-ELECTRIC POWER

19. Water power. Running water has long been used by man. The force exerted by flowing water to turn water-wheels which drove simple mechanisms dates, in Britain, at least from medieval times. It was used in corn-mills to grind flour, in the textile industry to power the fulling mills, and in the iron industry to work the bellows. Industries grew up in many areas where running water could provide motive power.

Nowadays water-power is used primarily as hydro-electricity. The falling water turns turbines which drive dynamos that produce electricity. Hydro-electric power was first developed on a large scale in North America, but it is now widely used as a source of power and gigantic power projects are revolutionising the economic potential of many unpromising areas.

20. Favouring factors. The natural conditions favouring the large-scale development of hydro-electric power are:

(a) *Fairly heavy rainfall* evenly distributed throughout the year.

(b) *A constant and uniform supply of water* either from rivers or lakes.

(c) *Moderate temperatures* to prevent winter freeze-up or summer loss through evaporation.

(d) *Steep slopes* to provide a good "head" or fall of water.

(e) *Narrow, deeply-incised valleys* to assist dam construction.

(f) *Impermeable rocks* to allow for maximum surface drainage and to prevent leakage.

These various physical factors are of little use unless there is a demand for power; this is the crucial factor. Mountainous areas would appear to be most favourable from the physical point of view, but many such areas are inaccessible and remote from markets. Some of the finest potential power sites in the world are unlikely to be used, at least for a long time, because of this drawback.

21. Multi-purpose projects. The development of hydro-electric power projects is a very costly business and the capital outlay for dams, plant, transmission lines, is often prohibitive. The oft-quoted statement that water-power is cheap, since water is a free gift of nature, is something of a myth. If one ignores the initial capital outlay, then it is true to say that the running costs of hydro-electric plants are relatively low and the electricity produced is relatively cheap.

But it is because of the high initial cost that projects serving a variety of uses have been developed. Obviously, if two or more purposes can be served by the same project the costs will be cheaper: hence hydro-electric power is often associated with irrigation schemes and, sometimes, with transport or flood control measures. Such multi-purpose projects then become economic. For example:

(a) *The Aswan High Dam on the Nile* provides electric power (to be used in a new steel industry) as well as water for irrigation.

(b) *The Hoover or Boulder Dam scheme in the USA* provides power, irrigation water for the Imperial Valley of California, and water supplies for Los Angeles.

(c) *The Volta scheme in Ghana* is linked up with the bauxite resources of the country, but is to provide navigation and is to be developed as a fishery.

22. Potential and production. Water-power resources, like most of Nature's gifts, are very irregularly distributed. The following table gives the estimated potential for each of the continents:

Continent	Potential water-power in millions of horse-power
Africa	272
Asia	151
North America	87
Europe	69
South America	55
Australia-Oceania	23

Africa, which leads easily with over 40% of the world's total potential power, has its resources mainly in the tropical belt. Very little of this power has yet been realised. Asia has rich resources which are located mainly in the mountain zone where most of the continent's great rivers rise. Outside the Soviet Union, which has made substantial progress in the use of its hydro-electric power resources, the greatest development has occurred in Japan where all the best sites have already been harnessed. Quite spectacular developments have taken place in Europe and the leading producers are Norway, Sweden, Finland, France, Switzerland, Austria and Italy (Fig. 18).

The hydro-electric power resources tend to be most highly developed in those countries where coal and oil resources are lacking or in short supply.

In North America the resources are already very well developed and the United States and Canada between them account for slightly more than one-third of the total world output. In South America very few schemes have been developed, although the great Furnas Scheme in eastern Brazil is noteworthy, and another great scheme is projected at Salto on the Rio Uruguay. Australia has very limited resources but its Snowy Mountains Scheme is one of the most ambitious in the southern hemisphere. The Kariba Dam on the Zambesi provides power for Zambia and Rhodesia.

NUCLEAR POWER

23. Nuclear energy. Since, sooner or later, coal and oil resources are going to run out, it is important that man should look to the future and discover sources of energy.

Nuclear power is a very recent development and, although its contribution to world power resources is as yet small—a mere 3% at present—there can be little doubt that it will become a major source of power in the future.

The chief sources or raw materials of nuclear energy are the metals uranium and thorium, two radio-active substances. The energy released from their fission is controlled and used to generate electricity.

24. The importance of nuclear energy. Its importance lies in the fact that:

(a) *Countries which lack supplies of conventional fuels* can now develop industry.

(b) *It will lead to a greater dispersion of industry* since really for the first time, industry will no longer be restricted to areas with power resources.

Developments are not likely to come quickly, however, for nuclear power stations are very costly to construct and a high degree of scientific and technical know-how is required to build and run nuclear reactors.

In the reasonably near future nuclear energy is more likely to augment existing sources of energy than to displace and supersede them.

PROGRESS TEST 15

1. Explain the difference between fuel and power, and between energy income and energy capital. (1, 2)

2. Outline the relative importance of the chief sources of energy used at the present time. (5)

3. Name the chief varieties of coal, give their particular characteristics, and say for what purposes each is used. (8, 9)

4. Give an account of the distribution of coalfields in *either* Europe, *or* the Soviet Union, *or* North America. (10)

5. Give an explanatory account of the formation of coal, oil and natural gas. (7, 12)

6. Outline the sources and methods of distribution of petroleum, noting especially the major producing areas and the chief importing countries. (12–17)

7. What factors favour the development of hydro-electric power? Name *three* countries in which conditions are particularly favourable. (20, 22)

8. Explain what is meant by the term "multi-purpose project." Quote some examples of such projects. (21)

9. Compare the distribution of world coal resources with potential water-power resources. (10, 22)

10. Describe the sources, present importance and future prospects of nuclear power. (23, 24)

SUGGESTED PROJECTS

1. Using encyclopaedias and reference books, find out as much as you can about the uses of coal, writing up your notes under separate headings.

2. On an outline map of Great Britain mark in the sites of Britain's nuclear power stations. Comment upon their distribution.

PART FOUR

MANUFACTURING INDUSTRY

CHAPTER XVI

INDUSTRY AND ITS DISTRIBUTION

TYPES OF MANUFACTURE

1. Meaning of manufacture. Manufacture may be defined as the processing and altering of materials, whether in their raw or partly altered state, to make new products to serve new ends.

The materials used in manufacturing may be in their natural condition, *i.e.* the so-called "raw materials," such as ore, timber or wool, or they may be partly processed materials, such as steel, sawn timber and leather, which are used to make other things.

The finished product of one industry may be the raw material of another. For example, iron ore is used to make steel and steel is used in the making of machinery; in like manner, timber is used to make wood-pulp, wood-pulp is used to make paper and paper is the basis of the printing industry.

A principle of industrial manufacture is that the more processing and altering a material is subjected to, the more valuable does it become. In fact, one way of defining manufacture might well be "the processing of raw material to enhance its value."

2. Reduction of manufacturing costs. It is the task of the producer to reduce manufacturing costs to as low a level as possible consistent with satisfactory workmanship. This can be done by:

(*a*) *Mass production:* usually the greater the number of articles produced, the smaller is the unit cost of production.

(*b*) *Mechanisation:* the use of machinery can increase the numbers and speed of output of articles.

(*c*) *Reduction of labour costs:* the cost of labour is normally the largest single production cost.

(*d*) *Selecting an economic factory site:* a site which will give economies with respect to raw materials, fuel, transport costs.

3. Types of manufacture. Manufacturing falls broadly into three types or classes:

(a) Craft manufacture.
(b) Domestic manufacture.
(c) Factory industry.

The first two share many features and there is a certain amount of overlapping between them. Factory industry is distinct from the other two in many important respects.

4. Craft and domestic manufacture. The craftsman was the earliest industrial worker. He appears as soon as civilisation developed, that is, as soon as man began to live in communities and *specialisation of labour* became possible. The craftsman is still a common feature of the pre-industrialised and less industrialised countries as, for instance, in Iran, Nigeria and the Central American Republics. Indeed, even in the industrially advanced countries a few true craftsmen linger on, *e.g.* cabinet makers, silversmiths, and textile workers, together with a few quaint survivals such as thatchers and basket makers. The chief characteristics of craft industry are that the craftsman finds or buys his raw materials, fashions his articles and sells them himself.

Domestic, sometimes termed cottage, industry may be said to have grown up out of the difficulty which the craftsman had in disposing of his goods. In domestic industry the merchant comes into the picture: he delivers the raw materials to the worker and then collects the finished product at regular intervals. Thus the merchant, in effect, controls the output of the worker but not the premises in which he works. As with craft industry, production is mainly by hand and is carried on domestically. The wool and silk industries in Britain were originally organised on this basis, as was much of the present-day silk industry in the Lyons area in France.

5. Factory industry. Factory industry differs markedly from craft and cottage industries.

(a) *Size of factory.* Although factories vary greatly in size, many of them employ large numbers of people, sometimes several thousand.

(b) *Powered machinery.* Groups of people are employed

on an organised basis using powered machinery on a large scale.

(c) *Specialised production.* Firms tend to concentrate upon the production of a specific article, *e.g.* carpets or engines or cables.

NOTE: Today, with the introduction of automation, where machines are used to control machines, factory industry has advanced a stage further.

6. The Industrial Revolution.

Modern factory industry is the product of the Industrial Revolution which, developing slowly during the seventeenth and eighteenth centuries, may be said to have had its take-off in the 'seventies and 'eighties of the eighteenth century.

The Industrial Revolution was marked by:

(a) *Change* in industrial *methods*:

  (i) a change from handwork to machine production; and
  (ii) the use of power to drive machines;

(b) *Change* in industrial *organisation*:

  (i) the organisation of work in factories; and
  (ii) the centralised location of industry in particular areas.

The central and distinguishing feature of the Industrial Revolution may be said to consist of an entirely new relationship between men, machines and resources.

7. The Industrial Revolution in Britain.

The Industrial Revolution started in Britain. It is impossible to interpret the Industrial Revolution in terms of a single factor but one very important factor was that, with the growth in the numbers of people, the domestic system was incapable of meeting the growing demand for goods.

NOTE: In saying this we are implying that possibly it was the growth in the numbers of people that helped to trigger off the Industrial Revolution. This is contrary to the traditional idea that it was the Industrial Revolution which was responsible for the great increase in the population of this country during the nineteenth century.

Other favouring factors were that:

(a) Britain, unlike her continental neighbours, had enjoyed a long period of peace and internal development;

(b) she had acquired colonies which supplied her with raw materials and provided her with expanding markets; and

(c) she had abundant supplies of coal and iron ore, the two pre-requisites for industrial development.

Added to these favouring factors, ingenious and inventive Britons devised a whole series of technical inventions and innovations in the eighteenth and early nineteenth century which made possible shaft coalmining, the large-scale production of iron and steel, and the mechanisation of textile manufacture.

8. The spread of the Industrial Revolution. The Industrial Revolution spread from Britain to the European continent: first to Belgium, then to France, then to Germany and later to Italy. From Europe the revolution then made its way to the United States, Japan and Russia. In recent decades it has spread widely throughout the world and many countries, such as Australia, South Africa, Brazil and Mexico, are currently undergoing their Industrial Revolutions.

Britain led the world in industrialisation until the beginning of the present century. Although Britain remains a major industrial nation, ranking after the United States, the Soviet Union and possibly West Germany, she is relatively much less important. Before the First World War Germany had overtaken Britain and after that war the United States rapidly forged ahead to become the greatest industrial nation on earth. In this she was greatly helped by her astonishingly rich resources of fuels and minerals.

MAJOR INDUSTRIAL REGIONS
OF THE WORLD

9. The pattern of industry. The pattern of world industry, that is the distribution of the major regions of industrial development, as shown in Fig. 21, shows some interesting features:

(a) two large areas of industrial concentration in mid-latitudes;

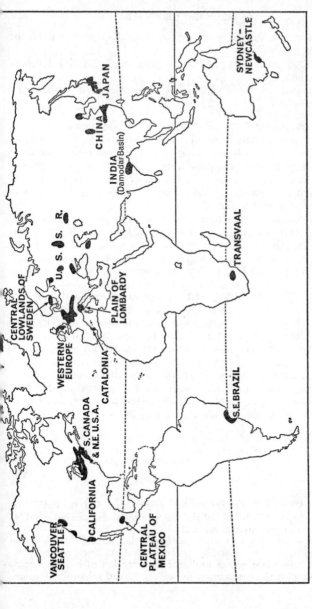

FIG. 21.—*World distribution of industry*

The four main centres of industrial development are the eastern USA, Europe, the USSR and the Far East. This zone in mid-latitudes is known as the Power Belt. There are some minor centres of industry outside this zone, but they remain relatively unimportant, though some countries are developing more rapidly.

(b) about a dozen small and widely dispersed clusters of industry;

(c) large areas devoid of any significant industrial development; and

(d) an almost total absence of industrial areas within the tropics.

10. The Power Belt. Most of the world's industry—in terms of the value of manufactured output, about 85% of it—is to be found in what is often referred to as the *Power Belt*, the zone extending in mid-latitudes from the Mississippi in North America across the eastern seaboard and Europe to the Ural Mountains in Eurasia. This zone is called the Power Belt because *it accounts for something like* 90% *of the world total energy consumption*—from coal, oil, natural gas and water power. The predominance of this industrial zone is illustrated by the fact that *it produces the bulk of the world's output of heavy industry*, of iron and steel, machinery, vehicles, ships and chemicals (*see* XVIII, Heavy Industries).

11. Outside the Power Belt. There are about a dozen subsidiary centres of industry elsewhere, some already of comparatively long standing, as in Japan, others of relatively recent development, as in California. The most important of these subsidiary industrial areas are in Soviet Asia, China, Japan, India, Australia, South Africa, Brazil, Mexico and western United States. With the exception of Japan, these subsidiary industrial centres are relatively small, though in some cases, as in north China and south-eastern Australia, they are expanding rapidly.

12. Features of the pattern. Closer examination of the world pattern of industry reveals some interesting and significant features:

(a) Most of the industry generally is concentrated on or near coalfields.

(b) Most of the *heavy* industry is associated with the coalfields.

(c) Much of the industrial development is concentrated in coastal areas and around ports.

(d) A high proportion of the industrial development is to be found in areas colonised by, and occupied by, European peoples.

(e) There is a rather limited concentration of industry compared with the comparatively widely-spread mineral resources.

Some of these features are readily understandable. Because modern industry is dependent upon power resources, the coalfields naturally became magnets of industry, especially since coal was the first and most abundant and most easily worked source of energy. Concentration in and around ports is clearly linked with the import of raw materials essential to industry and the export of finished goods. The newer industrial developments outside the Power Belt often resulted from Europeans carrying their industrial expertise and managerial capacity with them to the newer lands in which they settled. Even in non-European lands, such as China, the first industries were largely the outcome of European initiative.

13. Industrial areas within the Power Belt. In the Power Belt industry generally, but heavy industry particularly tends to be concentrated in a few important areas. These areas are mostly linked to the coalfields, although there is an increasing tendency for industry to develop off the coalfields and for it to become more widely spread. The main reasons for this are:

(a) The availability of new sources of power, such as oil, water-power, natural gas and nuclear energy.

(b) Improved means of transport resulting from the development of roads and motor vehicles.

(c) The ever-increasing need to rely upon outside sources of raw materials.

The *chief industrial areas* within the Power Belt are:

(a) *In Europe:*

    (i) The axial belt of industry in Britain.
    (ii) The Franco-Belgian Coalfield.
    (iii) The Ruhr–Westphalian region.
    (iv) Saxony and the Silesian Coalfield.
    (v) The Plain of Lombardy.
    (vi) The Moscow region of Russia.
    (vii) The Donbas region of the Ukraine.
    (viii) The central lowlands of Sweden.

(b) *In North America (cf. Fig. 16):*

    (i) The Lake Peninsula area of Canada.
    (ii) New England.
    (iii) The Hudson–Mohawk Valley.

> (iv) Lake Erie shores.
> (v) The Baltimore–Philadelphia region.
> (vi) The Chicago–Gary area.
> (vii) The Pennsylvania Coalfield.
> (viii) The Birmingham district of Alabama.

14. The dispersed subsidiary areas. These, widely scattered, are sometimes based upon coalfields, sometimes upon newer sources of power.

(a) Soviet Central Asia: the Urals and Kuzbas regions.
(b) South Manchuria: Anshan, Fushun, Mukden (Shenyang).
(c) The lower Yangtse and delta region: Wuhan, Shanghai.
(d) Japan, the Tokyo Plain and Inland Sea: Tokyo–Yokohama, Osaka–Kobe and northern Kyushu.
(e) Damodar–Calcutta area: Calcutta, Howrah, Jamshedpur.
(f) South-east Australia: Sydney–Newcastle area and Whyalla.
(g) Transvaal, S. Africa: Johannesburg, Vereeniging.
(h) São Paulo region of Brazil: São Paulo, Rio de Janeiro, Volta Redonda, Belo Horizonte.
(i) Central Plateau of Mexico: Mexico City, Puebla, Guadalajara.
(j) California, USA: San Francisco and Los Angeles.

Although one or two of these areas had their origins before the turn of the century, mostly they are of relatively recent growth and some have only become important industrially since the Second World War.

FEATURES OF MODERN INDUSTRY

15. Factors affecting the spread of industry. Industry has spread widely over the face of the earth even if in many parts it is only sporadically developed. Today, many countries, formerly engaged almost exclusively in the production of primary products, *e.g.* Argentina, Mexico, Australia, possess manufacturing industries, industries which sometimes are dependent upon imported raw materials and fuels.

The reasons for this industrial development are mainly twofold:

(*a*) During the two World Wars many countries were cut off from supplies of manufactured goods and this meant either they had themselves to make the manufactured articles they required or do without them. Several of Brazil's industries developed for this reason.

(*b*) Many countries see in industrialisation a means of making themselves more self-supporting and independent and, also, of absorbing their surplus populations and raising standards of living.

16. The expansion of light industry. There has been a tremendous expansion in the secondary, light and consumer goods industries. Although some countries, *e.g.* the USSR and China, give the basic or heavy industries priority, most countries beginning an industrialisation programme develop the lighter type of industries, *e.g.* textiles, food processing, first. In countries which have well developed industrial manufacture and high living standards, the demand for luxury and sophisticated products, as distinct from purely utilitarian products, grows apace. The variety, output, and value of the secondary industries now reach staggering proportions.

17. Size of modern industrial plants. A distinctive feature of modern industry is the vast size of many industrial plants, *e.g.* the Ford motor works at Dagenham, ICI at Billingham, Margam iron and steel works. These factories, highly capitalised, use modern methods of mass production. Large, integrated plants are more economic to run than smaller ones, for:

(*a*) production can be streamlined and rationalised;

(*b*) large-scale mechanisation can be applied;

(*c*) by-products of the basic industry can be used for other industries; and

(*d*) large concerns can employ their own research and training staffs.

18. Automation. The logical development of such major scale mass production is automation. Automation may be defined as the use of machines to control machines; in other words, electronic devices supersede man in the supervision and control of machinery. In automation, the bulk of the manufacture is done by automatic processes, and the need of human intervention and control is reduced to an absolute minimum.

The future will see an increasing application of automative techniques, but how quickly and to what extent, as well as with what results, it is impossible to forecast. All that one can say is: automation is bound to have far-reaching effects upon industrial production, organisation and employment.

PROGRESS TEST 16

1. Explain how manufacturing costs may be reduced. (1, 2)

2. In what way is modern factory industry the product of the Industrial Revolution? (6)

3. What factors favoured Britain as the home of the Industrial Revolution? (7)

4. Explain briefly the following terms: specialisation of labour; craft manufacture; the power belt; light industries. (4, 10, 16)

5. What are the chief features characterising modern industry? (15–17)

6. Locate in a broad way the chief industrial areas of the earth. (9–14)

7. Why is mechanised mass production the chief characteristic of modern industry? (17, 18)

8. Manufacture may be defined as "the processing of raw materials to enhance their value." What factors must be taken into account when considering the meaning of "manufacture"? (1)

CHAPTER XVII

LOCATION OF INDUSTRY

FACTORS OF LOCATION

1. Locating factors of industry. Although some industries have grown up by chance, usually there is a reason (or reasons) why an industry happens to occur in a particular place. This is more especially true of the older, long established industries.

Many factors—economic, historical, human, political and geographical—are involved in the location of industry. Some of the factors which originally were responsible for the setting up of the industry may no longer be of any consequence or may even have become forgotten.

In the past there has been a tendency to emphasise, perhaps even to over-emphasise, the role played by purely geographical factors in the location of industrial enterprises. While there is no doubt that geographical factors have sometimes played a major part in industrial location. we must be careful not to interpret the siting and growth of industries *always and only in terms of geographical influences.*

The most important of the geographical factors which affect the location of individual industries are:

(*a*) Raw materials.
(*b*) Power resources.
(*c*) Water supplies.
(*d*) Labour supply.
(*e*) Markets.
(*f*) Transport facilities.

GEOGRAPHICAL FACTORS

2. Raw materials. Nothing can be made unless the essential raw materials are available. Early examples of the influence of the availability of necessary raw materials are provided by:

(*a*) The old established pencil industry of Keswick owed its development to local supplies of graphite and timber, the two chief raw materials required in the making of pencils.

(b) The leather and footwear industries of such Midland towns as Northampton, Kettering and Rushden owed their origin to the availability of hides in a cattle-rearing area.

(c) The sweetmeat industry of Pontefract owes something to the former cultivation of the liquorice plant (originally by the monks) in the neighbourhood.

Industries which are based upon a few heavy, bulky raw materials, e.g. iron-smelting, brick-making, cement manufacture, are usually located near the supply of raw materials e.g.:

(a) The Frodingham–Scunthorpe iron and steel industry which developed from the local Jurassic iron ore deposits.

(b) The brickworks of Peterborough which are based upon the local supplies of clay in the clay vale.

(c) Cement-making at Rugby, Harbury and Long Itchington which is based upon the locally quarried beds of limestone.

However, it should be noted that in cases of this kind the factor which is really involved is *the deterrent effect of transport costs rather than the positive attraction of the raw materials*. Where raw materials are of the lighter kind, less bulky, and more valuable, the manufactured products are better able to stand transport costs.

A good example of an industrial area which is firmly based upon local raw materials is Tees-side. The Middlesbrough iron and steel industry was originally based upon the Cleveland iron ores (now exhausted). The chemical industry is closely linked with steel-making since the coking process yields ammonia, tar and benzole, three important by-products which form the basis of a whole range of processes. Moreover, the Triassic deposits contain anhydrite (sulphate of lime) and salt (sodium chloride) used for making chloride and caustic soda. All the heavy industries of Tees-side owe their origin basically to the occurrence of local raw materials.

3. Power resources.

All modern manufacturing industries are dependent upon some source of power. The particular nature of an industry may, however, affect the role of power as a locating factor, e.g.:

(a) The *iron and steel industries* which need large quantities of coking coal are frequently tied to the coalfields; note, however, that the growing need to import large quantities of iron ore is

causing many of the newer plants to move to coastal locations
(*see* XVIII, **1**, 8–13).

(*b*) The industries which are *greedy users of cheap hydro-
electric power*, such as the electro-metallurgical, electro-chemical
and wood-pulp industries, are closely tied to areas of hydro
power production even though these are sometimes in rather
inaccessible highland areas.

The character of the source of power is important: coal, as
we have already noted, is a heavy, bulky commodity and costly
to transport; petroleum and natural gas are more easily handled
and transported—they can be piped—hence the oil- and gas-
fields have not attracted industry to anything like the same
degree as the coalfields. On the other hand, we should recognise
the importance of the gas deposits in the Plain of Lombardy
and in Mexico in stimulating considerable industrial development in those areas.

The development of electricity (from hydro, thermal or
atomic stations) and its relatively easy transmission over long
distances by cable has made possible a greater dispersion of
industry.

For example, the growth of manufacturing industries in
Essex and the home counties of Britain generally has been due
primarily to two factors:

  (*a*) the development of the electric grid; and
  (*b*) the great flexibility of transport made possible by the
      motor vehicle.

4. Labour supply. A labour supply is important in two
respects:

  (*a*) *quantitatively*, *i.e.* large numbers are often required;
  (*b*) *qualitatively*, *i.e.* people with skill or technical ex-
      pertise are needed.

Supplies of unskilled labour are not hard to come by except
in areas of full employment or in areas of small population
where a shortage may, in fact, exist. Modern industry requires
large numbers of workers in spite of increasing mechanisation.
In many industries, especially where machines do most of the
work, little skill is required, *e.g.* repetitive assembly and packaging jobs. Industries of this kind are often attracted to large
urban centres. In such cases, the availability of a labour

supply is often the only predisposing factor, for the employees can be easily and quickly trained.

Skill in a particular craft or trade, especially in the days of domestic industry, was often important. James Watt's early attempts to produce steam engines were greatly handicapped because he could not find engineers sufficiently skilled to make the precision parts he needed. New engineering firms will often set up in engineering areas simply because they require workers with experience of engineering work.

The so-called traditional skill in an industry was often an operative factor, *e.g.* in the woollen textile industry where, in fact, it still counts for much. There are cases where the tradition of an industry and an intimate knowledge of an industry—for there is no such thing as traditional skill: all skills have to be learnt—have accounted for the continuance of an industry or the establishment of an associated industry in a locality where the original physical advantages it had have long since disappeared.

5. Water supply. Supplies of water fall, in a sense, under the category of raw materials needed by industry, but water is of such great and growing importance that it deserves special mention. The use of water in industry, neglecting for the moment its role formerly as a source of power, is important in two respects:

(*a*) *Quantity of water supply*, since some industries, such as the paper-making, food processing and chemical industries, are prolific users of water; access to large water supplies is frequently essential.

(*b*) *Quality of water supply*, *i.e.*, whether it is clean, hard or soft, free of chemical impurities; this is especially important in some industries such as brewing, paper making, textiles.

NOTE

(i) *Water quantity:* the electricity industry provides a good example of an industry requiring copious water supplies. Since most power-stations make use of direct cooling, enormous quantities of water are needed for this purpose. A station of 300-megawatt demands approximately 12 million gallons an hour for direct cooling. This explains why power-stations have river-side sites. Many of the atomic power stations have river or coastal locations because of their very heavy demands upon water supplies.

(ii) *Water quality*: the whisky industry of Scotland provides a good and interesting example of the significance of the quality of water. Whisky-making requires plentiful supplies of water which has drained through peat: this basically determines the quality of the spirit. Of the hundred or so distilleries in Scotland about forty are to be found around the Moray Firth area with the major concentration occurring in the lower Spey valley. Water quality is, likewise, of tremendous importance in the brewing of beer.

6. Markets. The sole purpose of industry is the production of goods for sale and there is little point in producing goods unless there is a market for them. The market is dependent upon two main things:

(*a*) the *size* of the market, *i.e.* the number of possible purchasers;

(*b*) the *purchasing power* of the market, which is tantamount to saying the standards of living of customers.

The following nations illustrate the importance of these two factors:

(*a*) The *United States* offers an excellent market for goods, for it has a population of some **210** millions, most of whom enjoy a very high standard of living; hence the desire of European countries to break into the American market.

(*b*) *China*, with its population of 800 millions, ought to provide an enormous market, but because of the low living standards its market value is relatively small; yet *its potential value as a market is tremendous.*

NOTE: In talking about markets we should remember that markets are not always available or that they may be restricted because of tariffs, quotas and various other import restrictions. For example, in England imports from the USA have in the past been restricted because of a dollar shortage (*see* XXI, 14–16).

It is important to note that market demand will be the over-riding factor in manufacturing; as soon as demand begins to ease off production normally has to adjust itself. It is also important to note how the market may be stimulated by advertising. In order to encourage, develop and open up new markets most large organisations or firms these days have *market research departments.*

7. Transport facilities. Transport, whether by land or water or perhaps other means, is necessary:

(a) for the assembly of raw materials; and
(b) for the marketing of the finished products.

It is difficult to estimate how much a particular industry owes to the original transport facilities since there is a definite tendency for industrial development to foster and further improve communications facilities. One can quote one or two examples which illustrate, quite clearly, the benefits to industry of improved communications.

(a) The *Trent and Mersey Canal*, opened in 1777, enabled raw materials for the Potteries to be imported cheaply and in quantity and so greatly stimulated the growing pottery industry of North Staffordshire.

(b) The *advent of the motor vehicle* and improved road transport was an important factor in the growth of the varied light industries which became established in Essex.

(c) Most of the industrial development in Soviet Siberia clings to, and is dependent upon, the great communications line of the *Trans-Siberian Railway*.

Partly because of transport problems and costs many articles are often made in the consuming areas, *e.g.* agricultural machinery in farming areas, ships' engines and boilers in the shipbuilding areas (XVIII, 17).

NON-GEOGRAPHICAL FACTORS

8. The importance of geographical factors. We have emphasised the purely geographical factors influencing industrial location, but there are other factors of an historical, economic, political and human character which have exerted a great influence. These, nowadays, often overshadow completely any geographical influence.

Because of modern scientific and technological developments, the ubiquity of communications and the ready availability of electric power, not to mention the mobility of labour and the possibility of using alternative raw materials, one is tempted to think that geographical factors are no longer of any significance. The importance of many have, in fact, been reduced, sometimes completely nullified.

In some respects, however, their importance remains as great as ever and man cannot afford to ignore them. Two examples will illustrate this.

(a) *The nuclear power industry*. The generation of power in nuclear stations demands vast quantities of water for cooling purposes: so much so that the location of nuclear plants is tied very closely to sites providing abundant water supplies, *e.g.* Berkeley, Hinkley Point, Bradwell, Calder Hall.

(b) *Uruguayan industrialisation*. After the Second World War Uruguay embarked upon a programme of varied and rapid industrialisation, but this was undertaken with little regard to supplies of raw materials, power, and industrial expertise. At first this went reasonably well for it was financed by the rich profits Uruguay had made during the War. But when the money ran out, Uruguayan industry found itself in very serious trouble. Simply put, the Uruguayans had flouted geographical considerations.

9. Capital. Many factors are not strictly speaking geographical, although *they have geographical repercussions*. Perhaps the most important of the non-geographical factors is capital. Supplies of merchant capital helped to make possible early industrial enterprises. The availability of investment capital is just as important today. It is largely because capital is available in cities such as London, Paris and New York that these cities have become major centres of industry. Most of the underdeveloped countries lack domestic capital on a scale sufficient to promote industrial development and are, accordingly, largely dependent upon outside investment.

10. Management. Management involves many things but it includes:

(a) organisational ability;
(b) effective leadership;
(c) industrial expertise; and
(d) knowledge of markets.

The success or failure of an enterprise is to no small degree dependent upon the quality of its management. Many firms and undertakings have flourished because of the unique qualities of their founders—one can think of Henry Ford, Lord Nuffield, Josiah Wedgwood or present-day successful management, as at Unilever or Imperial Chemical Industries.

Industrialisation in the underdeveloped countries is frequently handicapped by shortages of managerial skill.

11. Government activity. Governmental interference, direction or control may be responsible for industrial location and development. An obvious example of this is provided by the Trading Estates set up in Britain. Political considerations, such as the desire to attain national self-sufficiency or at least a more nicely balanced economy may lead to the establishment of industries for which there are no obvious natural advantages. The role played by governments in industry is increasing in importance. This is perhaps inevitable, with the growing need to conserve and allocate resources at the present day, and the necessity to redress regional economic imbalance.

12. Personal factors. Some factors are difficult to classify since the establishment of an industry may have depended largely upon chance or the whim of an individual. As the *P.E.P.* (Political and Economic Planning) *Report on the Location of Industry*, 1939, suggested, the siting of a factory may be related to the managing director's addiction to golf. The classic example of the human factor may be said to be the great shirt and underwear industry of Albany in New York State, USA, which owes its origin to the simple fact that a local parson invented the first shirt to have a detachable collar!

DEVELOPMENT AND DISTRIBUTION OF MODERN INDUSTRY

13. Characterising features of development. Three important features may be said to characterise industry at the present time.

(a) *Industry has spread to almost all parts of the world.* Less than a century ago practically all the factory industry in the world was concentrated in Western Europe and most of this was in Britain. Now manufacturing industry is widely dispersed and countries which formerly were concerned with primary production now possess some industry. Even the most backward of the underdeveloped countries usually have some manufacturing industry.

(b) *There has been a tremendous expansion of the secondary, light and consumer goods industries.* Although some countries, *e.g.* the Soviet Union and China, give the basic or heavy industries priority, most countries beginning an industrialisation programme develop the lighter type of industries, *e.g.* textiles, food processing. Such industries make less demands upon capital equipment, industrial skills, technological know-how. The variety, output and value of the secondary industries now reach staggering proportions.

(c) *Modern industrial plants are now often of vast size, e.g.* the Fiat motor works in Turin, the giant steelworks at Margam in South Wales, the ICI plant at Billingham, the Phillips electrical works at Eindhoven in Holland. Modern methods, including mass production techniques, are employed by big firms. This involves heavy capital investment. To be economic such plants must be kept in production. The logical development of this large-scale mass production is automation.

14. The pattern and distribution of industry. The pattern of world industry, that is the distribution of the major regions of industrial development, was described in the previous chapter (XVI, **9–14**), which listed the industrial centres of the Power Belt in the mid-latitudes, and the more dispersed centres outside this belt, many of which are of fairly recent development.

If one compares this distribution of industry with the world distribution of coalfields, one should see a close correlation (*see* XV, **10**).

Industry is most weakly developed in the southern hemisphere: this is clearly indicated by the fact that the southern hemisphere produces less than 5% of the world's energy output and less than $2\frac{1}{2}$% of the world's production of iron and steel.

PROGRESS TEST 17

1. List the geographical factors which affect the location of industry. (**1**)

2. Show how certain manufacturing industries owe their origin mainly to the availability of raw materials. (**2**)

3. Outline the importance of power supplies in the location of industry. (**3**)

4. "Labour supply has two aspects: quantity and quality of labour." Why are these aspects both important? (**4**)

5. What factors have assisted the industrial growth of London and the home counties? (**3**)

6. Quoting appropriate examples, show how water supplies may influence the location of industry. (**5**)

7. Compare the United States and China as markets: why do they differ so greatly? (6)

8. Describe the role of transport in manufacturing industry. (2, 7)

9. Discuss the importance (a) of capital, and (b) of management, in manufacturing industry. (9, 10)

10. Give some examples of the effects of government influence and interference in industrial development. (11)

11. Where is the "Power Belt" located, and what was the main reason for its growth? (14)

12. Give an account of the chemical industry in Britain. (2, 5, 13)

SUGGESTED PROJECTS

1. What factors have influenced the growth of the chemical industry in Britain? From your reading, give an account of the industry in any one region in Britain.

2. Make a visit to a local factory, seek the help of the management, and attempt to find out:

(a) where the raw materials used come from;
(b) what kind of power they use;
(c) how many employees the firm has;
(d) where their markets are; and
(e) the means by which the goods are marketed.

3. Find out the raw materials used in the manufacture of cement; pottery; linoleum; toothpaste; paint. Outline the manufacturing processes used for *one* of these products.

CHAPTER XVIII

THE HEAVY INDUSTRIES

THE IRON AND STEEL INDUSTRY

1. Beginnings of the industry. The iron and steel industry is
of fundamental importance to modern society. In fact it may
be said that we live in a "Steel Age," for steel is the basis of so
many things, *e.g.* the constructional, engineering and transportation industries, and a multitude of articles are made out of it.

The present-day steel industry has grown out of the old iron
industry. Prior to the Industrial Revolution, the iron industry
in England was located in three areas:

(*a*) the Weald of Kent and Sussex;
(*b*) the Forest of Dean;
(*c*) the Midlands.

In each of these areas ironstone was available locally and was
smelted by charcoal.

The Industrial Revolution brought a vastly increased demand for iron and the industry moved to the coalfields. This
was because of the need for large quantities of fuel for smelting
purposes and partly, also, because iron ore (the blackband
ores) was found in the Coal Measures. The Coal Measure ores
quickly became exhausted, however, and iron ore from other
areas (first, home areas and, then, from abroad) had to be
brought to the coalfields (*see* XIV, **5** and **6**).

A large modern blast furnace, in which the ore is reduced,
requires large quantities of coke and limestone (used as a
flux); hence, the most advantageous locations for an iron-smelting industry are those where coal of the coking variety,
iron ore and limestone are at hand, as at Birmingham, Alabama, or can be conveniently assembled, as in the Ruhr, West
Germany. Until the Cleveland iron ores became exhausted,
Middlesbrough was highly favoured in this respect.

2. Pig, cast and wrought iron. Iron ore which is reduced in
blast furnaces is converted into *pig iron*, so called because the

molten metal is run off into moulds or "pigs." Formerly pig-iron production exceeded that of steel, but with the growing use of scrap metal this is no longer true. Pig iron, which contains various impurities and is brittle, is of little value for industrial purposes and so is further treated to produce cast iron, wrought iron and steel.

Cast iron is made by remelting the pig iron and running it into required shapes or casts. But cast iron is brittle and cannot withstand shocks or blows, hence its usefulness is very limited.

Wrought iron, which is soft and malleable and which can be hammered and so shaped, is able to resist shocks: it is used in the making of cables and couplings and things such as ornamental gates.

Both cast and wrought iron are of little consequence nowadays.

3. Steel. Until just over a century ago the use of steel (which is really an iron-carbon alloy) was confined to the making of such small articles as springs, instruments and tools. In the 1850s an Englishman, Henry Bessemer, invented a method of steel manufacture which enabled it to be produced cheaply. As a result, steel began to replace iron in the latter half of the nineteenth century. Steel had many advantages over iron: it was harder, tougher, stronger and lighter.

4. Methods of steel-making. There are three main methods:

(*a*) *Bessemer's process* involved the blowing of air through the molten pig iron to rid it of harmful trace elements, such as silicon, sulphur and phosphorus, followed by the addition of carbon (usually in the form of anthracite), the whole operation taking less than 30 minutes.

(*b*) *Siemens–Martin process*. Shortly after the introduction of the Bessemer converter, Sir William Siemens, following up experiments made by a Frenchman, Pierre Martin, invented the *open-hearth* (*Siemens–Martin*) *process*. This method, which produces better-quality steel and which also has the advantage that scrap iron can be used, takes about twelve hours. Most British steel is made by this process.

(*c*) *Electric furnace*. This is the most effective, but also the most expensive, method of making steel. During the past ten years, there has been a big increase in production by the basic arc electric process, partly due to the increased demand for alloy steel.

5. Phosphoric ores. Some ores, such as the Jurassic iron ores of the English Midlands and the minette ores of Lorraine, in France, contain a high percentage of phosphorus which prevented their use. The problem of being able to use these phosphoric ores was solved by *Gilchrist and Thomas* in 1878. They lined the Bessemer converter with dolomite (a variety of limestone) which absorbed the phosphorus. This is called the *Basic Bessemer process*. The importance of this development lay in the fact that some of the largest and most accessible iron-ore deposits, hitherto unusable, could now be exploited. Moreover, the slag from the converter provides a valuable fertiliser.

6. Ferro-alloys. A modern development in the steel industry has been the production of special steels which are made by adding small, carefully controlled, amounts of alloy metals: the chief ferro-alloys are manganese, nickel, cobalt, tungsten, chromium and vanadium. For example, manganese gives a non-magnetic steel, nickel or tungsten an extremely hard, tough steel, vanadium a high-speed tool steel, chromium a stainless, corrosion-resistant steel (*see* XIV, **12**).

7. World crude steel production. World steel production continues to expand and in 1972 reached 626·3 million tons. The annual rate of increase in recent years has been about 5%. There is now a considerable world steel surplus and this should have the effect of slowing down the rate of expansion. The leading producers are shown in the table below:

TABLE V. STEEL OUTPUT IN 1972
(in million tons)

United States	120·875
Soviet Union	125·589
European Coal & Steel Community	108·000
Japan	96·9
United Kingdom	25·3
Rest of World	149·636
World Total	626·390

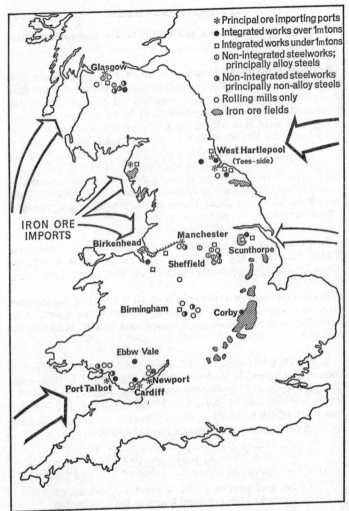

FIG. 22.—*Iron and steel in Britain*

The centres of iron and steel production were originally on the coal-fields since they used Coal Measure iron ores. As these became used up iron ore had to be brought from other iron ore fields or imported from abroad. For example, as the South Wales industry came to depend upon imported ores, the iron and steel centres moved to the coast. Some of the newer iron and steel centres, *e.g.* Scunthorpe, Corby, are located on the Jurassic ironfields.

8. United Kingdom. In the early days, roughly until the end of the nineteenth century, the United Kingdom led the world in iron and steel production; now she ranks fifth and takes second place to West Germany in Europe. Since the Second World War, output has steadily increased and her output of 27 million tons in 1965 was a record. The 1972 figure of 25·3 million tons shows a slight drop.

The two most important areas of iron and steel production are:

(a) *South Wales*, where the industry is now focused on the coast in large-scale plants at Port Talbot, Cardiff and Newport (except for the inland centre of Ebbw Vale), and where it is very largely dependent upon imported foreign ores; and

(b) *the North-east Coast*, where the industry is concentrated on Tees-side and at Consett, using home ores from Lincolnshire and foreign ores from Sweden and North Africa.

Both these areas produce about one-fifth apiece of the steel output (*see* Fig. 22). Areas of lesser importance are Scunthorpe–Frodingham, Sheffield, the East Midlands (Corby), and Lanarkshire.

Home resources provide only a small fraction of the iron ore used; we are dependent for about 90% of our needs upon imported ores from Sweden, Canada and North Africa in the main.

9. Western Europe. On the continent, the six countries of the Netherlands, Belgium, Luxembourg, France, West Germany and Italy became members of the European Coal and Steel Community (ECSC). The aim behind this co-operative undertaking was:

(a) to stop the participating members from running their own competitive iron and steel industries; and

(b) to enable them to make the best possible use of their combined resources through intelligent planned production.

The idea was proved to be a great success and the Community produces about one-fifth of the world's output of steel. Note that the United Kingdom only recently became a member of the Community.

There are three major areas of production (*see* Fig. 23):

(a) *The Ruhr region* in the Rhineland is the greatest centre of production and this makes West Germany the dominant partner

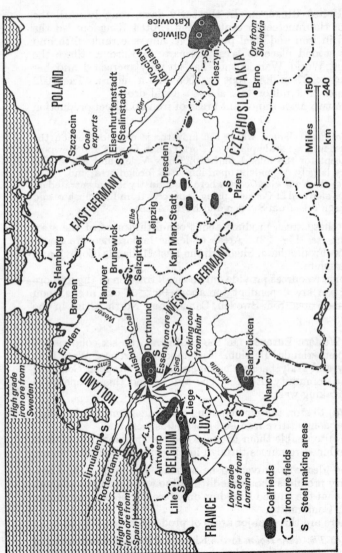

Fig. 23.—*Coal, iron and steel in Europe*

In earlier times the iron and steel industry was primarily coalfield-based using Coal Measure iron ores. Today many iron and steel centres lie off the coalfields, *e.g.* Hamburg, Salzgitter, Ijmuiden, Nancy; they are located on

in the Community. The Ruhr originally had many natural advantages—local iron ore, charcoal, running water—but the present industry is almost entirely dependent upon ore brought from Sweden up the Rhine, and from Lorraine, formerly by railway, but now, with the deepening and canalisation of the Moselle, by water also. The Ruhr's greatest asset is its excellent coking coal. German steel production is about 53 million tons.

(b) *The Lorraine region* has developed as France's premier steel-producing region, producing slightly more than half of the total output. Adjoining is the steel industry of Luxembourg which, like the French industry, is based upon the local minette ores. Some coal comes from the northern coalfield but much comes from the Ruhr via the Moselle in return for iron ore. French Lorraine and Luxembourg together account for a production of some 15 million tons of steel.

(c) *The Franco-Belgian Coalfield* (shown in Fig. 24 on p. 198) is the seat of the third main iron- and steel-producing area. Only some 2–3 million tons of the French output is based on the northern coalfield, but the field is the centre of the Belgian industry which is centred mainly in the towns of Liège and Charleroi (*see* Fig. 24 below). Belgian output is around 14 million tons a year. It is now dependent upon imported iron ore.

Ijmuiden is the centre of the Dutch iron and steel industry which has an output of slightly more than 3 million tons. The industry is based upon imported ores.

Fig. 23 shows the chief coal-, iron- and steel-producing areas in central Europe.

Production in Italy, now running at around 19·8 million tons a year, is mainly concentrated at a few large integrated plants on the coast. The chief centres are Cornegliano, near Genoa, at Piombino, opposite the isle of Elba, at Bagnoli, near Naples, and at the inland integrated unit at Aosta, north-west of Turin.

10. The United States.

The iron and steel output (120·9 million tons) of the United States is greater than the combined output of the European countries. The industry is mainly based upon large home supplies of both coal and iron ore. But, with the exception of the Birmingham, Alabama, region, coal and iron are not found close together (*see* Fig. 16).

The principal steel centres are:

(a) *The Pennsylvania Coalfield region* focused upon Pittsburgh (the greatest steel town in the world) and Youngstown. The

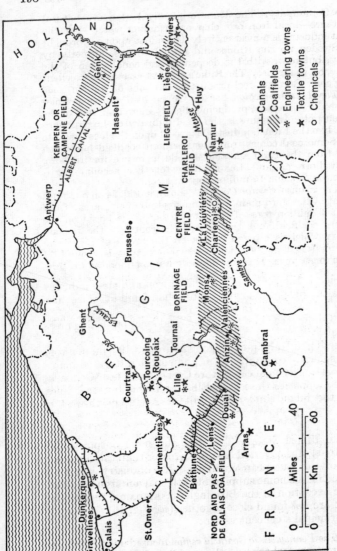

FIG. 24.—*The Franco-Belgian coalfield and its industries*

A coalfield extends from north-eastern France through central Belgium into southern Holland. The French coalfield region has almost every type of industrial activity, but the towns on the coalfield are concerned chiefly with mining, heavy engineering, chemicals and the generation of thermal electric power; the towns outside the coalfield with textiles, and light engineering. The Sambre-Meuse Coalfield of Belgium specialises in heavy original iron ores obtained from the Coal Measures have long since become exhausted and ore is brought from the Superior iron-fields and from Labrador.

(*b*) *The lakeside centres*. These include Chicago and Gary on Lake Michigan and Detroit, Cleveland and Buffalo on Lake Erie. These metallurgical centres depend upon ore shipped through the Lakes and Pennsylvanian coal.

(*c*) *The mid-Atlantic coast centres* such as the Sparrow's Point (Baltimore), Bethlehem and Philadelphia. These iron and steel plants are supported by coke from Pennsylvania and ores brought from Labrador, Venezuela and Chile.

(*d*) *Birmingham*, at the southern end of the Appalachians, has coal, ore and limestone at hand; unfortunately, its regional market is limited and, although Birmingham is a substantial producer, its early promise of becoming a major centre of production has never been fulfilled.

11. The Soviet Union. The iron and steel industry of the Soviet Union is of relatively recent development; certainly its tremendous expansion is a growth of the past quarter of a century. With an annual output of 125·5 million tons she now ranks first as a world producer, having overtaken the United States. The Soviet Union has plentiful indigenous coal and ore deposits.

There are three main steel-producing areas:

(*a*) *The Donbas region* in the Donetz basin of the Ukraine. Here, in southern European Russia, there exist close together the large iron-ore deposits of Krivoi Rog and the Donetz coal-field. The Donbas region has grown up to be the Soviet Union's largest iron and steel area, centred on the towns of Donetsk (formerly Stalino), Lugansk, Nikopol, Krivoi Rog and Kharkov.

(*b*) *The Urals region* is the second principal iron and steel region where Nizhni Tagil, Sverdlovsk, Chelyabinsk and Magnito-gorsk are the chief centres. The industry is based upon rich local supplies of ore and coal brought from central Asia.

(*c*) *The Kuzbas region* has developed upon the Kuznetsk coal-field. Although the Urals and Kuzbas regions are 1000 miles (1609 kilometres) apart, coal and ore are shuttled between them. This two-way traffic of fuel and ore has made the Urals iron-fields and the Kuznetsk coalfields into a giant *kombinat*, or combine.

12. The Far East. Three countries have iron and steel industries of note:

(*a*) *Japan*. Japan has a fairly long established industry in spite of the fact that she has little iron ore and lacks good coking coal. The Japanese iron and steel industry has grown by leaps and bounds during the past twenty years: production in 1965 was 40·5 million tons, in 1968 66·8 million tons, and in 1972 96·9 million tons. Her industry today is based almost entirely upon imported coal, iron ore and scrap metal. The great hub of the industry is in northern Kyushu centred in the towns of Moji and Yawata.

(b) *China*. China has had a small iron and steel industry for over half a century, but it is only within the past decade that rapid strides have been made in steel production which, in 1972, was estimated at about 23 million tons. The chief area is in the southern part of the central Plain of Manchuria, mainly in the towns of Anshan and Shenyang. Hankow, the traditional centre, has a growing steel industry.

(c) *India*. India's fifty-year-old industry is growing, but rather slowly, and the current production is around 6·5 million tons. The Damodar industrial region, to the west of Calcutta, is the major producing area.

13. The southern hemisphere. In the southern continents progress has been rather slow and none of the countries in the southern hemisphere is a major producer (XVII, **14**).

(a) In *Australia*, production in 1972 reached 6·5 million tons. The industry which is growing lustily, is based on home ores and coal and centred on Newcastle and Whyalla.

(b) In *South Africa* production, based on the Transvaal coal-field, has an output of 5·3 million tons.

(c) In *South America*, Brazil is the leading producer with 6·5 million tons; the steel industry is beginning to expand considerably. Argentina and Chile are small producers.

THE ENGINEERING INDUSTRY

14. Heavy and light engineering. The industry is very largely based upon steel and so is to be found in most steel-producing areas. A division is usually made into the heavy and light engineering industries.

(a) *Heavy engineering* is concerned with the making of large, heavy and bulky articles, such as girders and stanchions for bridges, railway engines and many kinds of machinery.

(b) *Light engineering* embraces the manufacture of small machines, implements, instruments, electrical components, etc.

Whereas heavy engineering is commonly associated with the iron and steel and coalfield areas, light engineering is less concentrated and may be widely dispersed, as it is in West Germany, for example.

15. Engineering in Britain. The chief areas of heavy engineering are:

(a) *Clydeside,* associated with shipbuilding and marine engineering;

(b) *Tees-side,* associated with ship-, bridge-, and railway-construction;

(c) *South Lancashire,* associated with mining and textile machinery;

(d) *West Riding of Yorkshire,* mainly concerned with textile machinery, boilers, etc.; and

(e) *West Midlands.*

Light engineering is fairly widely spread, but South Lancashire, the West Riding, the Midlands and the Greater London area are the principal regions.

16. Chief branches of engineering. Over and above this basic division into heavy and light branches, the engineering industry has many offshoots or sections, chief of which are shipbuilding, railway engineering, mechanical engineering, electrical engineering and the motor-car and aeroplane industries.

17. Shipbuilding. One of the major engineering industries, shipbuilding is dependent upon steel and so is located on navigable estuaries and along coasts usually in close proximity to supplies of steel (plates, girders, marine engines).

Today world shipping totals over 200 million tons. About half of it consists of oil-tankers, a telling commentary on the importance of petroleum in the world's economy.

The major ship-owning countries (Britain, the United States, Norway, Japan) are not necessarily the major shipbuilding countries. Britain was for long the world's premier shipbuilding country but was overtaken in 1957 by Japan.

(a) *Japan.* Japan's rise has been spectacular and during the past decade her output has increased tenfold. In 1972 her production of 12·8 million gross registered tonnage (g.r.t.)

represented over 50% of the total world output. Japanese success largely lies in the fact that her shipbuilding industry is a newly-developed one organised on modern lines and using new techniques of building. She is now building tankers of over 200,000 tons (*see* XX, 22).

(*b*) *United Kingdom.* Production has declined from some 2 million g.r.t. in 1913, when the United Kingdom accounted for about two-thirds of the world's output, to slightly over 1 million tons at the present day, which is about 5% of the total world output. The decline in the British shipbuilding industry has resulted from a variety of factors including cheaper production by foreign competitors, new shipbuilding techniques evolved by Japanese shipbuilders, strikes in Britain and late delivery dates. The most important areas for ship construction are Clydeside, the North-east coast, Merseyside, Belfast Lough and Barrow-in-Furness.

(*c*) *Other countries.* The other principal shipbuilding countries are West Germany, Sweden and the Netherlands. France and Italy are smaller producers. Note that the United States is not one of the major builders of ships. The Soviet Union, too, although building some vessels, is not an important producer.

18. Mechanical engineering. This is a highly complex branch of the engineering industry. It is concerned with the production of an enormous variety of articles, including mining, textile and printing machinery, engines of all kinds, machine tools and instruments.

A notable feature of the industry is the specialisation which takes place, a firm concentrating upon the making of ball-bearings or gears or office machines or motor engines as the case may be. Some firms have gained an international reputation for their products, *e.g.* the Italian firms of Necchi (sewing machines) and Olivetti (typewriters), the Swiss watch-makings firms of Omega and Cyma, the Swedish firms of Aga (cookers) and Electrolux (vacuum cleaners), the German firm of Zeiss (cameras), and the English firms of David Brown (tractors) and Platt Brothers of Oldham (textile machinery).

Many metals, besides iron and steel, are used by the mechanical engineering industry.

19. Electrical and radio engineering. This is a fairly recent branch of engineering, but it has expanded enormously during the present century with the ever-growing use of electrical goods and inventions such as radio, television and radar.

20. Motor vehicle and aircraft industries. Motor-cars and aeroplanes are very important products of the engineering industry; indeed, they are so important nowadays that automobile and aircraft engineering may be said to form separate branches of the engineering industry. As industries they are especially noteworthy because:

(a) *They make great demands* upon the products of the other branches of the engineering industry; essentially they are assembly industries using numerous components from other industries.

(b) The motor-car industry in particular has developed, at least in many countries, into an *important export industry*, *e.g.* in Britain, West Germany, and Japan.

21. Motor vehicle producers. The United States, Japan, West Germany, France, the UK and Italy in that order are the most important motor vehicle manufacturing countries.

In Britain, all the principal motor vehicle manufacturing centres, with the exception of a few such as Dagenham and Liverpool, are located in the Midlands, at Birmingham, Coventry, Derby, Luton, Oxford. The industry grew up here for a variety of reasons:

(a) The old-established engineering industries provided skilled workers for the new industry.

(b) There were good transportation facilities making the assembly of the component parts easy and assisting the export of cars.

(c) There were in some cases, notably in Oxford, large areas of cheap land available for the building of the great assembly plants.

(d) There were personal factors involved, *e.g.* the late Lord Nuffield who built the great Morris works at Cowley, near Oxford, probably chose this location because he was born and lived in Oxford.

During the past two years the British motor-car industry has been in a state of acute recession.

THE ALUMINIUM INDUSTRY

22. Growth. It is sometimes said that we are moving out of the iron and steel age and are on the threshold of a new metal age, the aluminium–titanium age. Whether this will prove to be true is impossible to say, but it is certainly true that the use of aluminium has increased by leaps and bounds during the last few decades. Not much more than a quarter of a century ago the use of aluminium was mainly confined to the making of cooking utensils. At the present time it has numerous uses, and, for example, the first all-aluminium ship has already been built. One of its most important uses is in aircraft construction.

23. Production. Aluminium is a light but strong metal which resists corrosion and conducts electricity. By using certain alloys it can be given additional strength and toughness. Aluminium is one of the commonest constituents of rocks, particularly of clay, but the chief source of aluminium is bauxite, a tropical red clay. Cryolite, mined in Greenland, is another source.

Aluminium is very difficult to extract from its raw material and high temperatures are needed for the reduction of the ore. Smelting can be carried on economically only where there is an abundance of cheap hydro-electric power; hence, the industry is most highly developed in those countries with plentiful water-power such as Canada, the United States, Norway, France and the Soviet Union. At Kinlochleven, in Scotland, where there is hydro-electric power, the smelting of bauxite is carried out on a small scale.

24. Some schemes. There are many centres of production but one or two may be noted.

(a) *Norway*. Ardal and Sunndal are the chief centres of aluminium production. The aluminium is produced from imported ore, and, in 1972, 548,000 tons were made. Norway, of course, has abundant supplies of cheap hydro-electric power and this greatly facilitates the electro-metallurgical industry.

(b) *The Kitimat Scheme* in British Columbia, not long since completed, provides power for the great smelting works constructed on the fiord harbour at Kitimat. To provide the necessary power an eastward flowing river was diverted westwards to the Pacific; this diversion involved the driving of a ten-mile-long tunnel through the Coast Range. The bauxite is imported from Jamaica. Canada produces 907,000 tons.

(c) *The Volta Scheme*, in Ghana, is another great project now going forward to enable local deposits of bauxite to be smelted.

THE CHEMICAL INDUSTRY

25. A key industry. The chemical industry is one of the key industries at the present day since many other industries depend upon its products. The chemical industry is, in a broad way, concerned with two processes:

(a) *Analytical processes*, *i.e.* it separates out the elements of raw materials, *e.g.* it breaks down coal by distillation to produce a wide variety of by-products; and

(b) *Synthesis*, *i.e.* it combines elements to produce new substances, *e.g.* synthetic fibres.

The chemical industry has two main branches: heavy chemical manufacture, and the production of chemical products, including pharmaceuticals.

26. Heavy chemicals. This involves the production of chemicals required in the manufacture of chemical products or for other industrial purposes. Acids, such as sulphuric, hydrochloric and nitric, and alkalis, such as caustic soda and carbonate of soda, are important products. Many of the old-established chemical industries were set up in areas where there were deposits of salt or potash or coal (since coal is a basic raw material of the industry) (*see* XVII, **2, 3**; XIV, **14, 15**). Two specialised aspects of the heavy chemical industry are:

(a) *Electro-chemical industries*, based upon the availability of hydro-electric power. Norway, Sweden, Switzerland and the Alpine region of France, for example, have all developed important chemical industries based upon water-power. The production of nitrates, ammonia, carbide, fertilisers and wood-pulp is closely associated with hydro-electric power.

(b) *Petro-chemical industries*, based upon petroleum and natural gas, are an even more recent development of expanding importance. The industries have grown up on or near to oil-fields and gas-fields or at the oil-refining centres. Petro-chemical industries are important in the United States, the Soviet Union, France, Italy, Holland and West Germany.

27. Chemical products. The products arising out of the chemical industry are numerous and astonishingly varied; some of the more important are:

(a) *The glass and pottery industry.* Glass is made by fusing sand (silica), soda ash and lime. The basis of most pottery glazes is white lead.

(b) *Soaps and detergents.* Soap is made from vegetable oils or fats and caustic soda and potash. Detergents use a similar base but also contain chemical solvents.

(c) *Artificial fertilisers* are essentially chemical fertilisers since they are phosphates, nitrates or potash, substances required by plants for their growth.

(d) *Dyestuffs* are produced from the distillation of coal and are widely used in the textile, paint and food-processing industries.

(e) *Synthetic fibre industry.* Some artificial or man-made fibres are derived from cellulose which is an organic base, *e.g.* rayon, but the non-cellulose fibres, such as nylon, Terylene and the like, are derived from coal or petroleum.

(f) *Pharmaceuticals.* Drugs, medicines, toiletries, are based on the chemical industry. Aspirin, for example, is a by-product of coal!

28. Main chemical producers. These are various European countries, the USA, the USSR and Japan.

(a) *Britain.* Britain's chemical industries are found chiefly on the coal- and salt-fields, as on Tees-side and Merseyside, and in the ports where raw materials can be easily imported. Imperial Chemical Industries (ICI) have great plants at Billingham and Wilton-on-Tees on Tees-side where plastics, synthetic fibres and a host of other products are made. The salt from the Cheshire salt-fields, combined with Lancashire and North Wales coal and vegetable oils imported through Liverpool have led to the great Merseyside chemical industry; here Port Sunlight is famous for soap, St Helens for glass, while Runcorn, Widnes and Warrington are chemical manufacturing towns.

(b) *West Germany.* The Germans, pioneers of the chemical industry, have built up one of the greatest industries in the world and have an important export trade in chemicals. The industry is based upon plentiful supplies of coal, lignite, salt, potash and imported petroleum. The Ruhr (Leverkusen), the Rhine Rift Valley (Ludwigshafen–Mannheim) and Hoechst, near Frankfurt, are the chief chemical areas.

(c) *Other areas in Europe.*

(i) France: Mulhouse, in Alsace, and Dombasle, in Lorraine, are important centres.

(ii) East Germany: the salt and potash deposits of the Stassfurt area have made Stassfurt an important centre of the chemical industry.

(iii) Holland: the chemical industry, largely based upon the oil-refining industry, has grown rapidly in recent years.

(iv) Sweden: here the industry is largely electro-chemical in its nature.

(v) Italy: the industry has largely grown out of the exploitation of its natural gas deposits.

(d) *United States.* She is the greatest producer of chemicals in the world and has a wide variety of products. The United States is fortunate in having large reserves of most of the raw materials required by the industry. The industry is closely associated with the main manufacturing regions. In the north-east the industry is linked with water-power resources; in California and on the Gulf Coast with the supplies of oil and natural gas.

(e) *Soviet Union.* There is no real shortage of any of the basic raw materials. The industry is well developed in certain aspects, *e.g.* fertilisers and explosives, but some sectors of the industry have been neglected.

(f) *Japan.* Very rapid development of the chemical industry has taken place since the end of the Second World War. Fertilisers are an important product. Tokyo and the manufacturing cities around the Inland Sea are the chief centres of chemical production.

29. The cement industry. Cement is an artificial mixture of clay and limestone which is burned and ground up extremely fine. When mixed with water, it becomes plastic but on drying out it sets or hardens. Cement in the form of concrete is widely used these days for structural foundations, bridges, buildings and even ships. Reinforced steel enormously enhances its utility.

Vast quantities are used nowadays and some 650 million tons are produced annually. The principal producers are the USSR (some 100 million tons), the USA (around 75 million tons), Japan (65 million tons), West Germany (45 million tons). The UK, France, Spain and Italy all produce between 20–30 million tons a year. China, India and Brazil are all fairly substantial producers with between 10–15 million tons annually.

The world demand for, and use of, cement seems bound to increase greatly in the future: during the past few years output has been increasing at the rate of 50 million tons annually.

PROGRESS TEST 18

1. Give a reasoned account of the development of the iron and steel industry in Great Britain. (1, 3, 4, 8)
2. Name and describe the three main processes of steel-making. (4)
3. Locate the main areas of iron and steel production in *either* Western Europe *or* North America. (9, 10)
4. Describe the iron and steel industry of the Soviet Union. (11)
5. Name the chief areas of engineering in the United Kingdom and state the particular branches of the engineering industry associated with each region. (15–21)
6. Outline and account for some of the changes in the ship-building industry during the past thirty years. (17)
7. Give an account of the production of aluminium, noting the factors which favour the establishment of the industry. (23, 24)
8. Give an account of the chemical industry, noting its raw materials, power and water needs, and its products. (25–28)
9. Locate the chief areas of chemical manufacture in Europe and indicate the factors which have given rise to these areas. (26, 28)
10. Explain carefully the following terms: electro-chemical industry; artificial fertilisers; Bessemer process; ferro-alloys. (4, 6, 26, 27)
11. Locate and give reasons for the development of the motor vehicle industry in the United Kingdom. (21)
12. Give a brief outline of (*a*) the iron and steel industry, and (*b*) the shipbuilding industry in Japan. (12, 17)

SUGGESTED PROJECTS

1. Give a full account of the industrial geography of *either* Italy *or* Sweden *or* Japan, noting the factors which influenced industrial growth and any present-day developments and problems.
2. Write a detailed essay on *either* the electro-chemical industry *or* the petro-chemical industry. Draw a sketch map of one of the main centres, indicating why the industry developed there.

CHAPTER XIX

THE LIGHT INDUSTRIES

NATURE OF LIGHT INDUSTRY

1. Meaning of light industry. The term "light industry" covers a very wide variety of manufacturing industries which differ from the "heavy industries" in the fact that their products are, literally, lighter in weight than most of those produced by heavy industry; they are also very largely based upon *materials which have already been partially processed, e.g.* footwear is based on the leather industry. Finally, they produce *goods which are made for consumption* and hence they are sometimes called, alternatively, consumer goods industries.

Light, secondary and consumer goods industries are, for all intents and purposes, synonymous terms. Strictly speaking, however, these three terms are not always exactly comparable, not all light industries are consumer goods industries; for example, one may quote the furniture industry which produces "durable consumer goods" as they are sometimes termed; again, the house construction industry produces houses which fall into the category of capital goods. But, in a general way, the terms may be taken to be synonymous.

2. Classes of light industry. Since the manufacturing industries are so varied it is difficult to group them into classes that are all inclusive. The following classification embraces the most important items:

 (*a*) the food industries;
 (*b*) the textile industries;
 (*c*) the leather industries;
 (*d*) printing and publishing;
 (*e*) household goods;
 (*f*) building construction.

THE FOOD INDUSTRIES

3. Foodstuffs. One of the largest and most varied of the light industries is that of food processing. It embraces the preparation, processing and preservation of animal and vegetable produce. A fourfold division of the food industries may be made:

(a) *The processing of foodstuffs.* These industries, mostly based on agriculture, include flour-milling, sugar-refining, oil-seed-crushing, and the processing of the beverage crops, *e.g.* the drying and fermenting of tea. Some of the industries are carried on in the areas where the foodstuffs are produced, *e.g.* sugar-beet refineries are found in villages and towns in rural areas as at Brigg in north Lincolnshire and Ely in Cambridgeshire. Note that such developments have the effect of carrying industry into the countryside. Flour-milling and oilseed-crushing are largely based in the ports importing grain and oilseeds, *e.g.* Hull.

(b) *The food preserving industries.* These include the drying and canning and freezing of fruit, vegetables and fish, the extraction and bottling of fruit juices, jam-making and meat-packing. Such industries are necessarily located near the source of the foodstuff that is to be preserved, hence the *frigorificos* and *saladeros* of Argentina and Uruguay are situated in the cattle and sheep areas, the fish canneries of British Columbia are on or at the mouths of the salmon rivers, while in Britain many of the great jam-making firms are in the midst of the fruit-producing areas, *e.g.* Chivers at Histon, near Cambridge.

(c) *The manufacture of proprietary foodstuffs.* Of these there is, of course, an enormous variety, but included among them are such things as breakfast cereals, custard and kindred powders, soups, extracts and patent invalid foods. Included within this group is the sweet- and chocolate-making industry. Branded and patented foodstuffs are usually made in, or near to, large centres of population and most towns have one or more firms engaged in the production of such commodities.

(d) *The bread and confectionery industries* may be placed in a separate category. These cater for local demand and are more especially concerned with the preparation of foodstuffs which must be eaten fresh. In contrast to the soft bakery goods (bread, cakes, pies) are the hard bakery goods such as biscuits, which will keep for long periods without deterioration; such commodities are much less dependent upon immediate markets and some of them in fact may enter into the foreign export trade.

4. Drink. A rather specialised aspect of the food industry is the preparation of drinks, intoxicating and soft drinks. The production of wine, the distilling of spirits, the brewing of beer and the making of cider fall into the category of intoxicants; the manufacture of fruit squashes, mineral waters, Coca-Cola, soda water, ginger ale and the like fall into the category of soft drinks.

The making of intoxicating drinks is sometimes related to specific geographical factors: cases are provided by the whisky industry which is linked with peaty waters and the beer brewing industry of Burton-on-Trent which was greatly assisted by the peculiar character of the water supply derived from the Keuper rocks. The wine industry has already been referred to (XI, 31) but here we may note that the port wine industry seems to be intimately linked with the grapevines which grow in the soils derived from the schist rocks in the Douro valley.

THE TEXTILE INDUSTRIES

5. Chief textile industries. The chief textile industries are the cotton, wool, linen, silk, jute (XIII, 2–8), rayon and synthetic fibre industries. Wool and flax appear to have been the earliest fibres used by man, and the Ancient Egyptians made woollen and linen cloth. Cotton cloth was also produced early on in India. Cotton, however, did not become dominant until the nineteenth century. In terms of the quantity of cloth produced, cotton is still the most important textile. The present century, however, has seen the very rapid growth of artificial, man-made or synthetic fibres in textile production.

Changes in textile production have been related to two main factors:

(a) *The development of colonies* (in which plantations were set up) and to the growth of international trade, which made raw cotton supplies available to the manufacturing countries of Europe in the eighteenth and nineteenth centuries.

(b) *The development of science and technology* which made possible the production of artificial fibres such as rayon, nylon, Terylene.

6. Influencing factors. The successful carrying-on of textile manufacture requires, like most other industries, certain conditions; there must be:

(a) readily available supplies of raw material;

(b) ample supplies of soft, good-quality water for processing;

(c) power supplies to work the machinery;

(d) a plentiful supply of efficient, skilled labour;

(e) good transport facilities for the assembly of the raw materials and for the disposal and export of the finished goods; and

(f) easily accessible markets.

7. The woollen and worsted industry. The woollen and worsted industry of the West Riding of Yorkshire well illustrates the importance of these factors. Sheep reared on the Pennine hills provided supplies of raw wool in the first place. The streams running over the millstone grit provided soft, clear water for the washing of the raw wool and the finished cloth and, at the same time, through their swiftness of flow powered waterwheels which drove the machinery. Later, local coal from the Yorkshire coalfield was used to generate steam power. And, finally, the rivers and, later, the building of canals provided transport. These conditions encouraged the growth of the wool industry, at first as a small-scale domestic activity and subsequently as a factory industry.

8. The West Riding industry. Located chiefly in the Aire, Calder and Colne valleys, the industry has developed a certain specialisation:

(a) *the woollen industry*, mainly at Bradford and Halifax, producing such things as blankets and carpets;

(b) *the worsted industry*, mainly at Huddersfield and Bradford, producing high-quality suitings; and

(c) *the shoddy industry*, based on rags, clippings and wool waste, at Batley and Dewsbury.

Bradford is the great marketing centre and has a Wool Exchange. Leeds, the largest city of the wool district, plays little part in the actual manufacture of wool, but is a great centre of ready-made clothes and tailoring and also makes textile machinery. Over 75% of all the woollen and worsted operatives in the United Kingdom are found in the West Riding. Even so the industry is in a state of acute recession.

9. The cotton industry. There was a domestic woollen industry in Lancashire as well as in Yorkshire, but with the growth of trade between Western Europe and the Americas cotton was introduced and displaced wool. With the late eighteenth century invention of the spinning "Jenny," the way was opened up for mass production and in the nineteenth century the cotton industry boomed. The factors operating in the case of the wool industry applied here but three points may be emphasised:

(a) *Liverpool* was a convenient importing port since it was within easy reach of the cotton manufacturing district and in the early days most of the cotton came from the United States.

(b) *The building of the Manchester Ship Canal*, opened in 1894, allowed raw cotton to be shipped right into the heart of the cotton region.

(c) *The development of the Merseyside chemical industry*, providing dyes and bleaches, greatly assisted the textile industry.

During the nineteenth century, cotton manufacturing became the chief textile industry of Britain and cotton goods became the country's leading export. A pronounced degree of specialisation developed:

(a) *The spinning towns* (Bolton, Bury, Rochdale, Oldham, Stockport) are grouped in a semicircle around Manchester.

(b) *The weaving towns* lie mostly to the north of the Rossendale Fells in the Ribble Valley (in Preston, Blackburn, Burnley, Darwen, Nelson, Colne and Accrington).

(c) *The bleaching, dyeing and printing processes* are undertaken mainly to the south of the Rossendale Forest, outside the main towns because:

(i) here are large supplies of soft water needed in the finishing processes; and

(ii) the finishing centres are within easy reach of Manchester, the great marketing centre.

The Lancashire cotton industry, however, has fallen on hard times and, largely owing to foreign competition, the industry has greatly contracted during the past half century. Both in its consumption of raw cotton and in its output of cotton cloth Lancashire has been reduced to less than one-quarter of its 1913 figure.

10. Artificial fibres. The development of, and change-over to, artificial fibres—whether cellulose fibres such as rayon or truly synthetic fibres such as nylon—has been a powerful factor affecting the traditional textile industries. By changing to other textiles the former advantages of location may be retained but the manufacture of rayon, nylon, and other synthetics is not confined to the older textile areas. The United States, West Germany, the United Kingdom and Japan are the chief producers of artificial fibre textiles.

11. The world's chief textile areas. Many of the older-established woollen industries elsewhere (*e.g.* in north-eastern France and New England, USA) changed over, at least in part, to cotton as did Lancashire. The main textile producers are found in the USA, Europe, Japan and some of the developing countries.

(*a*) *The United States.* Although some of the New England textile towns, such as Providence, Lowell, Lawrence and Holyoke are still interested in woollens, cotton manufacturing is more widespread in the area. With the growth later on of cotton manufacturing in the south of the United States in the cotton-growing belt (*see* Fig. 13 *above*), the character of the New England industry changed. In the south the cotton was immediately to hand and labour costs were cheaper; this made it possible to produce cheaper manufactured cotton goods. As a result, New England was unable to compete in the production of cheap cottons and had to specialise in top-quality goods which the southern region was unable to produce.

(*b*) *Europe.* The European textile industry is very varied, of large dimensions, and widely spread. It includes the spinning and weaving of cotton, wool, flax, hemp, silk and man-made fibres. Although widely dispersed, there are three areas of particular importance:

(i) *The Flanders region* which extends from north-eastern France (Lille, Roubaix, Tourcoing) across Belgium (Ghent, Bruges), where cotton, wool and flax are the chief fibres used.

(ii) *The Westphalian region* of West Germany which manufactures cotton, wool, linen and artificial fibres; the chief centres are Aachen, Krefeld, München-Gladbach, Wuppertal, Herford and Minden.

(iii) *Northern Italy* which deals with silk and hemp as well as the other fibres; the chief centres are Milan, Turin, Biella, Como, Bergamo, Brescia, Alessandria, Cremona and Padua.

(*c*) *Japan.* Japan, which early developed an important textile industry, especially in cotton goods, came to be Europe's chief competitor in the world market. All her cotton is imported. Recently she has begun to develop the wool textile industry and is Australia's best customer for her raw wool. Japan's traditional textile industry is silk; she ranks as the world's second greatest producer of raw silk. Japan is one of the major producers of man-made fibres and her artificial fibre textile industry is flourishing. The chief textile centres are Tokyo, Yokohama, Osaka, Kobe, Nagoya, Kanazawa and Niigata.

(d) *Other areas.* The relative ease with which textiles, especially cotton, can be manufactured has enabled many of the underdeveloped countries, *e.g.* China, India, Egypt, Brazil and Mexico, to set up substantial textile industries.

OTHER INDUSTRIES

12. Leather. The leather industry, the curing and tanning of hides, has tended to develop in or near to areas of animal rearing. In many countries, *e.g.* India, Morocco, Italy, there is a traditional leather-working industry. In England, the boot and shoe industry of the Midlands, based on Northampton, Kettering and Rushden, is derived from the cattle-rearing industry of that area. In the United States one-third of the workers in the leather-goods industries are concentrated in the Boston, Lynn and Brockton area of Massachusetts. Leather tanning began here soon after colonisation and was based upon local hides and tan bark. Newer and growing centres of the industry are Chicago and St Louis which are near the great cattle ranching areas of the west.

13. Printing and publishing. The printing industry is widely spread in the developed countries and every town will have one or two small printing firms. Every medium-sized town is likely to produce a local newspaper. The bigger towns are usually centres of publishing, especially the capital cities and often the old university towns. Some cities have earned international reputations as printing and publishing centres, *e.g.* Leipzig, in East Germany, which for long had a famous book fair.

14. Household goods. Many industries, *e.g.* pottery, furniture, fall into this category of industries producing household goods. In earlier times pottery was often produced locally but high quality ware has become focused in a few great centres, *e.g.* Worcester, Sèvres, Meissen, Copenhagen. The pottery towns of Staffordshire, *the* great centre of the industry in the United Kingdom, produces large quantities of cheap pottery, including toilet equipment. The furniture industry is widely spread. As in the case of pottery, high quality, often hand-worked furniture is produced in small workshops, often scattered in rural areas, while mass-produced furniture is produced in most large centres of population.

15. Building construction. This is a universal industry and little need be said about it except, perhaps, that sometimes it uses local materials and develops local building styles. But, at least in England, brick buildings are largely swamping the landscape—largely because of the cheapness of bricks.

PROGRESS TEST 19

1. Define and classify light industries. (1, 2)

2. Give an outline of the food processing industry. (3, 4)

3. What factors may influence the location of textile industries? Relate these to the growth of the cotton industry of Lancashire. (6, 9)

4. Give a brief account of the wool textile industry of the West Riding, noting the factors which assisted the development of the industry and its specialised branches. (7, 8)

5. Analyse the specialisation in the cotton industry of Lancashire. (9)

6. Locate the chief textile areas in Western Europe. Choose any *two* areas and give a brief account of the textile industries and towns engaged in these industries. (11)

7. Write a general account of the textile industry of the United States. (10, 11)

8. Show, by reference to specific examples, how the leather industries are closely associated with supplies of raw materials needed for leather working. (12)

9. Which textile industries are associated with the following towns; Bradford; Blackburn; Lowell; Ghent; Osaka; Oldham; Lille; Krefeld. (8, 9, 11)

10. What are the chief artificial or synthetic fibres? Which countries are the chief producers of artificial fibre textiles? (5, 10).

CHAPTER XX

THE MAJOR MANUFACTURING REGIONS

MANUFACTURING REGIONS

1. Introduction. In Chapter XVI we listed the main areas of manufacturing industry in the world and in Chapters XVIII and XIX we surveyed briefly the important heavy and light industries. Now we turn to the principal manufacturing areas; the industries within these areas are many and often complex and all we can do here is to give in summary form the main points of note: the *location* of these areas, their *industries*, and the *chief towns* engaged in the industries.

Each of the major areas has its own individual characteristics and industrial structure. Though there may be similarities between one area and another each has its own peculiar resources, industries, specialisations and problems.

EUROPE

2. Western and central Europe. The major zone of industrial activity in Europe—the so-called axial belt of industry—runs from Britain, through north-eastern France and the Low Countries, across West and East Germany, to southern Poland. Here is concentrated most of the industry, which is closely linked with the coalfields. Outside this axial belt there are subsidiary centres in central Sweden, in Switzerland, in northern Italy, in south-eastern France, and in the Barcelona district of Spain.

Since Europe is broken up into many national units, there is much duplication of industry, although it should be noted that the Common Market is an important attempt to create economic unity and has succeeded, in no small measure, in integrating the individual economies of its nine member states.

3. The chief industrial regions. The six major regions are:

    (*a*) The United Kingdom.

    (*b*) The Franco-Belgian coalfield.

(c) The Lorraine–Luxembourg–Saar area.
(d) The Ruhr–Westphalian area.
(e) The Saxony–Silesian area.
(f) Northern Italy.

These are further treated in paragraphs 4–9 below.

4. The United Kingdom. Industry is fairly widely spread in the United Kingdom but tends to be concentrated on, or near to the coalfields, with the exceptions of the London area and the Belfast area in Northern Ireland. The Lanarkshire, Northumberland and Durham, and South Wales coalfield areas are the chief centres of heavy industry, e.g. iron and steel, engineering, shipbuilding. Chemicals are concentrated in the Tees-side and Merseyside areas. The cotton industry, much less important than formerly, is concentrated in south Lancashire, the woollen and worsted industry in the West Riding of Yorkshire, and linen in Northern Ireland.

The light industries have witnessed an enormous expansion in south-east England, stimulated by the large domestic market of the London area but helped by the electric grid and the development of motor transport. Light industries have also been introduced into most of the traditionally heavy industry areas, owing to the decline in some of the heavy industries and in coal-mining, e.g. the Trading Estates of South Wales. The former export staples of coal and cotton have been replaced by motor vehicles, engineering products, chemicals and electronic equipment.

5. The Franco–Belgian coalfield. The coalfield is the seat of important iron and steel and engineering industries at Dunkerque, Anzin and Valenciennes in France and Liège and Charleroi in Belgium. Motor car production is absent. The heavy chemical industry is highly developed in the Sambre-Meuse coalfield and glass is particularly important, Belgium producing nearly a quarter of the world output.

Newer industries, expanding rapidly, are being established in Kempenland and in Flanders, e.g. at Lille and Courtrai. Flanders, of course, is the traditional seat of the textile industry. Cotton is the pre-eminent textile but linens and woollens are also produced. The industries of the Franco-Belgian coalfield are shown in Fig. 24.

6. The Lorraine-Luxembourg-Saar area. Industrial development here is mainly based upon the minette iron ores and other mineral deposits. A valuable coalfield exists in the Saar basin but coking coal is brought from the Ruhr. The chief iron and steel centres are Metz, Briey, Nancy, Thionville and Longwy. There are several centres in southern Luxembourg, the largest of which is Esch-sur-Alzette. Natural deposits of salt in Lorraine are the basis of an important chemical industry but coal and oil and potash deposits in Alsace, together with slag, gases and other by-products from the iron and steel industry have assisted the growth of the chemical industry. The chemical industry also supplies bleaches, dyes and agents for the cotton industry on the western side of the Vosges located in St Dié, Epinal, Remiremont.

7. The Ruhr-Westphalian area. This, the largest and most important industrial area in Europe, owes its significance to two geographical factors in the main:

(a) the highly productive *Ruhr Coalfield* which possesses good coking coal; and

(b) the *Rhine waterway* which greatly facilitates imports of raw materials and the export of manufactured goods.

There are three principal groups of industries in the *Ruhr area* (*see* Fig. 25):

(a) *Iron and steel and heavy engineering.* The Ruhr produces most of West Germany's steel output (some 53 million tons) and accounts for about half the European Coal and Steel Community's output. Although some local ore still comes from the Sieg valley, south of the Ruhr Coalfield, most is imported either from Lorraine or Sweden. The steel centres are Duisburg-Ruhrort, Oberhausen and Dortmund; heavy engineering is focused in Essen, Dortmund, Duisburg and Düsseldorf. Solingen and Remscheid, in the Wupper valley, specialise in machine tools and cutlery.

(b) *Chemicals.* The industry has expanded rapidly in this area since the Second World War. The chief centres are Duisburg and Leverkusen, both on the Rhine, and the new centre of Marl-Hüls in the north of the Ruhr which uses natural gas piped from the Ems gas-field. Cologne also produces chemicals as well as "eau de Cologne" and has three large oil-refineries.

(c) *Textiles.* Cottons are manufactured at Barmen and Elberfeld (the conurbation is now styled Wuppertal); woollens are made at Aachen and at Wuppertal; linen, an old industry,

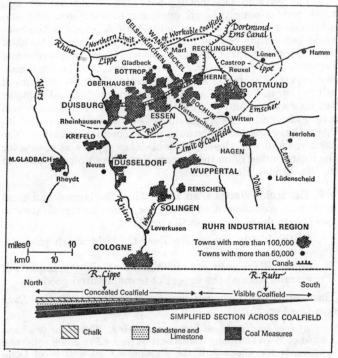

FIG. 25.—*The Ruhr industrial region*

Most of the coal mining is now carried on in the northern part of the region, near the Lippe valley. Essen is the great metropolis of the Ruhr and is now a great centre of heavy engineering. Dortmund has blast furnaces, steelworks and engineering shops. Duisburg is a great river port with iron and steel works. In the Wupper valley, Solingen has special steels and makes tools and cutlery, while Wuppertal is a great cotton and rayon manufacturing centre.

further north at Münster, Bielefeld and Lippstadt; and silk, velvet and man-made fibre textiles at Krefeld, München-Gladbach and Rheydt. Cologne and Düsseldorf produce man-made fibres.

8. The Saxony–Silesian area. An important, if rather discontinuous industrial area, occurs in the adjacent parts of

East Germany, Poland and Czechoslovakia. Here is the important Silesian coalfield and the smaller fields of Saxony and Bohemia. Considerable industrial growth has taken place in this region since the end of the Second World War when these countries became Communist dominated. Many of the pre-war industries of the area suffered badly from the War and its repercussions, but industrial production now far surpasses the pre-war level. Heavy engineering, chemicals and textiles are the most significant branches of industry. The chief industrial towns are Zwickau, Karl Marx Stadt (Chemnitz), Dresden and Meissen in East Germany, Wroclaw (Breslau), Gliwice, Zabrze, Katowice and Bytom in Poland, and Prague and Plzeň in Czechoslovakia.

9. Northern Italy. Though lacking in coal and possessing little iron ore, Northern Italy has water-power and natural gas and a wide range of vegetable crops. A flair for design has also helped the Italians in industrial success. There are iron and steel plants at Aosta, and at Cornegliano, near Genoa. Shipbuilding is carried on at Genoa and Spezia. Locomotives, rolling-stock, aircraft and hydro-electric turbines are made at Turin, Savigliano, Milan and Brescia. Many Italian products have found their way into the world market, and such names as Fiat and Ferrari (motor cars), Olivetti (typewriters) and Necchi (sewing-machines) are already world renowned. Turin is *the* great centre of motor car production.

A great chemical industry has grown up using Italian sulphur, borax, limestone, methane, and producing a wide range of products, *e.g.* acids, synthetic rubber, fertilisers, artificial fibres. The chief centres of the chemical and cement industries are Milan, Ferrara, Venice, Ravenna.

The textile industry is important and there is a wide range of textiles produced including cotton (the most important) at Milan and its satellite towns, Chieri, Bergamo, Brescia and Udine, wool at Biella, Alessandria and Vicenza, silk at Como and Milan, hemp at Bologna, Modena and Ferrara, jute at Turin and Padua. Synthetic fibre manufacture, especially rayon, is very important and is carried on in Turin, Milan, Pavia, Cremona and Padua.

AMERICA

10. The American manufacturing belt. This manufacturing region in the central eastern part of North America extends from the western shores of Lake Michigan to the Atlantic seaboard and from the River Ohio to the Lake Peninsula of Canada; because of its shape, it is sometimes referred to as the "American manufacturing quadrilateral" (*see* Fig. 26). It is an industrial region of exceptional productivity and a very wide range of goods is produced including heavy and light industries. The area, however, exhibits considerable regional specialisation: in the west there is an emphasis upon diversified metal industries and transport equipment, in the centre heavy industries, especially steel and engineering, in the north-east textiles, leather goods, and light engineering, and in the south-east, steel, ships and chemicals.

The eight chief sub-regions of this large and complex industrial area are described below, with the addition of a ninth separate region, California. The letters in brackets refer to the regions on the map in Fig. 26:

11. New England (A). Traditionally the area is important for its textile, leather and light engineering industries. It lacks supplies of coal, oil and iron ore (though coal can be brought in from the Appalachian fields), but is favoured with water-power and raw materials from the forests. Its coastal location also enables raw materials, such as cotton and hides, to be imported relatively easily. It was the first region in the Americas to develop manufacturing industry and this historical factor has been significant. New England offers a good example of *geographical momentum*.

Cotton textiles are chiefly centred in Lowell, Lawrence, Fall River, Manchester and New Bedford; Lawrence and Providence are the leading wool towns making woollens, worsteds and tweeds. Metal-fabricating works are a feature of the Lower Connecticut Valley. The towns of New Haven, Hartford, Springfield and Bridgeport manufacture office machines, rifles, locks, watches—articles needing little raw material but considerable skill in their production. Shoes and leather goods are important at Boston, Lynn, Brockton and Haverhill. Paper is made at Holyoke.

12. The Hudson–Mohawk Valley (B). The importance of this communications thoroughfare, together with the location of New York at its southern end, was bound to lead to industrial development. Manufactures, however, tend to be of the light type. New

York has manifold industries but the clothing industry is of special importance. Albany is a great centre of shirt and underwear manufacture. Syracuse, Troy, Schenectady, Amsterdam, Utica, have clothing, electrical, photographic, scientific instrument, paper and chemical manufactures.

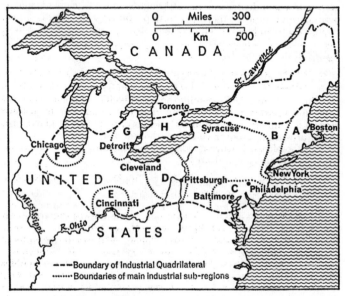

FIG. 26.—*Industrial regions of the United States*

This area with its concentration of industry is known as the "industrial quadrilateral." The letters on the map refer to the regions described in the text.

13. The Mid-Atlantic coast (C). The large port cities of Baltimore and Philadelphia (on the Delaware) are important centres of industry. Iron and steel, small metal goods, ships, aircraft, chemicals, electrical goods, as well as a wide range of consumer goods, are manufactured in this region. Linked to the area and conveniently taken with it is the inland area of south-eastern Pennsylvania which has important iron and steel and leather industries. Other important towns besides the ports are Wilmington (explosives), Binghamton (leather goods), Trenton (pottery) and Chester (ships).

14. The Pittsburgh–Cleveland area (D). This region is dominated by its heavy industries and especially iron and steel. Coal, oil, limestone are here in abundance and, formerly, there was iron ore. The iron ore now comes mostly from the Superior region and Labrador (*see* Fig. 16 *above*). There is good water and rail transport. The making of iron and steel and its use in heavy engineering dominate the industrial scene, although chemicals, cement, glass-making and oil-refining are all important. Pittsburgh is *the* great steel town but Wheeling, Youngstown, and Johnstown share the industry. The lake-shore steel towns include Cleveland, Toledo, Lorain and Erie.

15. The Ohio–Indiana region (E). This is an area of diversified metal industries. Here are the towns of Indianopolis, Columbus, Dayton, Cincinnati, Evansville and Louisville. Fuel is near at hand and there is a variety of raw materials, including iron, lead and zinc, timber, farm products and clay, which have given rise to metal-working, motor vehicle parts and other light engineering goods, chemicals, leather goods and the processing of foodstuffs which is especially significant.

16. The Lake Michigan area (F). This area mainly focuses upon the great city of Chicago and nearby Gary. Milwaukee and Rockford are not far away. Chicago is a lake port of importance and a great railway focus and these two communications factors have played a great role in its growth. Heavy industries (iron and steel, shipbuilding, locomotives, chemicals) and secondary industries (clothing, furniture, paper, paint and food processing) characterise the region. The area has witnessed spectacular growth and its industrial development seems likely to continue to grow apace.

17. South-eastern Michigan (G). Specialised manufacturing is the keynote of this region. Detroit and other nearby cities, such as Flint and Pontiac, are primarily concerned with the manufacture of motor vehicles. Detroit is the headquarters of the Ford and General Motors Corporations, and manufactures half of all the motor-vehicles made in the United States. Industries ancillary to the automobile industry, such as glass, rubber and paint manufacture, have grown up. There are chemical industries at Port Huron. Food processing (flour-milling, meat-packing, dairy products) is important.

18. Lake peninsula of Ontario (H). Geographically the most favoured part of Canada, the region has become important both agriculturally and industrially. Its advantages for industrial development include a lakeside location and access to the sea, hydro-electric power supplies, nearness to the rich forest and mineral resources of the southern parts of the Shield, a large agricultural output (which has favoured the food processing industries), and a populous market with a high purchasing power. The chief manufacturing towns are Toronto, Hamilton, Brantford, Kitchener, London and Windsor. There are both heavy and light industries in the region. Among the most noteworthy are motor vehicles (Windsor), steel-making (Hamilton), chemicals (Sarnia), agricultural machinery (Brantford), food-processing (London).

19. California. This region lies away from the manufacturing quadrilateral of the east but is, of course, part of the United States. Industrial development here has been phenomenal: most of the growth has taken place since 1940. It is one of the fastest growing industrial areas in the world. Some of the industries are derived directly from primary occupations, e.g. the canning of fish, and fruit and vegetables, saw-milling, oil-refining; some are based upon imported commodities, e.g. rubber, sugar, vegetable oils; some developed during the Second World War for wartime needs, e.g. the shipbuilding (San Diego), and aircraft (Los Angeles) industries; while some have developed to serve the expanding Californian market, e.g. the motor vehicle (Oakland and Los Angeles), clothing and electronics industries.

THE USSR

20. The Soviet Union. After the United States the Soviet Union is the greatest industrial country in the world. Although Russia had a measure of industrial development before the First World War, the astonishing growth of industry has occurred since about 1930 and especially since the Second World War. Emphasis has always been upon heavy industry and although more consumer goods are now being manufactured they are, in both quantity and variety, small and frequently of poor quality. The most important sectors of industry are iron and steel production, engineering, chemicals and textiles. Industry in the Soviet Union is state-owned and state-run. Industry has been rationalised in relation to both raw materials and internal markets. This has led to a wider dispersion of industry and to the building of smaller plants; (in the early days of industrial development, and this applied especially to the iron and steel industry, the Soviet planners set up a few large-scale plants, thereby achieving low-cost production). It should be noted that the Soviet Union is rich in coal and oil supplies and has many valuable minerals, including iron ore, and great forest wealth.

The chief industrial regions are:

(a) The *Leningrad* region: textiles, shipbuilding, printing, wood-pulp.

(b) The *Moscow* region: textiles, machinery, machine tools, printing, chemicals.

(c) The *Donbas*, (*Ukraine*) based upon the Donetz coalfield (Fig. 27): steel, vehicles, farm machinery, electrical machinery, hardware, chemicals, food processing.

(d) The *Caucasus*: oil-refining, chemicals, steel, ferro-alloys, textiles.

(e) The *Urals* region: iron and steel, ferro-alloys, chemicals, tractors, railway rolling-stock, engineering.

(f) The *Tashkent* area: textiles, engineering, food processing.

(g) The *Karaganda coalfield* area: machinery, copper-smelting, iron and steel, food processing.

(h) The *Kuzbas*, based on the Kuznetsk coalfield: iron and steel, heavy engineering, chemicals, cement.

(i) The *Irkutsk* region: with aluminium-smelting and timber industries.

(j) The *Khabarovsk* region in the Far East: with oil-refining, engineering, chemical and timber processing.

The following *features of Soviet industry* should be emphasised and well noted:

(a) The paramount *importance of the Moscow and Donbas* areas (the industries of the Donbas are shown in Fig. 27);

(b) The great *spread of industrial development to the Asiatic part* of the USSR;

(c) *The dispersed and fairly well-balanced distribution of industry*;

(d) The *absence* (in the more *northerly parts* of the USSR), as yet, of any important *industrial developments*;

(e) The great *emphasis upon heavy industry* and the slow growth of the consumer goods industries.

ASIA AND THE SOUTHERN HEMISPHERE

21. Japan. The growth of industry in Japan has been nothing short of spectacular and is a product very largely of the present century. She is poorly endowed with coal and oil,

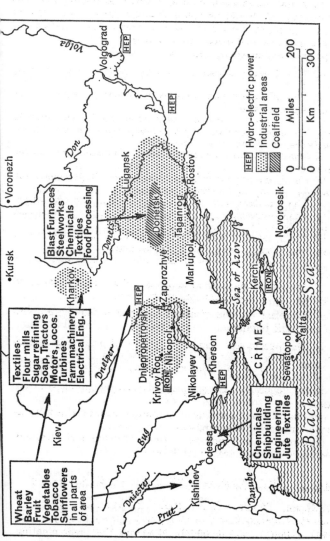

FIG. 27.—*The Ukraine (Donbas) industrial region*

This is the Soviet Union's greatest industrial region. It is the most important iron and steel area; the industry is based on the Donbas or Donetsk Basin Coalfield and the ironfields of Krivoy Rog and Kerch (in the Crimea).

iron ore, wool and raw cotton and yet, in spite of this poor industrial base, she has prospered. This is largely because:

(a) She had plentiful resources of *hydro-electric power*.
(b) She was able to *import her coal needs* and many of her raw materials from nearby countries.
(c) She had a *large and cheap labour force* (this no longer applies).
(d) She *gained markets* in the oriental (and western) world.

22. Japanese heavy industry. Japan's industrial development has moved from the production of cheap light goods, such as cottons and toys, to heavy manufactures. This is a startling, and largely unforeseen, development. A generation or so ago, no one would have prophesied that today Japan would be the world's largest shipbuilder producing over half of the world's tonnage or that her steel output would have reached 95 million tons, treble that of the United Kingdom.

(a) The success of the shipbuilding industry has been due largely to:

(i) new techniques of mass production;
(ii) quick delivery dates;
(iii) relatively cheap labour costs; and also
(iv) the big demand during recent years for oil tankers.

Her iron and steel industry has expanded rapidly, partly because of the demands of the shipbuilding industry for steel but also because of the growth of her heavy engineering industry generally. The problem of securing supplies of iron ore has been solved to some extent by the importation of large quantities of scrap iron: Japan is, in fact, the world's biggest importer of scrap.

(b) *Japan's chief industrial region* is around the Inland Sea but four main areas may be recognised:

(i) The *Kwanto Plain, the* most important industrial area, focusing upon Tokyo, Yokohama and Kawasaki. Here is a great variety of light industry but there is also shipbuilding and ship repairing and a new iron and steel plant at Chiba.
(ii) The *Kobe–Osaka region* is next in importance. Textiles, metal industries, and shipbuilding are the predominating

activities. Kyoto is the home of light craft industries, *e.g.* silk, porcelain, lacquer goods.

(iii) The *northern Kyushu region* bordering the Strait of Shimoneseki has become the most important specialised heavy industrial area of Japan. Yawata is the seat of the largest iron and steel plant in the country and Nagasaki is the second largest shipbuilding centre.

(iv) The *Nagoya industrial region* is predominantly engaged in textile (cotton, wool and silk) manufacturing but there are other industries mainly of the lighter type, *e.g.* pottery, paper, vegetable oil refining.

23. China. Since 1949, the year in which the Communists secured control of China, industrial development has been rapid. In the words of the First Five-year Plan (1953–8) the long-range goal was "to transform China from an agricultural into an industrial nation" (*see* IX). The transformation has been pursued with vigour and ruthlessness but not without difficulties and setbacks.

(*a*) The general aims have been to:

(i) accelerate industrial growth generally;
(ii) press forward the development of heavy industry;
(iii) create a greater dispersion of industry throughout the country.
(iv) rationalise industrial production.

(*b*) The chief industrial areas are:

(i) *Central and southern Manchuria*, the centre of coal-mining and iron and steel production, *e.g.* at Anshan, Fushun, Shenyang.

(ii) The *Tientsin–Peking area* and the Shansi coalfield: here are several iron and steel works, engineering shops and chemical factories.

(iii) The *Shanghai area*, focusing on the great port of Shanghai itself: textiles are most important, *e.g.* at Wusih, Soochow and Shanghai, but there are also engineering, shipbuilding and chemical industries.

(iv) The *mid-Yangtze basin* focusing on the Wuhan conurbation: iron and steel and textiles are dominant here.

(v) The *Szechwan basin* has varied resources, including coal, iron ore, salt and Chungking is a major manufacturing centre with textiles, chemicals and engineering industries.

(vi) *Canton* has shipbuilding, engineering, textile, glassware, soap and food products industries.

24. Australia. Industry in Australia is very largely confined to the south-east in the coastal areas of New South Wales and Victoria. Most of the coal and water-power resources are concentrated in the south-east. The Hunter Valley coalfield feeds the iron and steel industry of Newcastle and the Illawarra field the metal industries of Port Kembla. Sydney, Wollongong and Lithgow share the industries of this New South Wales region, which include oil refining, chemicals, engineering and motor vehicles, bricks, cement and pottery. The industries of Victoria, mainly located in Melbourne and Geelong, chiefly depend upon electricity generated from the brown coal deposits of the Latrobe valley; the manufactures include textiles, clothing, leather goods, motor vehicles and agricultural machinery. A new centre of industry is growing at Whyalla, in South Australia, where there are blast furnaces and steel works and the largest shipbuilding yard in the continent.

25. South Africa. Quite spectacular industrial development has occurred in the Republic of South Africa during the past generation. The southern Transvaal is the chief industrial area, although the Bloemfontein area of the Orange Free State and the Durban area of Natal are significant subsidiary centres. The production of iron and steel (3·2 million tons of steel in 1966) is established in four localities: at Pretoria, on the Rand at Johannesburg and Benoni, at Vereeniging and at Newcastle. Expansion of the industry is likely to be handicapped by the inadequate reserves of coking coal and water supplies. Mining machinery, railway equipment, tin plate for use in the canning industries and motor vehicles are also made. The port of Durban has oil refineries, chemical and soap factories, textile mills and many food-processing factories. Although, like Australia, still only a minor industrial country, South Africa has considerable potential and its manufacturing activities are likely to grow appreciably in the near future.

26. South America. Industrial development in South America is growing and there have been notable advances since the time of the Second World War. The chief handicap, certainly from the viewpoint of heavy industry, is the continent's poverty of coal supplies. There is much dependence upon oil and electricity. There are really only four areas where there is an industrial activity of any note:

(*a*) The hinterland of *Rio de Janeiro*, in Brazil.
(*b*) Around the *Plate estuary*, especially in Buenos Aires and Montevideo.
(*c*) In central *Chile*, around Concepcion.
(*d*) In *Colombia*, notably in the towns of Medellin and Manizales.

The Brazilian "heartland" region is the most important industrial area in South America. Rio de Janeiro, São Paulo and Belo Horizonte are the chief manufacturing centres. Manufactures include textiles, metal products, chemicals, footwear, soap and many other light industrial products. At Volta Redonda is Brazil's great iron and steel plant using local iron ore but relying upon imported coking coal.

27. India. From the point of view of total manufactured output, India has long been a significant industrial country, usually ranking about sixth in the world. Apart from her cotton textile industry, most of the industries were concentrated in India's ports. Since the Second World War India's industrial expansion has been considerable and many new industries and many new centres have been established. However, there are two principal industrial areas:

(*a*) *Calcutta and the Damodar Valley area:* here is to be found coal, iron ore and other minerals, and hydro-electric power is available; important industries are iron and steel, engineering and jute manufacture.

(*b*) *Bombay and the surrounding region:* the cotton textile industry, oil-refining, engineering, leather, soap and glass manufactures, heavy machine-tool making, ship repairs and railway workshops are all present. Hydro-electric power is supplied from stations in the Western Ghats.

PROGRESS TEST 20

1. What and where is the axial belt of industry in Europe? (2)
2. Give in outline a reasoned geographical account of the industries of the Ruhr–Westphalian region in West Germany. (7)
3. Name and locate the chief industries of Northern Italy. (9)
4. What is the "American manufacturing quadrilateral"? Why is this area so important as a manufacturing region? (10)
5. Name the chief sub-regions of the American manufacturing belt. Select any *one* region and give a brief outline of its industries. (11–18)

6. "Industrial development in California has been phenomenal." Explain this development and give an account of California's industries. (19)

7. What principal features mark Soviet industry? How does Soviet industry differ from that, say, in the United States? (20)

8. Account for Japan's industrial development. (21–22)

9. Locate Japan's chief industrial regions and indicate the nature of the manufactures carried on in each region. (22)

10. Outline the industrial geography of China. (23)

11. Locate the chief industrial areas of *either* Australia *or* South America and describe the nature of the manufactures carried on in the continent of your choice. (24, 26)

12. What important industries are associated with the following towns: Cologne; Düsseldorf; Turin; Pittsburgh; Detroit; Kyoto; Whyalla; Wuhan? (7, 9, 14, 17, 22–24)

PART FIVE

TRADE AND TRANSPORT

CHAPTER XXI

TRADE AND EXCHANGE

THE BASES OF TRADE

1. The beginnings of trade. In the very earliest times people had to depend upon the things, whether they were foodstuffs or raw materials, that were available in their own locality. But very early on primitive man learned to exchange or barter articles with his neighbours. We know, for instance, that even Stone Age peoples bartered stone weapons while the backward and isolated Indian tribes of the Amazon Basin engage in simple exchange. Thus, even when man lives an almost self-sufficient existence at subsistence level some trade takes place. As society developed in the early centres of civilisation, such as Sumeria, Egypt and the Indus Valley, specialisation of labour evolved; potters, carpenters, smiths, gradually emerged, especially in the early village communities and first towns. Hence, besides growers of food there grew up makers of things; and food could be bartered for things and vice versa.

As these early peoples advanced in culture and as their standards of living increased their requirements increased in variety and quantity. To procure their more sophisticated needs, people were prepared to travel farther afield in order to get them. We know that the early Egyptians journeyed to the far off land of Punt for certain luxury commodities that were not to be had in Egypt. It may be noted that trade in early times was mainly of a luxury nature, although it was not entirely so, for there is clear evidence of trade in corn and timber.

Gradually, however, the character of trade has changed and nowadays the really important items of trade are foodstuffs, oil, ores, timber and the like rather than perfumes, gold dust and fine feathers. Moreover, the volume of trade has expanded enormously; between highly-developed countries trade is of a very varied, complex and large-scale character. The items which Britain, for instance, exports and imports each month forms a lengthy list, while the value of the exports and the imports runs to between £1500–2000 million per month (*see* I, **7, III, 1,** etc.).

2. The bases of trade. The main bases of trade are:

(*a*) a differentiation of products;
(*b*) a surplus of products;
(*c*) a demand for commodities;
(*d*) differences in culture;
(*e*) adequate transport facilities;
(*f*) suitable world conditions.

The differences in the natural resources of countries, resulting from differences in climate, soil, vegetation and geology, form the most important and the one enduring basis of trade between countries (*see* II, IV). This explains the large amount of trade between the tropical lands and the temperate lands of the northern hemisphere. A surplus of products is not always necessary for trade to take place, neither does a surplus always mean that trade will take place; but, by and large, a surplus will tend to promote exchange. There must be a demand for a commodity before it can enter into trade. Differences in the culture of a people cause differences in production. The skill, initiative, and inventive capacity of a people may enable a country to make more rapid technical progress than its neighbours and so forge ahead of them in the production of manufactured goods; then, it is likely that manufactures will be exchanged for foodstuffs and raw materials.

The exchange of primary products for manufactured goods forms the most important aspect of present-day trade.

The development of adequate transport facilities is, clearly, another necessary factor for trade. Another necessary condition for the carrying on of trade and commerce is the normal functioning of social life and stable political conditions; war, for example, is a great disorganiser of trade.

3. The effect of demand. A point to be emphasised is that there is no automatic development of trade. Simply because there are regions with deficiencies and regions that are capable of making good these deficiencies, this is no guarantee that trade exchange will naturally follow. In the first place *economic demand must be present* and, if this is sufficiently

strong, a country will then set about trying to satisfy this demand. It will take the initiative and seek supplies; it will go even further and help to organise those supplies. This can be illustrated by the development by Europeans of plantations in tropical regions: this was a deliberate attempt to ensure the sufficient supply of much needed or essential tropical commodities such as rubber, vegetable oils and sugar. Another example is provided by oil production in the Middle East. Before the trade in petroleum could be developed, countries such as Britain and the United States had to finance, explore and develop the oilfields.

4. Primary and secondary products. The commodities entering into world trade may be said to fall into two main categories:

> (a) *primary products, i.e.* foodstuffs and raw materials; and
> (b) *secondary products, i.e.* manufactured goods.

There is a great flow of primary products towards the highly developed, industrialised and well-populated countries. Foodstuffs, such as cereals, meat, fruit and beverages, are imported in large quantities, for home supplies are insufficient to meet needs. Raw materials, such as ores, textile fibres, vegetable oils, timber and petroleum, are imported to sustain the manufacturing industries since home supplies are either deficient or non-existent. Conversely, there is a movement of surplus manufactured goods to various parts of the world which do not make them in sufficient quantities to supply local requirements or which are incapable of manufacturing them.

A point worth emphasising is that trade does not occur only between countries with differing types of production; there is, for example, an important interchange of manufactured goods between the United States and Western Europe, both manufacturing areas. This is usually due to specialisation in certain types of manufactured goods, but sometimes even the same products are interchanged, *e.g.* motor cars, watches.

5. Primary producers. While there is an appreciable flow of trade between primary producers and secondary producers, as, for example, between Britain and Sri Lanka, and between one secondary producer and another, as, for example, between the United States and West Germany, there is seldom much trade between primary producers. Any interchange that does occur is usually in foodstuffs, *e.g.* the export of rice from Thailand to Malaya. Trade does not normally develop between primary producers.

This fact can be illustrated by reference to the countries of Latin America which are basically primary producers; for example, not much more than 10% of Argentina's exports go to Brazil and Chile, her near neighbours and best customers while Bolivia, notwithstanding the fact that it is a land-locked state, exports a mere 10% of its products to other Latin American countries. Another observation we might usefully make is that primary producing countries have frequently developed as *single-crop* or *single commodity* countries—think of Ghana (cacao), Cuba (sugar), Brazil (coffee), Bolivia (tin). While this dependence upon one item is breaking down and a greater diversity of economy is developing, it can still be said that many countries rely upon one main economic prop.

THE PATTERN OF TRADE

6. Types of trade. Generally speaking, the trade of any country falls into two parts: the *home trade*; and the *foreign trade*. The older textbooks often distinguished a third type of trade, the colonial trade, which was distinct from foreign trade because it was intimately bound to that of the home country and because it usually enjoyed preferential treatment. For example, the system of "imperial preference" still operates between the United Kingdom and the members of the British Commonwealth.

(a) *Home trade* is the internal trade of a country. It refers to the buying and selling of goods by the individuals of the community. The volume of the internal trade varies widely from country to country. Much depends upon the size of the country, the variety of its resources, the numbers of its population, the standard of living of the people and the degree to which the internal communications, transport facilities and marketing organisations are developed. In countries such as the United Kingdom and the United States there is much internal exchange; in countries such as Egypt, Burma and Peru there is little internal trade. The internal trade of a country should not be neglected or under-estimated; in the case of the United Kingdom, for example, the home trade accounts for some 75% of the total trade.

(b) *Foreign trade* is the external trade of the country. It connotes the exchange of commodities—foodstuffs, raw materials and manufactured goods—between one country and another. Again, the significance of the foreign trade varies greatly from country to country. The United Kingdom's trade, for many decades, has been of major proportions partly because it depends upon other countries for more than half of its foodstuffs and for the greater part of its raw materials, and partly because the country has lived upon the export of manufactured goods. The slogan "export or die" has a very real meaning for countries such as the United Kingdom and Japan. On the other hand, some countries which are large, possess great variety of resources, and live a largely self-sufficient existence, such as the Soviet Union, have not a well-developed foreign trade.

7. Aspects of the foreign trade. Foreign trade has two separate aspects: the *import trade*, which involves the bringing of goods from abroad into the home country, and the *export trade*, which involves the sending of goods to external countries, either neighbouring countries or overseas countries, for sale. A country such as West Germany, for example, carries on a large export trade with her immediate neighbours (especially her Common Market neighbours) but she also exports goods to distant countries such as the United States, Canada, Brazil, India.

Countries try to balance their imports against their exports. If they can export more in terms of value than they import, they are in a favourable position; but if they import more than they export they are likely to find themselves in financial difficulties.

8. Classes of trade. *Foodstuffs, industrial raw materials* and *manufactured goods* comprise the three main classes of commodities involved in exchange. Cereals, meat, dairy products, beverages and fruit are the most important foodstuffs entering into world trade. The United Kingdom, incidentally, accounts for a considerable proportion of these: she is the world's greatest importer of food products.

Among the wide variety of raw materials involved in trade, petroleum, mineral ores, textile fibres, timber, wood pulp and vegetable oils are the most important. It is interesting to note that petroleum is now the most important single commodity entering international trade. Coal, which fifty years ago was a major item, is now of little significance (*see* XIII, XIV, and XV).

Manufactured goods are tending to become increasingly important in international trade. This is largely the result of increasing specialisation, of the higher spending power of peoples, of the development of many backward countries, and of the effects of advertising and publicity. The greatest volume of manufactured goods continues to flow, as it has long done, between North America and Europe.

In terms of value, over one half of all international commerce is made up of manufactured and semi-manufactured goods, approximately a quarter of foodstuffs and beverages, and the remainder, roughly another quarter, of raw materials including fuels.

9. The direction and volume of international trade. For over a century now the general pattern of world trade has consisted of a flow of primary products, such as grain, vegetable oils, rubber, minerals, from the tropical regions and the "new" lands of the southern hemisphere to the industrialised countries of the northern temperate zone and, conversely, of a return flow of secondary products or manufactured goods, such as machinery, vehicles, textiles, chemicals. One has only to compare the import and export trade of two representative countries such as West Germany and Argentina to see the difference in the character of the trade. The percentages refer to the value of each item in the total value of the exports or the imports.

(*a*) *West Germany.*

(i) *Exports:* machinery (22·2%), steel (13·9%), vehicles (13·4%), chemicals (11·6%), electrical equipment (8·9%), textiles (5%), coal and coke (4·3%).

(ii) *Imports:* textile raw materials and clothing (11%), petroleum (7·7%), fruit and vegetables (7·1%), iron ore (6·5%), machinery (6·2%), chemicals (5·1%), cereals (4·3%), ores (3·7%), timber (3·3%), pulp and paper (3·2%).

(*b*) *Argentina.*

(i) *Exports:* cereals and linseed (28%), meat (19%), oil-seeds and vegetable oil (14%), wool (12%), hides and skins (7·5%).

(ii) *Imports:* machinery and vehicles (54%), iron and steel goods (11%), fuels (7%), chemical products (6%), textiles (3·5%), paper products (2·5%), rubber goods (2%).

The exception to the general north-south flow of trade is provided by the east-west traffic between Western Europe and North America. The historical, ethnic and cultural links between these two great regions have helped to forge intimate economic contacts and the greatest volume of trade flow in the world is actually between these two.

Finally, let us draw attention to one important point. We have stressed the importance of international trade but, to put it in its true perspective, let us emphasise that, in terms of its total value, it is only equal in magnitude to the gross national product or total national income of the United Kingdom, *i.e.* around £50,000 million.

10. The benefits of international trade. Trade between the countries of the world brings benefits of various kinds to all concerned.

(*a*) It allows people to enjoy products which they cannot produce themselves; *e.g.* Britain imports tea, bananas, pepper and other tropical produce.

(*b*) It enables some commodities, which otherwise would be available only seasonally, to be procurable the year round; apples, salad crops, for instance, in Britain.

(*c*) It makes possible a greater choice of commodities and provides a wider range of designs and styles; *e.g.* Paris fashions, Danish furniture, Italian typewriters in Britain.

(*d*) It often makes it possible for countries to obtain goods more cheaply than they could produce them themselves.

(*e*) It permits economic specialisation or, in other words, it enables countries to produce those commodities for which their particular resources best suit them.

(*f*) Trade is, as it always has been, one of the greatest agents in the dissemination of ideas and so helps to promote cultural advancement.

In sum, a thriving international trade promotes better standards of living the world over and promotes economic and cultural development.

BRITAIN'S PATTERN OF TRADE

11. Britain's place in world trade. For more than two hundred years Britain has been one of *the* leading commercial countries in the world. Indeed, from the eighteenth century until the eve of the First World War Britain was the leader in world trade. In the inter-war period Britain was compelled to yield pride of place as the world's number one exporter to the United States, although she continued to be the world's greatest importer. Today the United Kingdom ranks next after the United States as the world's greatest trading country; she accounts for approximately one-tenth, by value, of the world's total export and import trade. Although the United Kingdom continues to increase the volume of her exports, she has a declining share of the total world export trade.

12. Reasons for Britain's trade. The United Kingdom is a major trading country because:

(*a*) Her 56 million inhabitants rely for nearly one half of their foodstuffs upon overseas suppliers.

(*b*) As an important industrial country she is dependent to a very considerable extent upon a wide variety of imported raw materials.

(*c*) Her traditional role has been to import foodstuffs and raw materials and live by the export of her manufactures.

(*d*) She built up the world's greatest mercantile marine and today with 31·5 million metric tons ranks third in the world after Liberia and Japan.

(*e*) Her former great colonial empire which stimulated trading activity.

13. The scale and pattern of Britain's trade. The following tables show the imports (£15,854 millions) and exports (£12,455 millions), roughly itemised, for 1973. The figures refer to the value in £ million.

Imports	£ million
Food and live animals	2,714
Beverages and tobacco	383
Raw materials (*e.g.* ores, timber, textile fibres)	1,954
Basic manufactures (*e.g.* refined copper, textile yarns, paper)	3,383
Machinery and transport equipment	3,293
Mineral fuels	1,727
Chemicals	897

Exports	£ million
Machinery and transport equipment	4,777
Basic manufactures	3,258
Miscellaneous manufactures	1,149
Chemicals	1,272
Food and live animals	512
Beverages and tobacco	363
Mineral fuels	370

The chief imports are foodstuffs and raw materials for Britain's manufacturing industries. The main exports are manufactured goods—vehicles, machinery, electrical goods, chemical products and textiles. Some items are both imported and exported; often this is because the raw material is imported and the refined product exported, *e.g.* as in the case of petroleum.

Most of Britain's exports have been to her neighbours in Europe, the United States and the English-speaking members of the Commonwealth. It was hoped that by joining the Common Market our exports to the member countries would greatly increase. This benefit has not so far materialised and Britain is, in fact, importing substantially more from the E.E.C. than she is exporting to it. Our exports to other areas in the world, *e.g.* the Soviet Union and the Eastern European countries, the Far East, Africa and Latin America are only small. Perhaps Britain's greatest success has been with the countries of the Middle East where important new markets have been captured.

BALANCE OF TRADE AND
BALANCE OF PAYMENTS

14. The balance of trade. A nation, as with an individual, must live within its income, that is it must not spend more than it earns, or else it is heading for bankruptcy. Most countries, therefore, desire to balance the cost of their imports against what is earned by exports. If more is earned than is spent, a favourable balance of trade exists; if more is spent than earned there is an unfavourable balance. Britain, for a long time now, has been spending more on imports (£15,854 million in 1973) than she has been earning from her exports (£12,455 million in 1973). The difference between expenditure and income on visible trade—the manufactures, raw materials and foodstuffs exported or imported—was £3399 million in 1973. This, the *crude trade gap*, resulted in an adverse balance of trade. Since 1973 the situation has worsened as a result of the O.P.E.C. countries putting up the price of oil. Britain's oil bill alone is now running at several thousand million pounds a year. Clearly, if this situation was continually repeated Britain would quickly be in financial difficulties. Fortunately, this is not the whole of the financial picture.

15. Invisible exports. In addition to the actual visible exports, there is a further source of income, known as *invisible exports*, which is not included in trade returns. These invisible exports consist of services: these include among other things earnings from shipping, air transport charges, banking and insurance charges, brokerage dues, royalties, interest on investments, tourist receipts. These invisible items may be of considerable importance and in the case of the United Kingdom they are of major significance for it is by them that the country usually "closes the gap" in its trade. In other words, the income from the invisible exports raises the value of the visible exports up to the level of the imports and until recently has enabled the United Kingdom to pay its way.

16. Balance of payments. The *balance of payments* is a statement of income and expenditure on international account.
Payments and receipts on international account are of three
kinds:

    (*a*) the visible balance of trade;

    (*b*) invisible items; and

    (*c*) capital transfers.

The balance of payments shows the relationship between the
United Kingdom's total payments to all other countries and
its total receipts from them. An adverse balance of payments
can be met in a variety of ways, *e.g.* by borrowing, by selling
investments abroad, by exporting gold, but these expedients
cannot go on indefinitely, as will be realised, and the only real
solution is for the country to export more to meet the deficit.

PROGRESS TEST 21

1. Outline and explain the bases of trade. **(2)**

2. Explain the meaning of (*a*) primary products, and (*b*) secondary products, and quote examples of each. **(4)**

3. Why is there an important interchange of manufactured
goods between Western Europe and the United States, especially
since both these regions are manufacturing areas? **(4, 8, 9)**

4. Distinguish between the home trade and the foreign trade of a
country. **(6)**

5. Explain the meaning of the following terms: single commodity
countries; imperial preference; balance of trade; invisible exports.
(5, 6, 14, 15)

6. Give reasons for the fact that the United Kingdom is a major
trading country. **(12)**

7. Explain why a large proportion of the world's trade is between temperate and tropical lands. **(2–5)**

SUGGESTED PROJECTS

1. Draw (*a*) *pie graphs* to illustrate the *exports* of West Germany and Argentina, and (*b*) *bar graphs* to illustrate the *imports* of West Germany and Argentina.

2. From a book of reference such as *The Statesman's Year Book* or *Whitaker's Almanack* find out, and list, the chief imports and exports of the United Kingdom.

DISCUSSION TOPICS

1. Britain must export or die.

2. A greater volume of international trade should be the aim of the governments of the world.

CHAPTER XXII

TRANSPORT NEEDS AND PROBLEMS

IMPORTANCE OF TRANSPORT

1. Transport as part of production. To the economist, transport is a phase in the production process: production is not complete until the commodity, after treatment or manufacture, is in the hands of the consumer. For example, wheat in an elevator at Port Arthur or meat in a *frigorifico* in Buenos Aires, which is destined for shipment to Europe, can be said to be still in the process of production. In the same way, eggs in an egg-packing plant in the Fylde district of Lancashire or shoes in a Northampton footwear factory can be regarded as being in the productive process.

2. Importance of transport. Specialised economic activity, whether it be in the field of agriculture or manufacture, is dependent upon trade and this exchange, in its turn, cannot be carried on without transport. Except among a few backward communities, economic self-sufficiency is a thing of the past and most people are, to a greater or lesser extent, dependent upon supplies of foodstuffs and manufactured articles brought from outside their immediate locality. It will be readily appreciated that:

(*a*) Inadequate transport facilities will hinder and slow down supplies of raw materials to factories or consumer goods to shops; and

(*b*) Inadequate transport will be likely to put up the costs of carriage and so increase the price of raw materials or finished goods.

3. Transport considerations. In the carriage of goods or passengers a number of considerations have to be taken into account, the most important of which are:

(*a*) the cost of carriage;

(*b*) the speed of carriage;

(c) the quantity or load factor;

(d) the packaging factor.

Some of these considerations are closely inter-related; for example, the greater the degree of packaging required, the more costly will transport be, while the greater the load, the slower, generally speaking, will be the speed with which it is carried.

SPEED AND COST

4. Cost of carriage. The cost of transport is obviously a very important consideration and it may be said to be closely related to four factors:

(a) the distance the goods or passengers have to travel;

(b) the speed at which carriage is undertaken;

(c) the care and attention devoted to packaging, loading, checking;

(d) the means of carriage adopted.

Trade almost always follows the cheapest routes. The cheapest route is not necessarily the shortest route; neither is the quickest route always the shortest. Natural obstacles along the line of route may have to be avoided and a more circuitous route taken, although journeys round such hindrances may in fact take a shorter time than those through or over them. Sometimes a short route, though quicker than a longer one, is more expensive because of the need to use special equipment or vehicles whose running costs are heavy. In mountainous country, for example, rack railways, more powerful engines, bridging and tunnelling, mean higher transport costs.

5. Use of routes. The use of routes is primarily determined by cost of carriage and this is dependent upon four factors:

(a) the distance over which goods have to be transported;

(b) the means of transport used for carriage;

(c) the obstacles and handicaps to free movement; and

(d) the nature of the goods carried.

6. Cheapness in transport. Cheapness in transport is secured by:

(a) uninterrupted carriage over long distances;
(b) increasing the size of the carrying agent;
(c) using level and direct routes as far as possible;
(d) having full cargoes in both directions.

7. Time factor. When the time factor is involved, such as getting perishable commodities like fish or fresh fruit or flowers to market, the quickest routes are commonly chosen, even though these on the face of it appear to be the most expensive; such routes are, in actual fact, the cheapest since perishable goods quickly lose their value once they begin to deteriorate.

If time is of little or no consequence, as in the case of most non-perishable commodities, such as coal, ores, timber, more leisurely routes can be followed.

Similarly with regard to passenger traffic: if time is no object, the traveller from Britain to the United States, for instance, is likely to go by sea; but if time is important he is likely to travel by air. Frequently to business men "time is money"; when this applies, quicker travel, though perhaps more costly, is, in the final reckoning, cheaper.

8. Speed in transport. Speed in transport can be achieved in a variety of ways:

(a) By using new and more powerful methods of propulsion; e.g. jet engines.

(b) By improving trackways to facilitate speedier movement, e.g. dual carriageway roads.

(c) By guaranteeing full cargoes which enables transport to be organised to schedule.

(d) By improving terminal facilities which allows a quicker turn round.

(e) By inventions, such as radar, automatic signalling, radio communication, which facilitate movement.

LOADS AND PACKAGING

9. Size of load. Generally speaking, the larger the load that can be carried the less is the cost per unit carried; for example, while it may cost £1 to carry a unit over a distance of 100 miles, it may only cost £60 to carry 200 units over the same distance. This explains why nowadays so much "bulk carrying" is undertaken. Bulk carrying, in turn, leads to the development of specialised forms of transport, *e.g.* bulk milk-carriers, re-frigerator ships.

The importance of the load factor is well illustrated in the case of oil tankers. In the early days petroleum was trans-ported in metal drums. With the increasing demand for oil, special ships, called tankers, were built to transport it in bulk. While a decade ago most tankers were up to about 50,000 tons in size, nowadays 100,000-ton tankers are not uncommon; in Japan an oil tanker of over 200,000 tons is in production and very much larger tankers are being planned.

The use of such monster-size vessels inevitably brings problems, *e.g.* of loading and unloading, and routing. Special deep-water terminals are required (*e.g.* as at Milford Haven) for handling these great tankers. Traditional routes, such as the Red Sea–Suez Canal route, become impossible because of the limited size of the vessels the ship canals can accommodate.

10. Packaging. Many imperishable and unspoilable com-modities, *e.g.* ores, coal, gravel, timber, can be carried in open trucks or barges. The large-scale carriage of liquids, such as milk, oil, acids, must be carried in bulk containers. In general terms, such bulk carriage appreciably decreases transport costs.

Miscellaneous items usually require independent, careful packaging. If they are of a fragile nature, such as glass and china, or perishable, such as flowers and market garden produce, very careful packaging is required. The amount of packaging needed and the care required to prevent contamina-tion, spoilation or deterioration increases substantially the cost of carriage.

NOTE: This increased cost results from:

    (i) the need to use special containers, *e.g.* bags, boxes, packing materials;

    (ii) the extra work occasioned by careful loading and un-loading and, perhaps, attention *en route*.

PROGRESS TEST 22

1. "Transport is part of production." Explain what this means. **(1)**

2. What considerations must be taken into account in the car-riage of goods or passengers? **(3, 7)**

3. Upon what principal factors does the cost of carriage depend? (4)

4. "Trade always follows the cheapest routes." What factors determine the cheapest route? (4, 7)

5. Cheapness of transport is very important. How is this cheapness secured? (6)

6. Indicate the ways in which speed in transport may be achieved other than by travelling more speedily. (8)

7. Explain what is meant by the following: time is money; bulk carriage; perishable commodities. (7, 9, 10)

8. In the transport of the following commodities which is more important—speed, cheapness, or packaging: timber; fresh milk; bananas; porcelain; tea; eggs; orchids; strawberries; coal? (7, 9, 10)

CHAPTER XXIII

MODES OF TRANSPORT

1. The chief modes of transport. The methods of transport used in the world at the present day vary widely from country to country and from region to region. This variation is the result of the influence of geographical, economic, social and historical factors. The modes of transport fall into nine different categories:

(a) Human porterage and human traction.
(b) Animal transport.
(c) Motor road transport.
(d) Railways.
(e) Air transport.
(f) Ropeways and cableways.
(g) Pipelines.
(h) Inland water transport.
(i) Ocean transport.

Here we cannot go into each of these in detail and attention will be directed only to the more significant points with regard to the more important forms of transport.

2. Human and animal transport. In spite of the remarkable developments in modern transport, the oldest forms of transport are still to be found in some parts of the earth, usually in rather remote and isolated areas far from railways, or where roads are poor or non-existent. Human porterage continues to be used in a few places, chiefly in parts of Africa and South-east Asia.

Animals are used:

(a) as beasts of burden;
(b) for draught purposes;

and animal transport (by horse, ass, mule, oxen, yak, camel, llama and elephant) is still important in some areas, but

252

mechanical transport is tending increasingly to displace animals the world over.

ROAD TRANSPORT

3. Roads. Metalled, *i.e.* hard-surfaced, roads date back to Persian and Roman times but such early good roads fell into disuse and disrepair and during medieval times most carriage was by pack animals along trails. Until the eighteenth century such highways as existed were mainly dirt trackways, dusty and rutted in summer, quagmires of mud in winter. When industrial progress demanded improved means of communication, Telford, Macadam and Metcalfe pioneered the metalled road. But it was the invention of the automobile which led to the great extension and improvement of roads. The astonishing growth of motor transport has presented us with a major problem at the present time. In order to keep pace with the rapidly increasing number of vehicles and to combat a growing congestion and death-rate on the roads, existing highways are being straightened, widened and cambered while special arterial roads, or motorways as they are called in Britain (*autobahnen* in Germany, *autostrada* in Italy), are being built for fast traffic.

4. Automobiles and their function. Motor cars, motor lorries and motor coaches play an important and ever-increasing role in the transportation of passengers and goods. So vital has motor transport become that many bus and coach terminals are as large and as busy as the bigger railway stations. During the past fifty years the automobile in its various forms has revolutionised methods of internal transport. *Road transport has the advantages of flexibility of service, greater speed over short distances and directness of communication over other forms of land transport.* In Britain, the motor lorry, by providing fairly cheap and rapid door-to-door transport, has made great inroads into the traffic formerly carried by the railways. Ideally, roads should act as "feeders" to railways but an increasing element of competition has developed between the two. There has been a growth of long-distance traffic by heavy lorry and trailer.

5. Motor transport in Britain. Britain possesses some 200,000 miles of roadway. Approximately half of this mileage consists of unclassified roads of only local importance, over 80,000 miles (128,000 kilometres) fall into the category of classified roads, 8600 miles (13,840 kilometres) are trunk roads and about 1200 miles (1930 kilometres) are motorways. Britain has one of the closest networks of roads in the world and, although our roads leave much to be desired, one of the best networks. The greatest weakness of our system was until recently a deficiency of high-speed arterial highways. Although the present system is still inadequate to meet modern needs, it is beginning to take the shape of a national network capable of carrying the vastly increased volume of motor traffic at high speeds.

In 1973 there were some 13 million private cars on the road and about 2 million commercial vehicles. The growth of road transport is shown by the following figures:

Year	Ton-miles
1952	19,000 million
1960	30,000 million
1965	40,000 million
1973	60,000 million

NOTE: A "ton-mile" is a composite unit representing one ton of goods carried for one mile.

Already 85% of all inland goods transport in Britain is moved by road.

6. Roads and road transport throughout the world. Road transport is very unequally developed throughout the world. Western Europe and North America have the greatest number of vehicles, the closest road networks and the most developed services. In these regions all towns and ports are linked by inter-communicating road systems and most have linking coach services. Most of the countries of Western Europe have well-developed arterial highways. The United States has half of all the cars in the world and coaches and lorries provide coast-to-coast services. In Canada, the recently constructed Trans-Canadian Roadway links St John's in Newfoundland with Vancouver in British Columbia. The Alcan or Alaskan Highway links Edmonton to Alaska.

Outside Europe and North America good roads and well-developed road systems are scarce. Beyond the immediate environs of towns, made roads often peter out and become mere dirt tracks. Even so, motor transport has helped to solve many transport problems in regions where railways are lacking.

In both Africa and Australia, where distances are great and settlements widely spaced, motor transport is much used. One of Australia's major road links is the trans-continental Stuart Highway which connects Birdum in Northern Territory with Oodnadatta in South Australia. Roads form important links between ports and their hinterlands in South America, and some countries, *e.g.* Brazil, Bolivia, Peru, are building great roads to assist national cohesion as well as economic development. The major road project in South America, largely financed by the United States, is the Pan-American Highway which now links up practically every South American State and, ultimately, will join together South America, Central America, Mexico and the United States.

RAIL TRANSPORT

7. The function of railways. The railway was in a very real sense the product of the Industrial Revolution: the revolution in industry demanded a new form of transport and the revolution made the railway possible. Prior to the First World War the railway was the predominant agent in inland transport in most regions.

(*a*) The advent of the steam locomotive, running on fixed rails, solved two important problems:

(i) It made possible the *economic carriage by land* of: materials in bulk; and heavy, bulky goods.

(ii) It made possible, for the first time, the *relatively rapid movement* of people, mail, commodities.

(*b*) In addition to its carrying function, the railway had two important effects:

(i) It helped to accelerate the process of industrialisation, and the most highly industrialised areas have the densest railway networks.

(ii) It served as the advance guard of civilisation in the underdeveloped "new lands" of the world, making possible their economic development and settlement.

(*c*) The railway development and mileage in any area is largely the result of four factors:

(i) the relief of the land surface;
(ii) the degree of progress in civilisation;
(iii) the density of the population; and
(iv) the degree of development of the natural resources.

Broadly speaking, *the stage of development, social as well as economic, of a region may be judged by the adequacy of its railway network*: in fact it has been said that "railroad mileage is an index of civilisation."

8. Characteristics of rail transport. The chief characteristics of rail transport are:

(a) The use of a fixed track which means that rail transport, unlike road transport, is not flexible.

(b) Routes operate between stations which are fixed terminals and transhipment is necessary at the end of the rail journey.

(c) Railways are best suited to the carriage of large consignments over long distances, especially heavy, bulky commodities.

(d) The cost of carriage for small consignments and short hauls tends to be high.

(e) Individual consignments on cross-country journeys may require several transhipments and so may take long to reach their destination.

(f) Capital, maintenance and operating costs are heavy.

9. Railway patterns. Railways can be grouped into three main types or patterns: lines of penetration, local networks and trans-continental lines.

(a) *Lines of penetration:* these are isolated lines, frequently running inland from a coastal port, to tap areas important for mineral resources or agriculturally productive areas. In Africa, Australia and South America there are many isolated stretches of line, e.g. the line from Cairns to Forsayth in Queensland, or the line from Fort Gouraud to Port Etienne in Mauretania built to exploit the iron-ore resources.

(b) *Local networks:* these are integrated meshes which often have a high density especially in industrial regions, such as the Ruhr, or in densely populated areas, such as the London Basin. Dense local networks, though they are now often being streamlined are also usually being improved, e.g. by electrification. Outside Europe and North America the chief networks are found in the pampas region of Argentina, in the São Paulo region of Brazil, in South Africa, India, Japan and south-eastern Australia.

(c) *Trans-continental lines:* these were constructed for both political and economic reasons. In North America the lines were built mainly to open up the West, although in the case of the Canadian Pacific Railway there was a political motive as well: British Columbia refused to join the confederation of Canadian

FIG. 28.—*The railways of Australia*

Note (a) the lines penetrating inland to mining or agricultural areas; (b) the beginnings of a network in the south-eastern portion of the continent; (c) the trans-continental line across southern Australia; and (d) the three different gauges which are used and which create difficulties of inter-communication.

provinces until a rail link with the east was guaranteed. The Trans-Siberian Railway was built to open up Siberia and link Moscow with Vladivostok on the Pacific. In South America Buenos Aires is linked with Valparaiso and a new trans-continental line will eventually connect Rio de Janeiro with Arica in northern Chile.

Fig. 28 shows these three patterns in one continent—the Australian network.

10. Beeching and British Rail. In countries with well-established and close networks, there is a tendency to close down unremunerative branch-lines and to use roads as feeders to the main lines. In Britain, the growing competition from road transport led to an increasing deficit on the railways. First, in 1947, the railways were brought under public ownership; then, in 1955 modernisation plans were initiated; and, finally, under Dr Beeching's management ruthless pruning was started. All these steps were taken in an attempt to solve the railway problem.

The Beeching Report outlined the steps to be taken to make the railways of Britain an efficient and going concern. Among the many recommendations were:

(a) The closure of many uneconomic lines.
(b) The elimination of many stopping passenger services.
(c) The rationalisation of duplicated routes.
(d) The improvement of many inter-city services.
(e) The speeding-up of many long-distance trains.
(f) The reduction of uneconomic freight traffic.
(g) The development of liner freight trains.
(h) The replacement of steam by diesel and electricity.

Dr Beeching may be said to have provided the blue-print for British Rail of the future. Many uneconomic lines and services have been withdrawn and many small stations closed. Many of the larger stations have been amalgamated and some of the railway workshops closed. Marshalling yards and other premises no longer of use are being sold (often they occupy valuable sites). The liner freight service has been launched and the new electrified fast services introduced. Even so, British Rail operates at a big loss and has to be subsidised by the state, and currently there is talk of further drastic pruning.

AIR TRANSPORT

11. Development of air transport. The most striking development in twentieth-century transport has been the invention of the aeroplane. Since the first successful flight—a distance of 300 yards—in December 1903 by the Wright brothers, aircraft have developed phenomenally in size, speed and flying distance. Because of its importance as a weapon of war, the aeroplane underwent a rapid development during the Second World War. Since then improvements have proceeded apace and it is difficult to envisage what the future will bring; but of one thing we can be sure, the aeroplane will play an increasingly important role in communications.

In passing, we might note that the airship or zeppelin, a rigid dirigible balloon, providing an alternative method of air transport to the aeroplane, had much less success; a series of experiments ended mostly in disaster with the result that developments on these lines were brought to an end.

12. The function of air transport. The function of the aero-plane (apart from its military significance) continues to be mainly concerned with passenger transport. It is true that more and more freight is being carried by air each year but it is equally true that air transport is only competitive for freight that is light and expensive. The cost of air transport limits its use mainly to small, costly, light-weight, perishable com-modities.

The sort of goods commonly carried by air include mail, precious stones, bullion, traveller's samples and, in some areas, high-priced fruit, early vegetables and flowers. In a few areas, usually where alternative modes of transport are lacking, more prosaic commodities are moved by air, *e.g.* carcass meat is flown from the interior of Guyana to the capital, Georgetown, and it has been known for machinery, tractors and motor vehicles to be shipped by air.

Air transport, however, is most important for passenger transport, especially when passengers wish to economise on time. Using modern jet-propelled aircraft, it is possible to travel several thousands of miles in a few hours. For instance, it is not uncommon for Britishers working in Kenya to fly home to London for the week-end. Aircraft also serve a very useful function by helping to open up remote and inaccessible areas by providing communications links—often the only links—with centres of civilisation. Many Canadian, Siberian, Australian and South American outposts are maintained by air links.

13. Advantages and disadvantages. The chief advantages of air transport are speed of transit, freedom of movement (though sometimes there are national restrictions), no need of track (though airfields are essential) and aircraft can often go where other forms of transport cannot. On the other hand, transport by air has certain disadvantages: the vehicle is of limited size and so it can carry only restricted loads, air travel is still expensive although the rates are becoming increasingly competitive and the dangers from air transport are still proportionately much greater than with other modes of transport. We should note, too, that in spite of modern devices (radar, etc.) air transport is more susceptible to interruption by bad weather conditions, *e.g.* fog or icing, than other forms of transport and that, as aircraft become bigger and bigger, larger and longer runways are required and these can, often, only be found farther and farther away from centres of population. Hence, the time saved on the actual flight is often offset by the time it takes to get from the airport to the city centre.

14. Air routes. There are two types of air service:

(*a*) Those operated by companies providing charter flights, *i.e.* air transport is desired for special purposes, such as the ferrying of tourists during the height of the holiday season or the carrying of equipment to, say, a mining camp; and

(*b*) Those services operated along regular routes where the aircraft fly to fixed schedules. In this latter group are:

(i) the short-distance internal flights operated within a country such as those between Glasgow and London, Dublin and Liverpool; and

(ii) the long-distance international flights such as those between London and New York and London and the Far East.

Increasingly air routes tend to radiate from the great capital cities and highly urbanised and industrialised centres, simply because it is these centres which provide the most traffic. As a result large and elaborate airports have grown up in or near to these centres. Such modern airports take up large areas of, frequently, very valuable land and are very expensive to build but *they must be near the areas they serve.*

World air routes tend to converge upon a limited number of geographically favoured centres which are well-equipped and possess good facilities, *e.g.* London, Cairo, Bangkok. The heaviest international traffic is that between Western Europe and North America across the North Atlantic and London Airport and Idlewild, New York, are among the busiest airports in the world. Finally, we should emphasise that aircraft, like ships, aim wherever possible to follow Great Circle routes (which mark the shortest distances between places), for in this way aircraft can economise in time and fuel.

SPECIALISED FORMS OF LAND TRANSPORT

15. New techniques of overland transport. In addition to the common methods of land transport, there are a number of specialised techniques which should be noted, chiefly ropeways and cableways, pipelines and transmission lines. Although there have been developments in the use of ropeways and cableways, this particular method of transport is not of any great significance except in a few fairly localised instances. On the other hand, the use of pipelines and transmission lines is increasing rapidly and already they are very important methods of transport.

16. Ropeways and cableways. We are all familiar with chair-lifts and cable-cars such as are used in the Alps, but it is seldom realised to what extent ropeways and cableways are used as a medium of transport. The main principle involved is that loads are suspended from overhead cables and carried clear of the ground. The great advantage of this method of transport is its ability to cross terrain, such as deep valleys, wide rivers, forests and glaciers, where no other form of transport is physically practicable or economically possible.

The use of aerial ropeways is not new, indeed some were in use a century ago, but the extent to which they are used at present is a new development in transport. Until 1939 rope-ways were mostly modest in both their length and carrying capacity but technical advances have made possible ropeways of up to 50 miles (80 kilometres) in length with carrying capacities of up to 500 tons. The Reynolds Bauxite Mines in Jamaica installed a ropeway which transports 160 tons of bauxite an hour.

17. Pipelines. Pipes have long been used to carry water, but in more recent times they have been used to carry a variety of other things including oil, natural gas, liquefied coal and even milk. The recent increase in the use of the pipeline "represents one of the most notable revolutions in the history of transport, and especially in the transport of energy." For many decades now the overland transport of oil has been effected by pipe-lines and many of them are hundreds of miles in length.

One of the most recent oil pipelines, and the longest built so far, is the 3000-mile (4828-kilometre) "Friendship Pipeline" which carried crude oil from the Ural-Volga oilfields in the Soviet Union to the Communist satellite countries of East Europe. Gas pipelines are very common in North America and the United States has a greater mileage of natural gas pipeline than she has of railways. In Europe, growing use of pipelines is taking place, especially for the purpose of moving oil inland from the great oil importing ports (*see* Fig. 20).

18. Transmission lines. Another important method of transporting energy or power is by electricity transmission lines. The landscape of Britain is already festooned with power lines held aloft by pylons, a constant reminder of the importance of electricity in our modern economy. These power lines link the consuming with the producing areas. In some areas, such as Scandinavia, power lines of up to 400 miles (643 kilometres) in length carry electricity from the water-power sites in the mountains to the towns and factories in the lowlands.

The problem of transmitting electricity over distances of two or three hundred miles—until recently the maximum distance over which it could be carried—is gradually being overcome. This development will enable electricity to be exported on a larger scale than at present, although even now there is a considerable international exchange of power, *e.g.* Sweden exports power to Denmark and Switzerland exports electricity to its neighbours.

INLAND WATERWAYS

19. Rivers. From the very earliest times inland waters have been used for transport and rivers, if they were navigable, have served as important lines of communication. In Yorkshire, in medieval times, for example, the Ouse and its tributaries provided *the* great artery of communications within the county and many riverside towns, such as Selby, York, Boroughbridge, were important ports. In those days, of course, ships were small and of shallow draught and, accordingly, were able to penetrate far upstream. The size of modern ships renders many rivers useless for navigation but some of the larger rivers, especially if dense populations congregate in their valleys, continue to be of great importance for interior communications.

Rivers, from the point of view of navigation, have several disadvantages: they often lack directness of route, they suffer seasonal variations in level, they may be impeded by natural obstacles and they are sometimes blocked by ice in winter. On the other hand, water transport is usually cheap. Large, bulky, heavy, low-value, imperishable commodities, such as coal, ore, timber, gravel, can be carried cheaply by water. Think, for example, of the Great Lakes of North America in this respect. Large rivers on which small ships or large barges can work still form very important means of transportation, *e.g.* the Rhine, St Lawrence, the Plate; rivers are also of great value in countries which are not yet well served with alternative means of communication, *e.g.* the Yangtse, or not yet fully opened up to modern commerce, *e.g.* the Amazon.

20. Canals. Many rivers, as noted above, have disadvantages for modern traffic and, to overcome these difficulties, artificial waterways or canals were often constructed. Canals have a long history (the first was built in Egypt long before the Christian era and the Grand Canal in China is, in parts, at least 2000 years old) but they are essentially a development of the last two hundred years.

The great era of canal building in England was 1750–1850 but the canals' importance was diminished by the introduction of railways. England was less suited to canal building than many parts of the Great Plain of Northern Europe. Level lands, easily excavated, facilitate canal building. The need of many locks not only makes canal construction more expensive but slows down passage. *Canal transport usually is cheap and suitable for heavy, bulky goods, but slow.*

The chief disadvantages of canal transport are: that carriage is slow and there are delays at locks, the maintenance of an adequate supply of water may be difficult and expensive, and canals, particularly in England, are of too small dimensions for modern requirements. Some canals, such as the North European canals, continue to be of great importance. They are probably most useful and most important where they link with, and are integrated with, navigable rivers and canalised rivers.

Fig. 29.—*Canals and waterways of Western Europe*

Western Europe has an extensive system of natural and artificial waterways. Water transport, by river and canal, is helped by (*a*) the levelness of the North European Plain, which seldom needs locks; (*b*) the presence of great east–west valleys, left by the Ice Age, which facilitate lateral links; (*c*) the soft rocks of the Plain which make excavation easy; (*d*) the heavy, bulky nature of many of the commodities requiring transport (water carriage is cheap); and (*e*) most of the rivers, are amenable to improvement and flow in the right direction, *i.e.* northwards towards the English Channel and the North Sea.

21. Water transport in Western Europe. In parts of Western Europe water transport is of more than ordinary importance and there is an extensive system of natural and artificial waterways; this is shown in Fig. 29. Water transport, by river and canal, is helped by:

(a) *The levelness of the North European Plain*, which seldom necessitates locks.

(b) *The presence of great east–west valleys*, left by the Ice Age, which facilitate lateral links.

(c) *The soft clay rocks* of much of the plain, which make canal excavation a relatively easy matter.

(d) *The heavy, bulky nature of many of the commodities* requiring transport; water transport, remember, has the advantage of cheapness.

(e) *Most of the rivers* which were amenable to improvement *flowed in the right direction*, *i.e.* northwards towards the English Channel and the North Sea.

Thus the rivers from the Seine to the Elbe or even beyond to the Oder, together with their inter-connecting canals, afford the best developed waterway system in the world. Water transport is particularly important in France, Belgium, Holland and Western Germany. The Rhine is *the* great artery of this European system and is of premier importance to the aforementioned countries and to Switzerland. Large barges can ascend the Rhine to Basel, Switzerland's great river port. The Rhine allows heavy imports, such as ores and oil, to be cheaply imported and serves as an export route for many Swiss, French and German manufactures. Together with its tributaries and canals, the Rhine links together several important industrial regions. The recent (1964) canalisation of the Moselle allows the interchange of coal and iron ore between the Ruhr and Lorraine.

OCEAN TRANSPORT

22. Advantages of sea transport. Sea transport presents the greatest combination of advantages:

(a) the "highway" is free;
(b) there is no "trackway" to maintain;
(c) large quantities can be carried; and
(d) carriage is cheap.

Sea transport is especially competitive in the case of low value, bulky commodities. The size of vessels may be said to be limited only by the accommodation available at ports and the dimensions of ship-canals. Until recently vessels of around 60,000 tons were the largest to be built but in the past few years tankers of 100,000 and 200,000 tons are being built, *e.g.* in Japan, and tankers of several times this size are envisaged in future. Bulk carriage of this magnitude should result in much cheaper transport. It is interesting to note that in the United States the average cost of transporting a barrel of oil over 100 miles is less than two cents if carried by tanker but is roughly eight times as costly by rail and about forty times as costly by road.

23. Types of vessels. From the very earliest times ships have been specialised in function. Mainly, in the past, ships were classed as warships and merchantmen. During recent times vessels have come to show greater specialisation and several distinct types of commercial vessel have gradually evolved. Today, five main types of merchant ship are recognised:

(*a*) *Liners* which are primarily passenger vessels operating on the main shipping routes. The passenger liner has faced strong competition from air transport and liner services have been drastically reduced. They usually carry mail and sometimes a little cargo.

(*b*) *Cargo-liners* combine the function of passenger and cargo transport. They carry commodities such as grain, meat, fruit, wool. Many of the vessels on the Australia–New Zealand run or the South American run are of this type.

(*c*) *Tramps* are small cargo vessels, picking up trade as they go, and following no set route. As ocean carriers they are becoming increasingly less important.

(*d*) *Tankers* are relatively new-comers to the scene: they are a product of the oil age. They comprise half the world's merchant shipping tonnage and, as a group, they are the largest vessels afloat.

(*e*) *Coastal craft* are mainly used for shipping heavy, bulky commodities, such as coal and ore, from point to point along the coast. Some countries, *e.g.* Britain, Norway, Japan, the United States, make much use of coasters.

24. Merchant fleets. Since the end of the Second World War a number of significant changes have taken place in the world's merchant fleets. Great Britain, which for long had had the world's greatest fleet (as much as 40% of it at the beginning of the present century), now ranks third. The other merchant navies of significance in world trade are those of Norway, France, Greece, Japan, Liberia, Panama, the USSR and the USA. Both Norway and Greece may be said to have developed their mercantile marines because of the poverty of their respective homelands. The earnings from their ships form a valuable invisible export. The inclusion of Panama and Liberia appears strange and occurs simply because their conditions of registration are less exacting than those in other countries, hence ships belonging to other nations may register in Liberia or Panama. In fact, Liberia with a gross registered tonnage of 55 million tons has the largest fleet in the world.

25. Shipping routes. The bulk of the world's ocean-going vessels follow regular routes. Many well-defined shipping lanes have developed and where ships follow these routes there is less risk of danger or catastrophe, for safeguards (in the form of lightships, lighthouses, weather-ships) are provided.

Since Great Circle routes are the shortest routes, shipping routes between two ports tend to approximate to an arc of a Great Circle. Departures from such routes normally occur only if there is a threat of danger, as on the North Atlantic route in late spring and early summer when icebergs floating southwards cause vessels to take a more southerly course. The density of shipping on any route is clearly related to the volume of traffic in both passengers and goods that is available and this is likely to be greatest in the most densely populated, most prosperous and most economically advanced areas. Thus, as one might surmise, *the most important and busiest routes are those spanning the North Atlantic.* Ocean terminals, or ports, mark the ends of shipping routes; these terminals should have, and usually do have, good facilities for handling ships, *e.g.* repair services, the supply of fuel and water, customs facilities, storage warehouses. In order to speed up loading and unloading and ensure a quick "turn-round", a vessel may prefer to travel an extra hundred miles to use a well-equipped terminal than put in at a port possessing inadequate facilities.

26. The chief shipping lanes. These are shown in Fig. 30 and described below:

(a) *The North Atlantic route* between Western Europe and eastern Canada and the United States, which is the busiest and most important of all the world's shipping routes and the most important passenger route.

(b) *The Mediterranean–Red Sea–Indian Ocean route* which leads to Australia and the Far East; this route carries passengers and a variety of commodities, including cotton, tea, rubber, wool, dairy produce and meat, but especially petroleum from the Middle East to Europe.

(c) *The Cape route*, via West Africa, to the Republic of South Africa and thence eastwards to Australia and New Zealand; this route carries passengers to Britain's southern Dominions and fruit, wine, wool, tobacco and meat come from these countries to Britain.

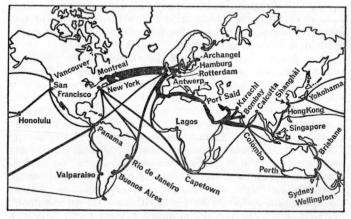

FIG. 30.—*World shipping routes*

Note the overwhelming importance of the trans-North Atlantic route and the importance of the Mediterranean–Suez–Red Sea route, the short cut to the Indian Ocean. Most of the world's major ports are shown. British ports are not indicated.

(d) *The South Atlantic route* to Brazil, Uruguay and Argentina; coal, machinery and manufactured goods provide the chief items of traffic on the outward journey, raw materials and foodstuffs (meat, coffee, fruit) the chief items on the return journey.

(e) *The Panama route* via the West Indies to the Pacific whence the route branches either to Hawaii and Australia, or to the western coast of North America or the western coast of South America.

(f) *The North Pacific route* between the western coast of

North America and the Far East; only a small volume of trade is carried over this route.

27. The ship canals. The Suez and Panama Canals, the two most important of the world's ship canals, are human attempts to overcome the inconvenient arrangement of the land masses. They both cut through narrow necks of land joining continental areas and thereby facilitate ocean shipping and save travelling time. Of the two the Suez Canal, opened in 1869, was the more important until its closure in 1967 through the war with Israel. The Suez Canal greatly shortened the sea route between Europe and the countries of the northern embayment of the Indian Ocean. Every year over 20,000 vessels with a net tonnage of over 200 million tons passed through the Canal. Three countries (Britain, Norway and France) dominated the traffic. The most important trade item was oil coming from the countries of the Middle East. Between 300,000 and 500,000 passengers passed through the canal annually. The Arab–Israeli War resulted in its closure but in late 1975, after 8 years, the Canal was re-opened. However, it seems likely that it will never be as important in the future as in the past since the passenger liner trade has gone and much of its former oil trade is now moved by supertankers (which are too big to negotiate the Canal).

The Panama Canal, opened in 1914, has six locks, in contrast to Suez which is lockless. The construction of the Panama Canal brought two main advantages: the long and difficult trip around Cape Horn was eliminated and the American coasting trade was greatly facilitated and thereby expanded. The total traffic of the Panama Canal is considerably less than that of Suez: slightly more than 14,000 vessels use the canal annually, while the cargo amounts to around 80 million tons. The west to east traffic is more than twice as great as that flowing westwards.

The need for a new sea-level canal across Central America has been recognised for several years in order to meet the increasing volume of traffic and the larger size of many vessels, notably oil tankers. There are four possible routes available but in 1966 it was announced that plans had been made for a canal through north-western Colombia. Vessels of up to 20,000 tons will be able to pass through it. Construction costs will be around $450 million. However, by 1975 no action had been taken.

PROGRESS TEST 23

1. Make a comparison of road and railway transport, noting the advantages and disadvantages of each. (4–8)

2. "Outside Europe and North America good roads and well-developed road systems are scarce." Explain the reasons for this. Is the situation changing in any way? (6)

3. Give an account of motor transport in Britain. (5)

4. Give an account of some of the great new road highways which have recently been built in different parts of the world. (6)

5. What are the chief characteristics of railway transport? (8)

6. Illustrate the different kinds of railway patterns which can be discerned upon a world railway map. (9)

7. What problems faced British railways and what were Dr Beeching's proposals for improving their efficiency? (10)

8. State the chief advantages and disadvantages of air transport. (13)

9. Describe the differing uses of pipeline transport. (17)

10. Compare rivers and canals as means of transport. What are the advantages and disadvantages of each? (19–21)

11. Explain why the Rhine is *the* major communications artery of Europe. (21)

12. Compare the Suez and Panama Canals from the viewpoints of (a) situation; (b) negotiation; and (c) nature of traffic passing through. (27)

SUGGESTED PROJECTS

1. Using an outline map of the world, mark in the shortest sea route (a) between London and Calcutta, and (b) Liverpool and Auckland (N.Z.). Mark in and name the chief ports of call *en route.*

2. Draw a sketch-map of South America and mark in the route of the Pan-American Highway. Name all the capital cities through which the road passes.

3. Consult *Whitaker's Almanack* and look up in the index "Merchant Shipping." From the statistics given of steamships and motorships owned in the world, draw bar graphs to show the total gross tonnage owned by the different countries listed.

DISCUSSION TOPICS

1. Britain's road transport problems.
2. The place of canals in a modern transport system.
3. Future developments in air transport.

CHAPTER XXIV

COMMUNICATIONS

MEANING AND IMPORTANCE

1. Meaning of communication. The terms transport and communications are usually used rather loosely in geography and are frequently taken to mean the same thing. Each term, however, has a precise meaning: *communication* may be defined simply as *the transmission of thought* by voice and message; *transportation* may be reserved as an expression for *the function of carrying*.

Often in the past, and sometimes even at the present time, the means of communication and the means of transport were the same: the carrying of messages by runners is a case in point.

2. Importance of communication. The communication of thought has been of tremendous significance since the very earliest days of human existence; today it is more important than ever before. Not even the simplest human societies can function unless men can communicate with each other. Today, communication, in the sense that we can translate or put across our ideas to someone else, is of prime importance: think for a moment of the term *democracy* and the interpretation which the West puts upon it and which the Soviet Union puts upon it.

Adequacy and accuracy of communication have tremendously important international implications. Moreover, we are all, to a greater or lesser degree, subjected to the impact of what we call *mass media*, *i.e.* newspapers, advertising, radio, television, with beneficial or harmful results. Think of the impact of "There's a tiger in my tank" or "My goodness, my Guinness"—highly effective advertising! And advertising may have very important geographical repercussions.

3. Early attempts at communication. Because primitive man wished to express his thoughts and feelings he used his vocal chords to produce a series of grunts and squeals which, in due course, developed into speech or language.

Wonderful as the voice is, it has its limitations: it cannot carry very far and, until very recent times when recordings could be made, the spoken voice was transitory. To enable him to communicate over long distances, man invented a variety of ingenious ways of sending messages. Most of the early methods involved sight and sound, *e.g.* drums, beacons, smoke signals. These were practical solutions devised by primitive man to overcome the problem that distance placed in the way of his need to communicate.

Somewhere about five thousand years ago, man invented writing so that he could perpetuate his thoughts.

4. Communication devices. Throughout human history man has invented a series of devices to facilitate and speed up communication. But developments in systems of communication were slow until just over a century ago; then, developments in electrical technology wrought a revolution. Quite suddenly communications were speeded up as never before.

(*a*) *The electric telegraph.* The invention of the electric telegraph by Samuel Morse, in 1844, ushered in a new era in communications. This new invention had two important results:

(i) communications ceased to be primarily dependent upon transportation; and
(ii) it led to the establishment of widespread communications networks.

Within a very short time all the important towns in Europe were linked together by telegraph cable. In 1866 the first trans-Atlantic cable was laid, and with it the time required to communicate between the two continents was reduced from weeks to minutes.

(*b*) *The telephone.* In 1875 the telephone was invented by Alexander Graham Bell and electric land telephones came into use. Now, for the first time, it became a practical possibility for the human voice to be heard from one end of the world to another. The telephone greatly facilitates the conduct of business and administration as well as having a useful social purpose.

(*c*) *The teletype machine.* Another useful development was the marriage of the typewriter with the telegraph to produce the teletype machine. Today, the teleprinter system is widely used and the British Weather Forecasting Bureau for example, relies upon it to a great extent. Recently a teleprinter link-up was installed between Washington and Moscow.

(d) *Radio*. The greatest development of all in communications was the coming of radio, mainly owing to the work of Marconi. Radio meant that messages could be heard instantaneously the world over. The speed, reliability and accuracy is matched by no other communicating medium.

(e) *Radar*. This is a process whereby distant objects can be detected and located by radio. A transmitter sends out waves in a particular direction: these detect objects and echoes of the radio waves are reflected back to the detecting apparatus. During the Second World War much use was made of radar, for it enabled enemy aircraft and flying bombs as well as submarines to be detected by night and in fog. It is much used by aircraft and ships at the present time, especially during darkness and in foggy weather.

(f) *Visual communication*. This came with the invention of the film, but the motion picture served entertainment rather than business ends. Television has joined the other means of communication but, like the film, its importance is still mainly in the field of entertainment.

In so far as communications are concerned, the conquest of space and time would seem to be complete, but there is no telling what new devices electro-technology will bring in the future. Within the past few years Telstar and Syncom have provided virtually instantaneous aural and visual links between one continent and another. Without doubt we shall see further refinements in communications.

5. The value of communications. The facility with which messages can be dispatched and received nowadays is significant geographically in many ways, *e.g.* in forecasting weather, in giving warnings of potential hazards, in securing information on market prices, in conducting business matters, in advertising for commercial ends, in international political relations.

(a) *Weather forecasting*. The ability to transmit information about weather conditions is of tremendous value to a host of people—farmers, sailors, aircraft pilots, lorry drivers. Frost warnings, gale warnings, fog warnings and the like may save lives as well as money. For example, the destruction and loss of life from hurricanes in the West Indies and the United States is substantially reduced by having advance warning of their occurrence.

(b) *Fore-warning of disasters*. Other potential hazards, such as flood, fire, eruption, locust infestation, can be guarded against if adequate warning is given. Speedy messages can help man to take due precautions. During recent years there have been many threats of floods in England but the fact that due warning has been given has helped man to mitigate disaster. Moreover, when disasters have occurred the news can quickly be made known and assistance promptly sent to alleviate the distress.

(c) *Business matters*. Information on the supply, demand and prices of commodities can be secured by business men which helps them to buy and sell and to plan for their markets. A good example of the value of communications is provided by the tramp steamer: in former times tramps called at port after port in the hope of picking up a cargo and time and money were often lost in seeking cargo; today the owners can cable or radio their ships and direct them to ports where a consignment awaits them.

(d) *Commercial advertising*. Radio and television have provided important media for advertising, to some extent taking over the functions of the newspaper. Advertising is an important adjunct of business these days. Communication media such as radio and television which began as entertainment media have now become useful tools of the business world.

(e) *Political ends*. Rapid communications are of tremendous consequence these days in the sphere of national and international politics. Leaders can speak directly to their peoples and communications can help to link together peoples, often widely dispersed. International crises may be solved by statesmen taking prompt action, itself only made possible as a result of speedily communicated knowledge.

LANGUAGE

6. Language. The development of speech and language is one of the fundamental developments of man's cultural evolution. Only by speech and gesture is it possible for man to communicate with his fellow men. Business, clearly, makes great demands upon communication, but language is especially important and the written word becomes essential. It is often said, and probably with much truth, that the Phoenicians developed the alphabetic system of writing because their business transactions necessitated written records.

7. The languages of commerce. Man has developed a multiplicity of tongues and these are, unfortunately, a great hindrance to easy communication between groups and especially to commercial intercourse. Largely for this reason, a few languages, mostly European languages, have come to be used as "the languages of commerce" and most international transactions are carried out in these commercial languages. Man prefers to do business in his own language or in one with which he is familiar.

The European languages have become predominant in international usage for two main reasons:

(a) because European peoples spread throughout the world conquering or colonising various parts and so taking their particular tongues with them; and

(b) because many of the new developments in communications were invented in Europe, a fact which tended to emphasise the importance of European languages.

8. The chief languages. These are:

(a) *English*. English is the most widespread of all languages for not only is it the mother tongue of the British peoples in the United Kingdom, Australia, New Zealand, Canada and Rhodesia, but it is the language spoken in the United States, South Africa and in most of Britain's former colonial territories.

NOTE: In eastern and south-eastern Asia "pidgin" English is spoken, a kind of mongrel English with Portuguese and Chinese words. The term "pidgin" itself is a Chinese corruption of the word business.

(b) *French*. Still very largely the language of culture and diplomacy in Europe, French is widely understood in North and Central Africa and South-east Asia although it has tended to lose its importance as France has declined as a great power and as it has lost its colonial empire. We should note the presence of a large French-speaking minority in Quebec province in Canada.

(c) *Portuguese and Spanish*. These two Iberian languages have currency throughout practically the whole of Latin America. Both, of course, are importations from Europe. With the major exception of Brazil, where Portuguese is the official language, Spanish predominates generally throughout Central and South America and is, therefore, the main commercial language.

German, though widely used in Central Europe and regarded as the "scientist's language," has not developed into an important commercial language. Russian, though growing in importance and spreading through the Soviet Union's Asiatic territories, is little understood outside the Soviet Union and is not commercially important.

9. Lingua Francas. Reference was made above to "pidgin" English which is a case of a *lingua franca*, a jargon composed of a mixture of languages used in trade intercourse. *Lingua franca* was originally a corrupt form of Italian used among the trading communities of the Levant. Another example is Swahili, a language derived from Bantu mixed with Arabic, English, Portuguese and Hindustani; it is widely spoken throughout Kenya and Tanzania and even by some of the Congo tribes.

The development of these *lingua francas* illustrates the need for some mutually intelligible mode of communication between peoples speaking different languages.

10. A linguistic comment. Language facilitates the cultural, as well as the economic, progress of man. It is unfortunate that many countries, especially the newly independent ones, are changing languages purely for the sake of nationalistic ends. India, for example, has attempted to promote Hindi, spoken by a minority only, in the place of English which at least had the advantage of being widely spread and understood even though it was not spoken by very many people. It is now reported that Tanzania proposes to drop English as the national language in favour of Swahili. This is somewhat of a retrograde step for, though Swahili has a wide currency in East Africa, it lacks the necessary vocabulary for any cultural advancement: furthermore, the cost of changing the written word, *e.g.* in the case of books, documents, place-names, will be great. One cannot help feeling that the money so used might well be more usefully employed for more constructive ends at this stage of the country's development.

PROGRESS TEST 24

1. Explain the meaning and estimate the importance of communication. (1, 2)

2. Write descriptive notes on any *four* communication devices. (4)

3. Outline the importance to man of communications. (5)

4. Which are the chief languages of commerce? Indicate the areas in which these languages are used. (**7, 8**)

5. Explain the terms: mass media; *lingua franca*; pidgin English. (**2, 8, 9**)

6. In what ways (*a*) did primitive man transmit messages; and (*b*) does modern man transmit messages? (**3–4**)

DISCUSSION TOPICS

1. Television does more harm than good.
2. Without language man would still be merely an animal.
3. The Russians are justified in compelling everyone within the Soviet Union to learn Russian.

CHAPTER XXV

PORTS AND THEIR FUNCTIONS

PORTS AND DOCKS

1. Havens, harbours and ports. These terms are often confused and it will be useful first to be clear as to terms:

(*a*) A *haven* is nothing more than sheltered water really, perhaps the sheltered side of a promontory or island although, of course, a harbour provides a haven; havens tend to provide temporary shelter;

(*b*) A *harbour* connotes some partially enclosed area, *e.g.* a creek, estuary or other inlet, providing shelter and safe anchorage; and harbours may be:

(i) *natural*, *i.e.* bays, inlets, river estuaries and the like which are provided by nature;

(ii) *artificial*, which have been created by man by the building of breakwaters or moles;

(*c*) A *port*, though it must in some degree have the qualities of a harbour, has docks, wharves and other facilities for handling ships and their cargoes.

Not every natural harbour forms a port. There are many excellent natural harbours in the world but, if they are to develop into ports, they must have an economic hinterland or productive area lying behind them.

2. Requirements of a port. Many factors are involved in the origin and growth of a port but a great commercial port must satisfy three principal requirements:

(*a*) It must provide *safe and sheltered anchorage* with sufficient depth of water to accommodate ocean-going vessels at all states of the tide;

(*b*) It must be *readily accessible* with easily navigable approaches in all kinds of weather; and

(*c*) It must be *linked by efficient means of communication with a hinterland* which is economically productive.

There are some ports, often of considerable importance, which do not have economic hinterlands, such as naval ports and ports of call, but these have specialised roles and a productive hinterland is not necessary in their case. But, let us emphasise, *a great commercial port cannot exist without an economic hinterland*.

3. Docks. The function of a port is to enable passengers or cargoes to be embarked or disembarked at convenient places. A port is a terminal just as an airport is a terminal serving aircraft or a station serves railways. To facilitate loading and unloading, ports have developed docks, artificially excavated basins in which operations may be carried out regardless of the state of the weather or the tide.

(*a*) *Dry docks* enable ships to be taken out of water to allow hull examination and repairs to be carried out. In the early days it was customary to beach ships, but as they grew larger this became impossible and it became necessary to provide dry docks.

(*b*) *Floating docks* serve the same purpose as graving (dry) docks but they are not tied to ports or harbours; they are movable and capable of operating anywhere so long as there is a sufficient depth of calm water.

4. The Port of London docks. London is one of *the* most important ports in the world. As it grew in importance increased facilities were needed and a series of docks were built during the nineteenth century. The present century has seen some notable additions and improvements. The need for docks arose out of two conditions:

(*a*) *The growing congestion* on the wharf-lined river resulting from the growth of trade; and

(*b*) *The high tidal range* of the estuary of the Thames which held up shipping.

The soft rocks—alluvium and London Clay—made the excavation of the docks a relatively easy matter. Each group of docks is located within a bend of the Thames, thus permitting two entrances to the systems, one on the upstream, the other on the downstream, side of the bend.

5. Development of the docks since the nineteenth century. In the development of the dock systems these points may be noted:

(a) The *gradual extension of the docks* farther and farther downstream;

(b) An *increase in the size of the dock basins* as one goes down river.

(c) The way various *docks tend to specialise* in the types of cargo they handle. Many of the older docks upstream from the Isle of Dogs have closed down and more and more traffic is being handled by the docks downstream, *e.g.* at Tilbury (*see* Fig. 31).

6. Containerisation. In the long history of transport every now and again some introduction comes along which has revolutionary effects: containerisation is one of these. The use of containers for goods is not new, but containerisation is a new form of packaging on a large scale. Containers are simply unit loads in, usually, metal packing cases of standard size which fit motor vehicles, rail cars and ships' holds and hence can be easily transferred from one kind of transporting agent to another. Loading and unloading can be quickly effected by mechanical means. Containerisation has many advantages but, in brief, it reduces the cost, the delay, the damage and the pilfering of goods in transit. Many ports now have container docks. Tilbury is the largest in Britain. Felixstowe, within the course of a decade, has developed from a minor rundown port into a flourishing and prosperous container port.

KINDS OF PORTS

7. Classification of ports. There are many different kinds of ports and they may be distinguished according to the specialised work they do. Very few ports, however, fall into hard and fast categories: frequently they combine several functions, like Hull which deals with general cargoes, is a fishing port and also has passenger services.

The chief types are:

(a) *Passenger ports.* These, such as Southampton and Cherbourg, are concerned mainly with passenger traffic. They are located at the termini of important trans-ocean routes and have good rail links with the interior offering speedy carriage to the metropolitan centres. They are deep-water ports since they must be capable of accommodating large passenger liners.

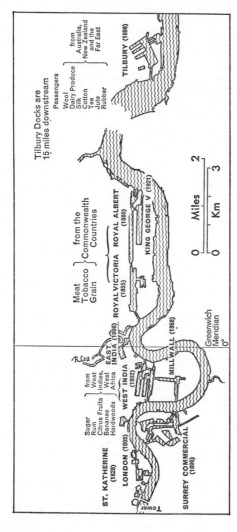

FIG. 31.—*Port of London docks*

London vies with New York and Rotterdam for first place among the world's ports. The Port of London extends from Teddington, the tidal limit on the river, some 70 miles downstream to the Thames estuary. Every year over 50,000 vessels visit London, nearly 60 million tons of cargo are handled and nearly a quarter of a million passengers embark or disembark. Note: the London, St. Katherine, Surrey Commercial, Millwall and East India docks are now closed.

(b) *Commercial ports.* These deal principally with the import and export of goods, though they may have certain passenger services or other functions (such as fishing). They may be large ports, such as Glasgow or Hamburg, or small ports, such as King's Lynn or Preston. Small ports dealing with coastal carriage are sometimes classed as a separate type.

(c) *Entrepôt ports.* Entrepôts are centres to which goods are brought for distribution to other countries rather than their own. They usually have ample storage accommodation for the temporary deposit of goods. Copenhagen, for example, has long been a collector of Baltic produce, which is then shipped elsewhere. Rotterdam is another great European entrepôt. Singapore is a notable Asiatic example.

(d) *Packet-stations.* Alternatively called ferry ports, these are almost exclusively concerned with the conveyance of passengers and mail over short-sea passages. The term "packet," note, has nothing to do with packages but derives from the boats, named "packets," which in earlier times carried State letters and dispatches. Packet-stations occur in pairs, facing one another across narrow seas, *e.g.* Dover and Calais, Newhaven and Dieppe, Larne and Stranraer.

(e) *Inland ports.* Though often located a considerable distance inland, through the agency of rivers or canals, such ports are accessible by certain types of sea-going ships and are usually served by barges and other specialised river craft. Usually they are commercial ports but often deal with a particular commodity. Notable examples of river ports are Duisburg on the Rhine, Memphis on the Mississippi, Hankow on the Yangtse. Chicago and Port Arthur are lake ports, Manchester a canal port.

(f) *Ports of call.* A number of ports have come into existence through their function as calling points on the main sea routes of the world; they are re-fuelling, watering and victualling points. Funchal (Madeira), Kingston (Jamaica), Aden, Honolulu are well-known examples.

(g) *Oil ports.* A new type of port which has come into existence in recent times is the port dealing with the shipping and processing of petroleum. The importance of oil in the modern world economy and the vast quantities consumed have given rise to certain specialist ports concerned almost solely with oil; these may be called *tanker* ports and *refinery* ports: Maracaibo in Venezuela, Skhira in Tunisia and Tripoli in Lebanon are examples of the former, Wilhelmstadt on Curaçao, Abadan on the Persian Gulf and Milford Haven in Wales of the latter.

(h) *Fishing ports.* These form a self-explanatory group. They vary greatly in size ranging from major fishing centres such as Grimsby and Bergen and Nagasaki in Japan, to small harbours such as Brixham, Concarneau in Brittany and Biloxi in the United States on the coast of the Gulf of Mexico.

(*i*) *Naval ports.* Located primarily for strategic purposes, they serve as bases for ships of war but may also sometimes undertake naval repair work. Spacious harbourage, shelter and good anchorage are necessary requirements. Unlike most other ports, the hinterland is of little significance. Examples of naval ports are Portsmouth, Toulon in southern France and Key West in Florida.

8. Outports.

Although outports are often taken as a special type of port and might form a further type in the foregoing classification according to function (7), they do not really form a separate type, for an outport may be a commercial or passenger port.

Outports are comparatively recent developments; they are deep-water ports, built farther downstream, serving "parent" ports which have become progressively inaccessible, owing to either silting or the growth in the size of ships.

Outports are very much a feature of north-western Europe and are to be found on the estuaries of rivers. Avonmouth is a classic example; it was built to help the trade of the old, and formerly important, port of Bristol, but it has now outgrown the parent port. Other well-known examples of outports are St Nazaire for Nantes, Bremerhaven for Bremen, Cuxhaven for Hamburg and Leixoes for Oporto.

9. Europoort.

Let us look for a moment at a new and extremely important port development—Europoort. This new port may in a sense be termed an outport of Rotterdam. Rotterdam is the biggest port in Europe and the second biggest in the world (coming after New York). Since the Second World War it has grown with great rapidity and trebled its trade between 1950 and 1962. Today it has a tonnage of around 100 million tons.

The old port of Rotterdam, called the inner port, lies on both sides of the Rhine. The construction of the New Waterway (1836–72) was the prelude to Rotterdam's growth as a port. Later docks at Pernis and then, farther along the Waterway, at Botlek were built. But the continuing growth of Rotterdam and the need for deeper water has led to the bold and imaginative construction of Europoort. Begun in 1958, it functions

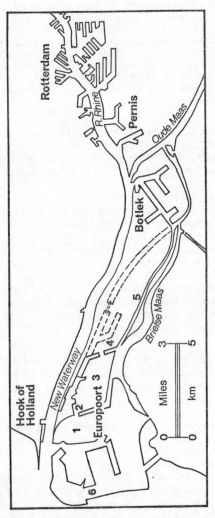

Fig. 32.—*Europoort*

The new port of Europoort is really an extension of the great Dutch port of Rotterdam. The numbers in the diagram explain the organisation of the new port: 1. Blast furnaces, iron and steel mills; 2. Storage depot for bulk goods; 3. Petroleum depot, distribution by pipeline; 4. Ship repair yard for large vessels; 5. Planned link with inland waterways; 6. Allocation and demarcation of this area are not yet fixed. Botlek and Pernis are largely oil ports.

as an ancillary port of Rotterdam. Fig. 32 shows the planned development of Europoort.

10. Port industries. To conclude, let us refer to the industries which are often associated with ports. Distinctive industries are associated with some ports. Since they have links with, and trade with, far off lands they frequently import commodities which are most easily dealt with at the point of entry.

Marseilles' chief function, for instance, has been to distribute imported "colonial" produce. Such commodities, *e.g.* vegetable oils, hides, sugar, esparto grass, have provided the basis for many of its industries, such as the manufacture of margarine, soap, sugar-refining, leather processing and paper making.

Similarly, Bristol with its centuries-old link with the West Indies, has imported tropical commodities such as sugar, cacao, tobacco, and these have given rise to the chocolate and tobacco industries of Bristol. Industries likely to favour a port situation are those based on colonial or tropical commodities which a country does not produce itself.

PROGRESS TEST 25

1. Carefully distinguish between the terms haven; harbour; dock; and port. (**1, 3**)

2. What are the principal requirements of a port? (**2**)

3. "A great commercial port cannot exist without an economic hinterland." Account for this fact. What ports are not dependent on a hinterland? (**2, 7**(*i*))

4. Give an account of the Port of London docks, naming the chief groups of docks and indicating the cargoes in which they tend to specialise. (**4, 5**)

5. Suggest a classification of ports and give examples of each type of port. (**7**)

6. What is an outport? Why have they grown up? What are their functions? (**8**)

7. Choose *either* London *or* Rotterdam and (*a*) describe its location; (*b*) indicate its importance; and (*c*) show how its port facilities have been improved. (**4, 5, 9**)

8. Distinctive industries are often associated with ports. Describe the nature of these industries and give examples of typical port industries. (**10**)

9. How may harbours and existing ports be improved and their

facilities increased? Quote examples of such improvements. (1, 3, 4, 5, 9)

10. Choose an example of each of the following types of port: an entrepôt; an oil port; an outport; and (a) give its precise location; and (b) state the area which it serves. (7, 8)

SUGGESTED PROJECTS

1. Draw sketch maps to illustrate the positions of Antwerp, Copenhagen, New York, Singapore and Suez.

2. Using reference books, trace the growth and decline of Venice as a port.

EXAMINATION TECHNIQUE

1. Three essentials. The examination candidate, if he or she is to be successful, must:

  (a) obey the rubric, *i.e.* the instructions;
  (b) understand the questions asked; and
  (c) arrange his or her material satisfactorily.

2. Read the instructions very carefully. Often the examination paper is divided up into sections and the candidate is asked to answer questions from specific sections. If one question has to be answered from each section, then answer one from each; it is pointless to answer two questions from a section if the rubric states that one only must be attempted. Furthermore, if the instructions say that four questions must be answered, this means four, not five; you will receive no credit for questions answered in excess of the number asked. If the paper has a compulsory question, this must be attempted; it may, indeed, carry more marks than the remaining questions you are asked to answer. Again, if a question specifically asks for sketch-maps or diagrams these should be given, for it is very likely that a proportion of the marks for that question has been set aside for the maps/diagrams. Try to make your sketches neat, accurate and to the point. Don't spend time wastefully by embellishing them.

3. Read the questions carefully. *Make sure you understand what the examiner is asking.* It is helpful to read the question through and to underline the key or salient points in the question. Take, for example, the following question: "Describe very briefly the origin of petroleum. Name the principal producing areas in the world. Indicate the chief methods by which oil is transported and the chief movements of oil in international trade." The chief points here are: *briefly—origin of petroleum—principal producing areas—methods of transport—movements of oil.* The examiner requires a brief account—a paragraph or so, not a page or more— of the origin of petroleum; he wants named the chief areas of production—not countries (though these may be named in addition to the areas); he asks for methods of transport (*i.e.* pipeline and tanker); and he wants to know the routes by which the oil is moved from the centres of production to the consuming centres. Note, too, the significance of *describe, discuss, explain, account for,* *compare* and *contrast* in questions: each has a different meaning; make sure you tackle the question in the way the question asks. For example, there is little point in giving a description of the West Riding wool industry if the question asks for the reasons which gave rise to the industry.

If a question asks for the "industrial geography" of a country, this means manufacturing industry not agriculture; if a question asks "either/or" this means one or the other, not both; if a question asks for "two of the following" it means two, not three; and so on. All these points seem so obvious but it is surprising how many candidates trip up on small points of this nature. Such stupid mistakes can mean only one thing—the student has not read the question carefully. Again, avoid superfluous and irrelevant "padding"; by padding, the student is not fooling the examiner, only himself. Obey the injunction: "Answer the question, the whole question and nothing but the question."

4. Arrange your material carefully. Organise the material of your answer in an orderly, systematic, and logical way. It is a good plan, after having read and understood the question, to jot down your ideas on a spare piece of paper or in your script and to arrange the main headings under which you intend to answer the question; see that you cover all the points. Be precise; give figures, if possible; give appropriate examples. Avoid such meaningless phrases as "a fertile soil," "the right type of soil," "a good climate," "cheap labour," "in many other areas." In describing rainfall and temperature figures required for the growth of a particular crop, give approximate levels of rainfall and degrees of temperature—not plentiful rainfall and high temperatures, for these can have different meanings under different circumstances. Likewise, in quoting cropping areas give precise locations: cacao in Brazil, jute in India, wheat in the United States, sugar-cane in Australia, coal in the Soviet Union, are almost valueless. The student should pay particular attention to those questions which ask him to deal with special areas of production of a commodity: in such cases the student must refer to what the conditions are *in the particular area* and not to what the commodity requires.

Sometimes a question is set which involves comparison and contrast, perhaps of countries, regions, crops or towns. In such cases, take a point at a time and consider the similarity or dissimilarity. Two quite separate and distinct descriptions do not necessarily constitute a comparison or contrast. Moreover, if the question specifically asks for a comparison, the candidate may be penalised if he does not fulfil the instruction.

5. Presentation. Finally, and this should not need emphasising, write legibly and neatly and use good English, paying some respect to grammar, punctuation and spelling. Avoid using slang, abbreviations and ungeographical expressions. Exemplify and amplify statements. The quality, not the quantity, of your answers matters to the examiner. Allot your time carefully so that you do not over-write on any particular question. The good candidate and the one who scores heavily in examinations is the one who can give that little bit extra, whether it be in information, argument or sketch-maps, which places him above the general run of candidates.

EXAMINATION QUESTIONS

1. For any *one* continent you have studied draw a sketch map to show the distribution of population. Explain the factors which have influenced this distribution. (*Welsh Joint Education Committee*)

2. What is meant by *natural resources*? Outline, and contrast, the natural resources of *either* Sweden and Italy *or* Chile and Egypt. (*Northern Counties Technical Examinations Council*)

3. Describe and give examples of *two* of the following: plantation agriculture; nomadism; perennial irrigation; dry farming. (*Northern Counties Technical Examination Council*)

4. Describe and explain the large-scale production of wool in Australia *or* beef in Argentina. (*Welsh Joint Education Committee*)

5. Both shipbuilding and vehicle-building are essentially "assembly" industries, but their geographical distribution in Britain shows great contrasts. Refer to the major localities involved and offer some explanation of the location factors which have contributed to this distribution. (*C.I.T.*)

6. Examine and describe the principal commercial and industrial characteristics of *two* major seaports in Great Britain. (*Institute of Bankers*)

7. Describe the geographical conditions favouring the cultivation of *either* wheat *or* coffee. Select *one* important area of production and give an account of the production of the crop *in that area*. (*Welsh Joint Education Committee*)

8. Examine the importance of irrigation in the agricultural development of the Indian sub-continent, and indicate some of the problems caused in this connection by political and social issues. (*Union of Educational Institutions*)

9. Give an account of the distribution of the coal resources in *either* Europe *or* North America. Select any *one* coalfield in the continent of your choice and give an account of the industries associated with it. (*Welsh Joint Education Committee*)

10. Give an account of the world distribution of copper ores. Name the chief producers of copper. What are the chief uses of copper? (*Welsh Joint Education Committee*)

11. Name three states in Europe that make great use of hydro-electric power and describe the conditions in *one* of them that make

cheap hydro-electric power possible. What industries are associated with hydro-electric power in the country you have chosen? (*I.C.S.A.*)

12. Give an account of *either* cereal production in East Anglia *or* dairying in the West Midlands. Show how factors of soil and climate and demand have influenced production. (*Northern Counties Technical Examinations Council*)

13. Discuss the geographical background of the export trade of Australia and New Zealand. (*C.I.T.*)

14. For any large country in the tropics which you have studied explain: (*a*) why it is backward; and (*b*) what measures are being taken to remedy this? Illustrate with a sketch-map. (*Institute of Bankers*)

15. Outline the world's major sources of timber supply. Explain why Britain is a large importer of timber. (*Welsh Joint Education Committee*)

16. Describe the industrial geography of *either* Tees-side *or* Clydeside. Draw a sketch-map to illustrate your answer. (*Northern Counties Technical Examinations Council*)

17. Write an essay on *one* of the following topics: (*a*) Californian industry; (*b*) Canadian forest resources; (*c*) Hydro-electric power in North America. (*Institute of Bankers*)

18. Discuss the importance of the Great Lakes of North America from the commercial standpoint. (*C.I.T.*)

19. Describe the power resources and their exploitation in *one* of the following: France; Canada; Brazil; India; Australia; Japan. (*Northern Counties Technical Examinations Council*)

20. Explain what is meant by soil erosion and indicate its causes. What measures have been taken by man to conserve the soil? (*Northern Counties Technical Examinations Council*)

21. Discuss *two* of the following statements: (*a*) the British fishing industry is declining; (*b*) population is growing more rapidly in south-eastern England than elsewhere in the British Isles; (*c*) the West Midlands are ideal for milk production; (*d*) the problem of adequate water supplies is gradually appearing in Britain. (*Welsh Joint Education Committee*)

22. Describe the world distribution of iron ores. Discuss the trade in iron ore, indicating the chief producers for export and the major importing countries. (*Northern Counties Technical Examinations Council*)

23. Describe, for any African state, the chief farming regions in that state and show how the differences in farming are related to differences of relief and climate. (*I.C.S.A.*)

24. Cacao, tea and sugar-cane are three important commodities grown under plantation conditions. For these three products: (*a*) draw sketch-maps to show an area of production in each case, and (*b*) in the case of *one* describe briefly the preparation and

processing of the crop ready for market. (*Associated Examining Board*)

25. (*a*) Describe the agricultural landscape in any *two* of the following areas: the polderlands of Holland; the Canadian prairies; Honshu (main island of Japan).

(*b*) Show how the geographical conditions in the areas of your choice have affected the type of agriculture practised. (*Associated Examining Board*)

26. During recent years oil refining and light industries have been established in parts of Great Britain formerly free from industrial development. Cite specific examples of these new developments and explain the choice of such areas. (*Northern Counties Technical Examinations Council*)

27. (*a*) Describe the geographical conditions favouring the production of *three* of the following: fruit in California; mutton in Argentina; dairy produce in New Zealand; early vegetables in southern France.

(*b*) In each case describe the methods of storage, transport and marketing. (*Associated Examining Board*)

28. Distinctive industries are usually associated with ports and capital cities. Give *two* examples of ports and *two* examples of capital cities and for each of one port and one capital city name *three* specific industries. For each describe the nature of these industries. (*Associated Examining Board*)

29. Choose *one* of the following industries: the chemical industry; the rayon industry; mineral oil refining. For any country of your choice, other than the British Isles, describe the industry under the following headings: (*a*) location of the main areas of manufacture; (*b*) the sources of the raw materials and power; (*c*) markets for the product and transport to them. (*Associated Examining Board*)

30. Discuss the statement, "The North Sea traffic route is the busiest in the world." (*C.I.T.*)

INDEX

INDEX

A

Absolute location, 8
Accessibility, 8
Afforestation, 12, 14, 31
Agricultural landscapes, 88–90
  production, 87, 93–5
  yields, 67–8
Aircraft, 9, 258–61
Air transport, 9, 258–61
Aluminium, 203–4
Animal life, 12–13, 27, 32–3, 70
Animals, economic importance of, 115
Anthracite, 158
Apples, 103, 108
Artificial fertilisers, 206
Artificial fibres, 211, 213–14
Asbestos, 151
Aswan High Dam, 79
Autobahnen, 253
Automation, 179–80, 189
Autostrada, 253

B

Balance of payments, 245
Balance of trade, 244
Bananas, 108
Barley, 97, 99–100
Bases of trade, 236
Bauxite, 148–50, 166

Beeching Report, 258
Bilharziasis, 18
Birth rates, 74
Bituminous coal, 158
Brewing, 99, 211
Britain, 3, 8, 15, 17, 21, 59, 63, 173–4, 201, 206, 241–4, 253–4

C

Cableways, 252, 261
Cacao, 103, 112–13
Canals, 263–5
Capital, 187
Cattle, 26–7, 41–7, 115–19
Cattle-rearing, 115
Cereals, 97
Cheapness in transport, 248–9
Chemicals, 205–7, 219, 221
Citrus fruits, 103, 108
Climate, 10–11
Coal, 10, 27, 156–61, 206
Coconut oil, 132
Coffee, 93, 103, 112
Colombo Plan, 69, 82
Common Market, 63
Communications, 9, 93, 271–4
Conservation, 30, 32–4
Containerisation, 280
Copper, 27, 146–7
Copra, 132
Cost factor in transport, 248

Details of some other Macdonald & Evans publications on related subjects can be found on the following pages.

For a full list of titles and prices write for the FREE Macdonald & Evans Business Studies catalogue and/or complete M & E Handbook list, available from Department A2, Macdonald & Evans Ltd., Estover Road, Plymouth PL6 7PZ

Labour Economics
J. D. S. APPLETON
This HANDBOOK is intended for students studying for "A" Level, professional, Higher National and degree examinations in which the papers invariably contain questions on labour economics for which the relevant information can seldom be found in one publication. The text analyses the structure of labour markets generally examining many specific topics in detail.

Managerial Economics
J. R. DAVIS & S. HUGHES
Specifically written for those studying for D.M.S. this HANDBOOK will also assist those taking H.N.C./D. and first-and-second year degree students of Business Studies. All the economic theory used is shown to be relevant in practice and coverage of the main decision areas of management includes choice of corporate form, demand analysis, cost analysis, pricing decisions and investment analysis.

Mathematics
for Economists
L. W. T. STAFFORD
The aim of this HANDBOOK is to help students of economics to handle the mathematical side of their work and to relate their mathematics to essential ideas of economic theory. Topics discussed include differential calculus, vectors and matrices, economic dynamics, and the techniques of regression analysis. Worked answers to most of the test questions in the book are given in a special appendix.

Modern Economic History
EDMUND SEDDON
A clear outline of British economic and social history for G.C.E., professional and university students, this HAND-BOOK traces the development of technology since the point of industrial "take-off" around 1760, and the parallel development of agricultural methods. The second edition contains extended information on the post-1945 period.

British and American Business Terms
RUDOLF SACHS

This book is a comprehensive guide to British and American business terminology. It explains the terms and conventions of all major fields of business and economics and gives a most valuable insight into the mechanics of international commerce. This book should prove valuable to all those engaged in banking, exporting, importing and insurance, to students of economics, and to the general reader interested in modern international commerce.

Development of the English Economy to 1750
PETER KING

This book, suitable for "A" Level and university students, gives the first modern detailed account of the development of the English economy from the earliest times to the start of the Industrial Revolution. It relates economic change to political events and the social life of the people, using cultural and literary evidence as well as the techniques of economic analysis.

Economic Theory and Organisation
A. G. McARTHUR & J. W. LOVERIDGE

This textbook has been written with a view to requirements of the Economics syllabuses of the B.I.M., I.W.M., I.B., H.N.C./D. in Business Studies, C.I.S., I.C.W.A. and A.C.C.A. . . . ."a high quality product . . . deserves a good share of the market which is its concern . . ." *Times Higher Education Supplement*
Illustrated

An Introduction to
Applied Economics
J. L. HANSON

This book is primarily intended for students taking a course in applied economics for the H.N.C./D. in Business Studies or Management Studies. It covers such topics as economic growth and the standard of living, the population problem, the European Community, the balance of payments and international monetary relations.
Illustrated

Monetary Theory and
Practice
J. L. HANSON

This book has proved of considerable value to three types of reader - specialist students of monetary theory, students of economics and the general reader who wishes to keep in touch with current economic events. For banking students, in particular, it covers the syllabus of the subject of Monetary Theory and Practice.
Illustrated